THE REVOLUTIONARY ROOTS OF
Modern Yiddish
1903–1917

Judaic Traditions in Literature, Music, and Art
Ken Frieden and Harold Bloom, *Series Editors*

1905: Zamlung (1905: Collection), edited by A. Yehudski and
E. Fininberg (Melukhe farlag fun ukrayne [State Press of the
Ukraine], 1925). This Yiddish-language volume, published in
the Soviet Union, commemorates the 1905 Russian Revolution
and contains essays, poems, and memoirs by such figures as
Trotsky, Lenin, Gorky, Sholem Aleichem, I. L. Peretz, Sholem
Asch, among others.

THE REVOLUTIONARY ROOTS OF

Modern Yiddish
1903–1917

Barry Trachtenberg

Syracuse University Press

CHAPTERS 1 AND 2 originally published in revised form as "The Revolutionary Origins of Yiddish Scholarship," by Barry Trachtenberg in *The Revolution of 1905 and Russia's Jews,* edited by Stefani Hoffman and Ezra Mendelsohn (Philadelphia: University of Pennsylvania Press, 2008), 174–84. Reprinted by permission of the University of Pennsylvania Press.

CHAPTER 4 originally published in revised form as "Ber Borochov's 'The Tasks of Yiddish Philology,'" *Science in Context* 20, no. 2 (June 2007): 341-52. Reprinted with permission.

The paper used in this publication meets the minimum requirements of American National Standard for Information Sciences—Permanence of Paper for Printed Library Materials, ANSI Z39.48-1984.∞™

For a listing of books published and distributed by Syracuse University Press, visit our Web site at SyracuseUniversityPress.syr.edu.

ISBN-13: 978-0-8156-3190-3   ISBN-10: 0-8156-3190-1

Library of Congress Cataloging-in-Publication Data

Trachtenberg, Barry.

The revolutionary roots of modern Yiddish, 1903–1917 / Barry Trachtenberg. — 1st ed.

p. cm. — (Judaic traditions in literature, music, and art)

Includes bibliographical references and index.

ISBN 978-0-8156-3190-3 (cloth : alk. paper)

1. Yiddish language—Russia—History—20th century.   2. Yiddish language—Social aspects—Russia.   3. Jews—Russia—Intellectual life—20th century.   4. Niger, Samuel, 1883–1955.   5. Borochov, Ber, 1881–1917.   6. Shtif, Nahum, 1879–1933.   I. Title.

PJ5113.T728 2008

439'.1—dc22

2008031740

Manufactured in the United States of America

For Paul Hoffman,

1947–2003

Barry Trachtenberg is assistant professor of European Jewish Studies at the University at Albany, SUNY. He was trained in Jewish history at the University of California, Los Angeles (PhD), the Hebrew University of Jerusalem, and Oxford University (postgraduate diploma) and also holds degrees from the University of Vermont (MA in U.S. history) and Rowan University of New Jersey (BA in English). He is the recipient (2008) of a grant from the National Endowment for the Humanities for his work on Yiddish in the twentieth century.

Contents

Illustrations

Acknowledgments

For their kind and constant support of this project, I thank my advisors and teachers at the University of California, Los Angeles, especially Professors David N. Myers and Arnold J. Band. The time, dedication, and patience they offer to their students are unparalleled and a model for me as I teach my own. Since first meeting David in 1996, he has continued to sharpen my understanding of Jewish history by encouraging me to look beyond the boundaries of accepted historiography, and to take risks in my thinking. My weekly tutorials with Professor Band in which we read modern Hebrew texts provided me with the type of training that I had long thirsted for as a student. I am also very grateful for the wisdom and guidance of Professors Saul Friedländer and Janet Hadda.

At the University at Albany (SUNY), where I now make my home, I am fortunate to have received support for my research from the Judaic Studies Department, Center for Jewish Studies, and College of Arts and Sciences. My colleague and friend Joel Berkowitz has been very generous with his critical feedback, guidance, and encouragement at every stage. Professors Bret Benjamin, Leona Christie, Toby Clyman, Jennifer Greiman, Stanley Isser, Eric Keenaghan, Martha Tuck Rozett, and Edward Schwarzschild offered helpful advice and support as I navigated through the many stages of the publishing process.

My editor at Syracuse University Press, Glenn Wright, and the editor of the Judaic Traditions in Literature, Music, and Art series, Ken Frieden, offered many valuable suggestions for revision and have been very encouraging throughout. Kay A. Steinmetz navigated the transformation of the manuscript into this book; Sheila Milden's copy edits clarified much of the prose; and Lynn Hoppel designed the wonderful cover. I deeply appreciate their support.

Research was conducted primarily at the YIVO Institute for Jewish Research in New York City, where I was the Maria Salit-Gitelson Tell Memorial Fellow for 2005. I have been fortunate to benefit from the friendship and expertise of Dr. Brad Sabin Hill (now of George Washington University) and Dr. Hershl Glasser. I am also grateful to the staff at the Jewish National and University Library in Jerusalem and New York Public Library's Dorot Jewish Division. Sharona Wachs and Carol Anne Germain of the University Library at the University at Albany were tremendously helpful in tracking down and suggesting many sources. Amy Lawrence (Harvard Law School), Shifra Kuperman (Universität Basel), and Mirjam Gutschow (Menasseh Ben Israel Instituut) very generously took their time to locate several hard-to-find sources.

Conversations with many colleagues both within and outside the field of Jewish Studies were of enormous value throughout the stages of this work. Mikhail Krutikov (University of Michigan) and David Shneer (University of Colorado) were generous readers who reviewed the manuscript in its entirety and whose critical suggestions have greatly improved the work. In addition to those already mentioned, I thank Merle L. Bachman (Spalding University), Doris Bergen (University of Toronto), Alisa Braun (University of California, Davis), Justin Cammy (Smith College), Mathew Coleman (Ohio State University), Gennady Estraikh (New York University), Jerold Frakes (University at Buffalo, SUNY), Alexandra Garbarini (Williams College), Yoshiji Hirose (Notre Dame Seishin University), Cecile Kuznitz (Bard College), Olga Litvak (Clark University), Alexandre Métraux (Universität Mannheim), Jared Poley (Georgia State University), Eddy Portnoy (Jewish Theological Seminary), Simon Rabinovitch (University of Florida), Adam Rubin (Hebrew Union College), Yankl Salant, Gayle Sulik (Texas Woman's University), Gary Steller (Community College of Vermont), Claudia Verhoeven (George Mason University), and Kalman Weiser (York University).

At the University at Albany, both Kathaleen Heinzl and Yoel Hirschfeld were of great help in navigating the many levels of University bureaucracy. My students Talia Ashworth, Michael Kupferberg, Liya Mikhaylova, Cynthia Roth, Jennifer Sacco, Erin Sawyer, Robert Titov, and Ashley Walters offered their time and skill to locate sources, and to maintain sanity and order around the office.

Many friends and colleagues scattered near and far shared their wisdom and friendship with me as I worked on this project. In addition to those mentioned above, I thank Elisa Albert, David Applebaum, Branka Arsić and David Wills, Karen and Bill Barlow, Kelly Barron, Craig and Elise Benjamin, Renee and Mark Benson, Benjamin Brown, Deborah Brown, Laura Carruth, Patricia E. Chu, Naomi and Michael Cohen, Anya von Cysewski, James and Sharon Danhoff-Burg, Manal Diab, Dan Dougherty, Sarah and Gareth Dowling, Rachel Dressler, Lynn DuFour, Gustav Erikson, Jeannie Masquelier and Tom Estgate, Mark Gilmore and Marcia Moriarta, John Genovese, Keith Gordon and Rachel Griffin-Gordon, Wolf Gruner and Sandra Gruner-Domic, George Haas, Pierre Joris and Nicole Peyrafitte, Gloria Kamler, Cricket Keating and Larin McLaughlin, Sonya Khoury, Micheline B. Levy, James Lilley and Lauren Sallata, Mary Jo Mastro, Gary McDonald, Lisa Moriyama and Stanley Wachs, Esther Nathanson, Linda Pardo, Beverly and John Petiet, Judy and George Robertson, Mazen Saalami, Helene Scheck, Barbara Schmutzler, Paul Schwabe, Victoria Stanton, Paul Stasi, Tim Talmage, Mary Thomas, Lisa B. Thompson, Laura Wilder, Gabriel Wishik, and Tamara Zwick.

I also wish to thank my parents, Eleanor and Harvey Trachtenberg, as well as my brother Robert M. Trachtenberg, my sister Fredda Ferris, and their families for their love and support.

I would like to express my deepest gratitude for the love, friendship, and patience shown to me by Jennifer Greiman. Life with her is my greatest joy.

Paul Hoffman was a dear friend and mentor who passed away just as I completed my graduate work. His intellectual curiosity, braveness, and honesty continue to inspire many of us who were fortunate enough to have known him. It is an honor to dedicate this book to his memory.

Author's Note

For Yiddish words, this work follows the orthographic standards of the YIVO Institute of Jewish Research, except in those instances where there exist commonly accepted spellings for proper names [hence Max Weinreich and not Maks Vaynraykh, Peretz and not Perets]. For Hebrew and Russian words, I have used the system of the Library of Congress. In the case of the many Yiddish titles of works, I have provided the English translation in the first instance and use the Yiddish title thereafter.

Because of the generational argument that I present in this work, the birth and death dates of the figures mentioned are provided in most instances. In the case of the Russian tsars and tsarina, the dates of their reigns are shown. Dates are cited according to the Julian calendar, which was twelve days behind the Gregorian calendar in the nineteenth century, and thirteen in the twentieth.

All translations, unless otherwise noted, are my own.

THE REVOLUTIONARY ROOTS OF

Modern Yiddish

1903–1917

Introduction

Yiddish as Instrument and Ideology

It was destined to me in my early years to stand at the cradle of our
new literature in the Jewish folk language and then later to observe
how this small child, which at the time was called "jargon," grew up
and received its proper name, "Yiddish."[1]
—Simon Dubnow

In 1929, the Russian-Jewish historian Simon Dubnow (1860–1941)
reflected upon the dramatic changes that had occurred within the Yiddish
language over the course of his lifetime. In a collection of essays entitled
Fun 'zhargon' tsu yidish (From Jargon to Yiddish), he traced how Yiddish had been transformed from an unnamed "jargon" without status or
honor into a dynamic language that was the foundation for a revitalized
literary folk culture. Dubnow, theoretician of a Jewish nationalist ideology known as Autonomism and author of a now classic multivolume
survey of Jewish history, was too comprehensive in his thinking to be
grouped into the particularist category of Yiddishist.[2] However, it was
among the early advocates for Yiddish that he found several of his greatest admirers, including those who committed themselves to the task of
elevating the stature of Yiddish much in the same way that Dubnow had
legitimated the study of Eastern European Jewry. Among Dubnow's most
important innovations in his study of the Jewish past was that he looked
beyond the religious, legal, and spiritual characteristics that had informed
prior histories, and he considered the demographic, ethnographic, and
material factors that shaped the Jews' development. In doing so, Dubnow identified the previously ignored masses of Eastern European Jews

1

as an authentic and necessary subject of inquiry after nearly a century of neglect by German-Jewish historians.

In his early years, Dubnow was a literary critic for the Russian-language Jewish press. Writing under the pseudonym "Criticus," he was among those who began to craft a tradition for Yiddish out of the works of writers such as Sholem Yankev Abramovitsh (1835–1917, who adopted the persona of Mendele the Bookseller), Sholem Aleichem (1859–1916, pen name of Sholem Rabinovitsh), Yankev Dinezon (1856–1919), and Shimen Frug (1860–1916), and helped to guide Yiddish into a modern literary language.[3] Looking back on these developments, Dubnow considered the changes that had occurred within Yiddish over the half century since he first wrote his literary criticism. The most influential catalyst for its growth, he argued, was the terrible violence that began in the spring of 1881, when for a year, pogroms raged throughout Jewish communities in the Russian empire and accelerated a culturally and politically inward turn among Jewish writers and thinkers.

Dubnow was also a leading figure among Jewish intellectuals who, in their youth, found themselves reassessing the Jewish Enlightenment, known as the Haskalah, an ideology that had been embraced by many Russian Jews in the name of modernizing themselves and their brethren.[4] The pogroms were the final and most compelling piece of evidence to those who believed that the Haskalah had failed to fulfill its promise of securing a place for Jews in the empire in exchange for their increased acceptance of Russian cultural and societal norms. In response, many Jewish youth began turning their attention to more radical alternatives that were gathering in strength, such as populism, socialism, and nationalism.[5] One important outcome of this ideological turn was a reconsideration of attitudes toward Yiddish. Despite a long history of sophisticated texts written in the language and the fact that it was spoken by nearly all Russian Jews (who numbered more than 5 million in the 1890s), in the last decades of the nineteenth century, Yiddish was nearly universally thought to be unfit for serious literary and intellectual pursuits, and as a barrier to Jewish participation in modern society. However, in their search for an alternative to Jewish acculturation, a small but influential number of writers began to explore its creative possibilities. They were among the first to turn readily to Yiddish and in so doing, made the first steps to adapt it for modern usage.

Dubnow was a part of what the scholar David H. Weinberg has identified as a "transitional generation" of Russian Jews who occupied a place between a traditionally religious-defined Judaism and a more revolutionary and nationalist one. Weinberg describes this generation as one faced with the challenge of maintaining the archive of Jewish knowledge while simultaneously refashioning Judaism in order for it to remain relevant in an increasingly secular world:

> On the one hand, there was the need to build a strong Jewish collective consciousness that would reconcile freethinking Jews with the deeply rooted values and beliefs of Jewish life. On the other, there was the challenge of developing a collective identity that would enable Jews to participate in the modern world despite the absence of the objective conditions of territory and sovereignty that characterized nation building in the nineteenth century.[6]

This book examines the maturation of Yiddish by the Jewish activists, scholars, and critics of the generation that followed Dubnow's. Born near the time of the 1881–82 pogroms, this generation grew up in an environment that was experiencing the rapid waves of modernization, industrialization, urbanization, and proletarianization that were leaving their mark on nearly everyone in the Russian empire. Moreover, they were born into a Jewish society whose ever-strengthening nationalist and socialist movements determined their ideological and intellectual boundaries. The defining moment of this generation was the unsuccessful Russian revolution of 1905, when both Jewish emancipatory expectations and anti-Jewish violence seemed to be at their zenith. By the time this generation reached young adulthood with the 1905 upheavals, they had fully invested themselves in the revolutionary currents sweeping across Russia. For many of them, Yiddish was not simply a form of poor German that had to be rejected in order to join the larger world; instead, it stood proudly at the center of a growing Jewish national revival. This was the first generation to take seriously the possibility that Yiddish could serve as a means through which to communicate the entire range of human thought, and in so doing, they helped to lay the intellectual and institutional foundations for a secular Jewish culture based on their spoken language.

In particular, this book is an investigation into the origins of the scholarly discipline known in Yiddish as *Yidishe visnshaft,* which can be translated into English as either Yiddish science, studies, or scholarship, and denotes a branch of Jewish studies dedicated to the study and development of the Yiddish language, its literature, and its speakers.[7] Although Yiddish has been an object of research since the sixteenth century, it was only in the beginning of the twentieth century that Yiddish-speaking Jews began to turn to their vernacular as both the subject and medium for its examination. Today, the Yiddish language and its culture is widely taught and researched in universities and academic centers in many countries; however, a century ago the very notion of Yiddish studies was hotly disputed, and its creation was an outcome of bitter ideological struggles over the future of Russian Jewry. Not only was the idea that scholarship could be conducted in and on behalf of Yiddish hotly contested, but even among its first practitioners, the agenda, assumptions, and strategies of *Yidishe visnshaft* were fought over as each sought to employ the tools and methodologies of scholarship to forge a Yiddish-speaking nation in a way that corresponded to their particular vision of the future. Similar to how the nineteenth-century German-Jewish project of *Wissenschaft des Judentums* (which began the field of Jewish studies) was shaped by "persistent tensions" between the demands of particularistic religious denominations and those of universal scholarly standards, the early twentieth-century project of *Yidishe visnshaft* was often defined by the competing demands of partisan politics and by the values of objective research.[8] The once stark divisions between mid-nineteenth-century Reform, Conservative, Orthodox, and secular Jewish scholars over the direction of Jewish studies in Germany often were echoed in equally tendentious disputes among early twentieth-century Zionist, Diasporist, Yiddishist, and Hebraist scholars over the meaning of Yiddish studies.

Despite its contested beginnings, the first practitioners of *Yidishe visnshaft* agreed that their task was to produce scholarly works written in the Yiddish language, and on the language, literature, and world of its speakers. Following the model set by other nationalist movements that were developing among the empire's minority populations, they were concerned with the standardization of Yiddish grammar, orthography, and word corpus, the establishment of a Yiddish literary tradition, the exploration of their history and folk traditions, and the creation of an institutional structure to support their language's development and hegemony over competing languages. In doing so, they hoped to refashion Russian Jewry as a modern nation with a mature language and culture that deserved the same collective rights and autonomy demanded by other nations in the empire.

This study considers the development of *Yidishe visnshaft* prior to the establishment of its brick-and-mortar institutions in the 1920s. It focuses in particular on the years 1903 to 1917, a time that began with a pogrom in the Bessarabian city of Kishinev in southern Russia, and ended with the successful 1917 Revolution. Although these years were often filled with extreme violence and uncertainty, the violence and the Jews' radicalized response to it prompted many activists and intellectuals to consider the possibility of their vernacular serving as the basis for a secularized national identity. From 1903 to 1917, many of the shifts in the functions of and attitudes toward Yiddish that had been set into motion since 1881–82 came fully into being as a younger generation assumed a greater role in their society's political and cultural affairs. Rather than accept the perceptions of the limits of Yiddish that had been assumed by prior generations of its speakers, many within the ranks of the new intelligentsia saw it as the most obvious language to sustain the Jewish society they hoped to create.

The entire period of 1903 to 1917 marks a decisive if overlooked moment in Russian-Jewish history and the development of modern Yiddish culture. Overshadowed by the violence of 1881 and 1882 on one side and World War I and the collapse of the tsarist regime on the other, the first attempt at revolution in Russia has been often viewed as an event of only transitional significance. However, in these years, Russian Jewry experienced the forces of modernity so profoundly that by the time of the tsar's overthrow in 1917, their life barely resembled its nineteenth-century existence. Once-isolated Jewish communities saw their populations migrate to urban areas, hundreds of thousands of Jews now labored in factories, and vast numbers abandoned their traditional religious practices in favor of secular Jewish identities. In addition, millions of Russian Jews were now living in the Americas, Europe, Palestine, South Africa, and beyond, joining a mass emigration that began two decades earlier.

Jewish life during the 1905 Revolution was marked by seemingly contradictory forces. In one respect, Jews endured some of the worst bloodshed in centuries. Not only did the Kishinev pogrom result in the death of dozens, but the riots that followed the granting of constitutional reforms in October 1905 left nearly nine hundred Jews dead.[9] For a time, all Jews in the empire were vulnerable to violence. Another consequence, however, was that for the first time in modern memory, many Jews became emboldened in their response, mobilizing into self-defense units, organizing political parties, joining in the cries for the tsar's overthrow, and imagining that a permanent solution to the questions regarding their status in the empire was on the near horizon.

Among the most important long-term consequences of Jewish involvement in the 1905 Revolution was the emergence of a new generation of Jewish leaders who were possessed of an ethos of Jewish self-determination that set the course of Jewish life for the next half century. The historian Jonathan Frankel vividly describes these leaders as

> extremely young in 1905, utterly committed both to the cause of revolution and to that of armed Jewish self-defense against the pogroms. Almost to a man they had become fervent Marxists by 1906, and even those who had not . . . now advocated (philosophically) a monistic determination and (politically) proletarian class war. By 1906, the revolution had absorbed their every waking moment, every ounce of strength and every hope. However, to them the revolution meant a struggle not only for social equality and political freedom, but also for national, for Jewish, liberation.[10]

Although the new generation's attempts to achieve Jewish national autonomy during the 1905 Revolution were unsuccessful once the tsar reasserted his authority in 1907, many continued their efforts to construct a revitalized Jewish national identity. With political avenues blocked, they increasingly focused their attention on the cultural aspects of their newly identified nation, in particular by developing its Yiddish and Hebrew creative and scholarly forms. Very quickly, questions of language, literature, and culture began to assume a central role in their discussions and debates.

For Yiddishists, the task before them was to elevate the stature of the language so that it could be accepted by its speakers as substantial enough to carry the weight of the Jewish nation.

This study appears at an important moment in the history of *Yidishe visnshaft*. In the words of the scholar Mikhail Krutikov, Yiddish studies is now entering into a period of "post-ideological scholarship."[11] This refers to the fact that although for most of its history, Yiddish scholarship was (and in some instances is still) practiced by scholars who saw themselves as participants in and advocates of a unique cultural heritage, an increasing number of studies are being written by nonnative Yiddish speakers who are less tethered to the various political, cultural, and linguistic assumptions and agendas that guided the discipline's earlier practitioners. As Krutikov diagnosed in a 2002 essay in which he provided a rough genealogy of the ideological impulses that have shaped modern Yiddish studies, one of the consequences of this most recent turn is that in the process of distancing themselves from the discipline's original intellectual assumptions, many contemporary scholars of Yiddish are simultaneously reluctant to reflect upon them. He cautions against what he sees as signs of an "ornamental" attitude toward Yiddish, as "our understanding of Yiddish literature risks soon becoming fossilized and fragmented, and turning into a repository of various images, metaphors, aphorisms, and phrases that can be used for any purpose" with nothing to unify them as a coherent discipline (Krutikov, 10). If during the first generations of Yiddish studies, the scholarly pendulum had swung far in favor of "positivist bio-bibliographical erudition," among later scholars, he argues, it is swinging too far into the realms of overtheorization and contextualization.[12] As a remedy, he proposes two tasks for future Yiddish research. First, Krutikov encourages scholars to tackle the "'big issues' of the previous, Yiddishist generation" (p. 8), and second, he suggests "Perhaps it's time now to revise the whole legacy of Yiddish criticism in the past century, from David Frishman and Bal-Makhshoves to Yankev Glatshteyn, from a 'post-ideological' perspective" (Krutikov, 10).

Krutikov's call for a reconsideration of the assumptions and truisms that have informed much of Yiddish scholarly research is an indication that the discipline of Yiddish studies is at a moment when its scholars can adopt an increasingly reflexive approach to its historical development. Although we still await the thorough reassessments of Yiddish writers such as Isaac Leib Peretz (1852–1915), Sholem Aleichem, and Dovid Bergelson (1884–1952) for which Krutikov has called, this book adds to a small but growing body of research that reconsiders the origins of Yiddish scientific research and the early years of the Yiddishist movement. Studies in recent years have begun to challenge many of the truisms of *Yidishe visnshaft* by expanding its focus beyond the circle of scholars tied to the Yidisher visnshaftlekher institut (Yiddish Scientific Institute, known as YIVO), by taking seriously the work of Soviet Yiddishists, by rethinking the extent of its relationship to partisan politics, and by placing it within the larger context of Jewish and European nationalism.[13]

Along with the changes currently underway in Yiddish studies, this work also appears at an important time in the study of Jewish nationalism. In the last two decades, Jewish—primarily Israeli—scholars have been identifying and reassessing the foundational myths of Zionism and the state of Israel. In particular, scholars identified (however reluctantly) with the post-Zionist movement have forcefully distanced themselves from historiographical narratives that follow the now well worn path of the "rise, fall, and rebirth" of Jewish sovereignty. In place of nationalistic renderings of the past, they have critically examined the formation of Jewish national consciousness, located its origins among late nineteenth-century minority populations in Eastern Europe, considered the consequences of importing their political, economic, cultural, and social ideologies to the Middle East, and explored Zionism's relationship to European colonization.[14] Despite the many differences in their approaches and conclusions, these works have paved the way for the possibility of a reassessment of other manifestations of Jewish nationalism—even those that were not similarly triumphant, but whose influence on modern Jewish history was profound—such as Diasporism, Autonomism, Territorialism, and most important to this study, Yiddishism.

The confluence of the postideological turn in Yiddish studies and the postnationalist moment in Zionist historiography allows for the opportunity to reflect upon the ideological underpinnings of *Yidishe visnshaft*.

In particular, it opens the way for a much needed investigation into the etiological myths that have informed its historiographical narratives and that have been reinforced and repeated since the Nazi Holocaust and the linguistic shift away from Yiddish by Jews in the Soviet Union, United States, and Israel. Such an exploration reveals that many of the attitudes about and defenses of Yiddish that continue to influence the discipline were originally articulated during the first two decades of the twentieth century in Russia when many within the ranks of the new Jewish intelligentsia began to understand themselves and their native language through the discourse of nationalism.

Although the first practitioners of *Yidishe visnshaft* saw their task as revolutionary, they also sought to locate it within a tradition of Jewish scholarly research. At the time of its inception in the early twentieth century, *Yidishe visnshaft*'s adherents understood their project as existing both as a corrective to the nineteenth-century German-Jewish scholarly project of *Wissenschaft des Judentums* and as an extension of it. Founded in 1819, *Wissenschaft des Judentums* was the name given to the enterprise of researching and legitimizing Judaism by examining it according to the presumably objective standard of science and in doing so, to support the movement for German-Jewish emancipation.[15] The year 1819 marked the infamous Hep! Hep! riots against German-Jewry, which resulted in a broad reconsideration of the legal status of Jews by both Germans and Jews. By this time, German Jews had relinquished many of the religious, linguistic, economic, and cultural attributes that differentiated them from German Christians and yet the riots suggested that they were no closer to realizing their goal of being accepted into public life. It was in this context that the Verein für Cultur und Wissenschaft der Juden (Society for Jewish Culture and Knowledge) was founded by a group of young university-trained scholars who sought, through a recourse to historical scholarship, to advance the struggle for Jewish emancipation while at the same time providing a means to continue Judaism's relevance in an increasingly modern age.

Immanuel Wolf's (1799–1829) 1822 essay, "Über den Begriff einer Wissenschaft des Judentums" (On the Concept of a Science of Judaism), introduced the Verein's ideology and articulates well the faith in *Wissenschaft* to convey the full scope of Judaism:

> The aim will be to depict Judaism, first from a historical standpoint, as it has gradually developed and taken shape, and then philosophically, according to its inner essence and idea. The textual knowledge of the literature of Judaism must precede both methods of study. Thus we have, first, the textual study of Judaism, second, a history of Judaism; third a philosophy of Judaism.[16]

The mission of the Verein was to unite German-Jewish intelligentsia around the study of Judaism and prove scientifically the viability of Jewish equality.[17] Its members were captivated by the spirit of intellectual renaissance within German universities that followed Prussia's defeat by France in 1806. The enthusiasm for method, the imperative to conduct original research, and the confidence in the objectivity of *Wissenschaft* were the hallmarks of this new standard, and they began a tradition of critical inquiry into Judaism that continues to this day. As the historian Ismar Schorsch has noted, for this first generation of scholars, understanding Judaism through the lens of secular scholarship was nothing less than the "intellectual equivalent of political emancipation."[18]

For the Russian-Jewish youths who first began to envision a *visnshaft* for Yiddish in the early twentieth century, their task was simultaneously much broader and much narrower than that of their nineteenth-century forebears. On the one hand, they adopted a wider range of methodological approaches. Along with literature, history, philology, and philosophy, they also looked to the modern sciences, such as linguistics, demography, economics, and ethnography. On the other, they restricted themselves to a more limited subject matter. Rather than claiming to embrace the totality of Jewish civilization, they kept their sights squarely on matters related to the study of the Yiddish language, and the history and culture of its speakers.

As much as they accepted the authority of science to substantiate and legitimate their conceptions of Judaism, the first practitioners of *Yidishe visnshaft* also sought to achieve very different ends than their German-Jewish predecessors. Although the efforts of the scholars of *Wissenschaft des Judentums* were linked in part to broader debates between Germans and Jews about the growing level of Jewish acculturation into German society, the purpose of *Yidishe visnshaft* was nation building and enforcing distinctions between Jews and non-Jews. No better evidence can be found for this than the languages in which the two groups of scholars conducted their work. Unlike the scholarship of *Wissenschaft des Judentums,* which was written in German, and therefore available to Jewish and non-Jewish readers alike, *Yidishe visnshaft* was composed for a Yiddish-reading audience, which by default, was nearly exclusively Jewish (and of Eastern European descent).

The first modern scholars of Yiddish understood their task in part as a corrective to the legacy of *Wissenschaft des Judentums.* As the linguist Nokhem Shtif (1879–1933) spoke of it in a 1925 blueprint for what became the YIVO, not only was Yiddish mostly ignored in the historical and philological studies of German-Jewish scholars, but in the few instances when it was addressed, it was done so in service of agendas that resulted in the further delegitimization of Yiddish:

> For 400 years, German scholars have studied the Yiddish language, and for the past 50–60 years in particular, German-Jewish scholars have likewise studied it. According to those who studied it (apart from 2–3 of them), the Yiddish language was a "Judeo-German": dead-book material from a bygone era, and none of them had the least idea of the living Yiddish national language or of the new Yiddish literature, since neither was of interest to them. Among the so-called *"Wissenschaft des Judentums,"* Yiddish research is merely a historical discipline, like Latin, in their eyes it is only an auxiliary source for Middle High German or for general German dialectology. Moreover, these fundamentally false methods have meant that Yiddish research has not been elevated to the level of an independent discipline.[19]

Since its origins in the beginning of the twentieth century, there has been little scholarly consensus as to the tasks and purview of *Yidishe visnshaft.* Unlike the situation in Berlin in 1819, for the first two decades of *Yidishe visnshaft,* there was no organized scholarly community, no Verein, no unified set of principles, and no agreed-upon agenda. Instead, Yiddish science developed in a more haphazard way, as young Russian-Jewish intellectuals began to consider the merits of adopting a critical approach to Yiddish with an eye to its development and enrichment. Some strove to emulate the intellectual rigor and objectivity of the Russian academy, while others tethered their research to political platforms. After World War I, *Yidishe visnshaft* was brought into service on behalf of a wide range of agendas, such as language reform and standardization, as a conduit for Sovietization, and in support of Jewish minority rights in Poland.

More recently, two definitions of *Yidishe visnshaft* have been proposed. In 1986, the scholar Dovid Katz spoke of modern Yiddish scholarship as "the literature *on* Yiddish and the literature *in* Yiddish," and also characterized it as "the modern literature *in, on,* and *for* Yiddish."[20] In 2007, Alexandre Métraux offered a corrective to Katz's description by suggesting that Yiddish scholarship is best understood as "scholarship written (and more than occasionally taught) in Yiddish."[21] Métraux considers his definition broader than Katz's in that it includes those works of scholarship written in Yiddish but which do not pertain to either Yiddish or Jewish subjects (such as medicine). At the same time, he views it as more exact than Katz's definition because Métraux's excludes the Yiddish works of "journalists, publishers, literary critics, popularizers, evening school lecturers, and other actors of *kultur-arbet*—i.e., activists engaged in promoting Jewish-Yiddish culture" that fall outside of the boundaries of scientific literature and institutions.[22]

For the purpose of this book, which focuses on the period from 1903 to 1917, *Yidishe visnshaft* (and its English equivalents) designates something somewhat different from the definitions offered by Katz and Métraux. Katz's description disallows those works of Yiddish scholarship not directly related to questions of language, such as the demographer Jacob Lestschinsky's (1876–1966) early studies of Jewish economic life in Russia and London or Noyekh Prilutski's (1882–1941) folkloric explorations. Métraux's characterization excludes both the preinstitutional phase of *Yidishe visnshaft* as well as the centrality of Yiddish literary criticism and history to the overall project. At the same time, it includes much work that fell outside the task of nation-building, which was of primary concern to the first proponents of *Yidishe visnshaft*. Following the example set by the founders themselves, in this book, when referring to the period of 1903 to 1917, *Yidishe visnshaft* refers to the scholarly and critical literature that was written in the Yiddish language, on the subject of Yiddish-speaking Jewry (in its broadest sense and irrespective of discipline), and on behalf of Jewish national development. This definition allows for a discussion of Yiddish literary history and criticism, language planning, and ethnographic and demographic research while acknowledging the particular nationalist imperatives that were central to its founders' efforts.

This book also suggests new ways to understand the origins of modern Yiddish scholarship, by locating them in the volatile days of the 1905 Revolution. Although recent studies have begun to consider the impact of 1905 on Russian-Jewish society and the development of modern Yiddish culture, its importance to the history of *Yidishe visnshaft* remains far less understood.[23] Instead, *Yidishe visnshaft* is most often spoken of as a phenomenon of the decades between the two world wars, and several important studies have appeared in recent years that examine its contours in the 1920s and 1930s in great detail.[24] By contrast, when the pre–World War I origins of *Yidishe visnshaft* are addressed, historians often consider them as but a prelude to the Yiddish scholarly institutions that emerged after World War I, and they repeat a narrative that overemphasizes certain moments as "seminal" and its founders as "pioneers."

According to a standard representation, scholarship on the Yiddish language for centuries was conducted by researchers who examined it in search of clues to the history and development of other Germanic languages.[25] Its early observers tended to view Yiddish not as a discrete language unto itself but only as a corrupted German dialect. This attitude was continued by German-Jewish scholars throughout the nineteenth century. Only in the last decades of the nineteenth century did Yiddish become a subject of interest to researchers in its own right, although their scholarship was conducted in languages other than Yiddish, such as German or English. The founding moment of a distinctly *Yidishe visnshaft* occurred at a Yiddish language conference held in 1908, when a linguist named Matisyohu Mieses (1885–1945) delivered the first Yiddish scholarly address, a defense of the integrity of the language against its Hebraist opponents. Five years later, while in exile from Russia, labor Zionist leader Ber Borochov (1881–1917) defined the "tasks" facing Yiddish philological research in a 1913 volume that was the first independent print forum for *Yidishe visnshaft*. In the same volume, he also published the first comprehensive bibliography of materials relating to Old Yiddish.[26] Then, in the interwar period, several Yiddish research institutions developed, the most important of them being the YIVO, which closely followed the agenda set by Borochov.[27]

This compact narrative elides the complicated origins of *Yidishe visnshaft*. By expanding the definition of *Yidishe visnshaft* beyond the field of linguistics, and considering the full scope of Yiddish scholarly activities conducted in the first decades of twentieth-century Russia, it becomes apparent that the route traversed by its founders was much more intricate, and cannot be compressed so neatly into a few particular moments. An investigation into its origins not only demonstrates the centrality of the 1905 Revolution to the development of modern Yiddish scholarship, but identifies *Yidishe visnshaft* as one of the achievements of the generation of Jewish political and intellectual leaders who rose to the fore of Russian-Jewish society in the first decades of the twentieth century.

Along with emphasizing the impact of the 1905 Revolution on the creation of *Yidishe visnshaft,* this study also draws attention to the many parallels between the Yiddishist movement and other forms of Jewish nationalism. Although Yiddishists (who tended to advance pro-Diaspora political solutions to the question of the Jews' status) often understood themselves in opposition to Zionist supporters of Hebrew, from the distance of a century, their particular differences are much less remarkable than what they held in common. All were part of a much larger transformation within European Jewry that was occurring at the turn of the twentieth century, and both groups held a similar diagnosis of the crisis facing the Jewish population, despite being divided, often bitterly, over its solution.[28] As the scholar Benjamin Harshav has noted, at their core, these movements participated in an ideology of rejection of the Jews' status in the empire, and the majority of Jewish intellectuals, artists, and activists hoped to bring about a fundamental change in their condition.[29] Regardless of their political affiliation, nearly all believed that their present situation was untenable, that the historical experience of the Jews was a unique one, that the nation was the highest ideal, that the agents of change would be an alliance of the Jewish intelligentsia and proletariat, and that this involved settling long-standing questions of language.

Such attention to language in the formation of national identities dates back to the beginning of modern European nationalism. In the late eighteenth century, romantic nationalists posited language as a defining characteristic of national cohesion and argued that the vocabulary and grammar of each language embodies the specific values and characteristics of its nation.[30] According to this formulation, languages contained the souls of the nations that spoke them and expressed each nation's particular *Volksgeist* (national spirit).[31] In the wake of such assertions, philologists and linguists played central roles in national movements by classifying, historicizing, documenting, and standardizing languages.[32] As the historian Benedict Anderson has noted, comparative studies of grammar ultimately exerted an equalizing force upon all languages, diminishing the status of classical ones (Hebrew, Greek, and Latin) while elevating vernaculars to the status of national languages. The result was that "the nineteenth century was, in Europe and its immediate peripheries, a golden age of vernacularizing lexicographers, grammarians, philologists, and litterateurs."[33] In time, and through the work of committed advocates, European vernaculars (Yiddish being among the last of them) were accepted by their speakers as mature languages, and as Alain Dieckhoff has argued, served as a "symbolic resource that signifies the primordial unity of the group."[34]

Although Yiddishists had many models for their program from which to draw, this book demonstrates how they had to overcome a series of obstacles that threatened to forestall their movement. Try as they might, Yiddish activists were forced to recognize that nationalism depended on a claim of autochthony, and Yiddish was clearly a language of a people without a homeland.[35] It had countless dialects and a vocabulary drawn from various languages, its speakers were scattered across the globe, and it had neither a defined structure nor a standard grammar. To reconcile its incongruent elements, activists developed a set of ideological assumptions and apologies for Yiddish. Yiddishists posited Yiddish as the most authentic language of the Jewish people, as the primary marker of the Jewish nation, as a key to unlocking its unwritten past, and as a justification for its political and cultural independence. Its philological exploration, classification, and standardization were therefore seen as among the most essential steps to bring about the necessary national "awakening." As Ber Borochov declared at the outset of his manifesto for Yiddish research, "of all sciences, philology plays the greatest role in the national revival of oppressed peoples."[36]

Drawing from primary source material as well as from recent scholarship, chapter 1 argues for the centrality of the 1905 Revolution in the creation of modern Jewish politics and culture and explains how the events of 1903–17 prompted a shift within Russian-Jewish leadership. It demonstrates how a new group of Jewish activists—the generation of 1905—attempted to liberate themselves by following the model set by other minority groups in the empire, and agitated for an array of radical socialist and nationalist platforms to settle questions of their legal, economic, and territorial status. It further reveals how, with the failure of the 1905 Revolution, many party activists turned with varying degrees of ambiguity toward the creation of a new national culture grounded in the Yiddish and Hebrew languages.

Chapter 2 sharpens this focus to discuss the uses and perceptions of Yiddish in the late nineteenth century, and to explain how the rapid expansion of Yiddish during the years 1903 to 1917 led to the creation of the new Yiddish science. Most often an object of scorn by eighteenth and nineteenth-century Jewish intellectuals, Yiddish only gradually came to be accepted as a language capable of expressing serious works of literature, pedagogy, and critical study. In the final decades of the nineteenth century, when Jewish leaders, activists, and intellectuals turned to Yiddish, it was most often with reluctance and out of necessity, as a way to spread their visions of enlightenment or revolution in the language of their audience. In doing so, they inadvertently expanded the range of what was possible to express in it. When a new generation of politicized youth began to consider the possibility of creating a viable, secular, modern Jewish culture out of Yiddish in the days leading up to the 1905 Revolution, there was already a small but powerful body of sophisticated works that could be employed to substantiate new intellectual, cultural, and political initiatives, and lay the foundations for a scholarly discipline dedicated to the language.

Chapters 3, 4, and 5 are biographically based discussions of the pre–1917 Revolution works of three prominent Yiddish activists, figures whom the Yiddish scholar Max Weinreich (1894–1969) once referred to as part of the "small core" that formed the new Yiddish scholarship: the literary critic Shmuel Niger (1883–1955), the Marxist Zionist leader Ber Borochov, and the linguist Nokhem Shtif.[37] By examining their work in the Yiddish press to transform the language, these chapters illuminate the passage of Yiddish through its different phases, and personify the various (and competing) ideologies that promoted its maturation. In focusing on these figures' early activity on behalf of Yiddish, these chapters show how for many of its first practitioners, the turn to *Yidishe visnshaft* was a consequence of their experiences in the 1905 Revolution.

Chapter 3 describes the literary critic Shmuel Niger's initial attempts to establish a new Yiddish literary canon, and to bring to fruition ever more artistic forms of the language. Niger, the most influential figure in modern Yiddish letters, played a role in almost every significant literary movement in Yiddish, from the beginning of the twentieth century until his death in 1955. More than any other member of the generation of Jewish leaders who came of age with the 1905 Russian Revolution, Niger was responsible for establishing many of the earliest forums for modernist Yiddish literature, and taught his audiences how to be sophisticated readers of it. He launched the organs in which many early Yiddish scholars first published their research, and brought the new discipline a much needed measure of legitimacy and support. From the 1905 Revolution until his arrival to the United States in 1919, Niger was guided by a three fold program for Yiddish culture: (1) overturning the assimilatory legacy of the Haskalah, (2) promoting sophisticated forms of literature that would serve the interests of the Jewish nation, and (3) forging that path by incorporating modernist literary forms into Yiddish. As both a strategic and ideological move in an era of great government censorship and growing Jewish national consciousness, Niger directed much of the Yiddish renaissance through his literary activism.

Chapter 4 is an examination of one of the best known figures in the 1905 generation, Ber Borochov. Already famous as the revolutionary who synthesized the seemingly irreconcilable ideologies of Marxism and Zionism,

and who founded the political party Poalei Zion (Workers of Zion), Borochov began to explore the possibilities of continuing with Jewish cultural
work once political avenues were blocked at the end of the failed 1905
Revolution. His essays crowned him as the discipline's chief ideologue,
whose activism brought Yiddish scholarship to a new level of sophistication, established several of its ideological foundations, and linked Yiddish
scholarship back to the revolution. As an alternative to the hagiographical
descriptions that often characterize Borochov's Yiddish activism, this chapter critically engages his efforts to create a scholarly discipline for Yiddish.
In doing so, it demonstrates that, in contrast to the oft-repeated depiction
of Borochov as the lone "pioneer" of Yiddish scholarship, he was in fact
very much a part of—and participant in—the larger social and intellectual
currents that were reshaping the Jewish world in the aftermath of the 1905
Revolution. As much as he was an innovator, Borochov was also a man of
his times, and accepted many of the assumptions of linguistic nationalism.
For Borochov, the study of Yiddish—with the goal of its standardization
and enrichment—was a weapon in the struggle for the Jewish nation.

Chapter 5 is a discussion of the critic, linguist, and literary historian
Nokhem Shtif. Like many of his peers in the generation of Jewish activists,
intellectuals, and artists who came of age with the 1905 Russian Revolution, Shtif advocated a wide range of political and cultural ideologies over
the course of his lifetime including Zionism, Territorialism, Yiddishism,
and Soviet Communism. A discussion of Shtif's work serves as a useful
counterweight to the ideologically charged agendas of Niger and Borochov,
as he (in his early period) insisted that only a rigorous application of the
highest standards of scholarship would provide the necessary legitimacy
to the burgeoning discipline. In spite of his intimate participation in creating the field of modern Yiddish studies, and his involvement with many of
the early important Yiddish journals to appear after the 1905 Revolution,
Shtif's attitude toward his work often placed him sharply at odds with his
fellow language activists, and he regularly moved between the center and
the periphery of the new Yiddish scholarly world. He insisted on inclusiveness during a time of intense partisanship, and refused to relinquish scholarly standards either for the sake of fashionable ideologies or the demands
of the marketplace. More than others in the Yiddishist movement, Shtif

never found a true institutional or ideological home from where he could give full expression to his ideas.

World War I and the 1917 revolutions in Russia forced a complete reordering of Jewish life in Eastern Europe. Once again, Jewish communities were the targets of extreme violence, often on an unprecedented and unimaginable scale. However, as with the 1905 Revolution, the aftermath of violence also brought about new opportunities. In the newly formed Soviet Union and independent state of Poland, *Yidishe visnshaft* at last gained the institutional structure and acceptance for which so many of its adherents had aspired. With government support for their efforts in the USSR, and with the legal right to pursue their cultural initiatives unhindered by government interference in Poland, it appeared for a time that the new science would come to define Jewish life and that a Golden Age of Yiddish culture had begun. For the next two decades, until the destruction of European Jewry and its culture in the Holocaust, Yiddish remained not only a means to access the Jewish past, but also a way to build its future.

1 The Jewish Revolution of 1905

A population of 150 million people, 5.4 million square kilometers
of land in Europe, 17.5 million in Asia. Within this vast space every
epoch of human culture is to be found: from the primeval barbarism
of the northern forests, where people eat raw fish and worship blocks
of wood, to the modern social relations of the capitalist city, where
socialist workers consciously recognize themselves as participants in
world politics and keep a watchful eye on events in the Balkans and on
debates in the German Reichstag. The most concentrated industry in
Europe based on the most backward agriculture in Europe. The most
colossal state apparatus in the world making use of every achievement
of modern technological progress in order to retard the historical
progress of its own country.
                    —Leon Trotsky, *1905*[1]

This chapter is a discussion of the modernization of Russian Jewry during
the late nineteenth and early twentieth centuries. In particular, it demonstrates how a combination of heightened emancipatory expectations and
crushing anti-Jewish violence during the years 1903–7 drove many Jewish political activists in the postrevolutionary period to concentrate their
efforts toward a variety of Jewish national cultural projects based upon the
Yiddish and Hebrew languages. After describing the 1905 Revolution and
its importance to Russia's various minority groups, it focuses on Russia's
Jewish population, which had been heavily invested in the 1905 Revolution's success and which suffered greatly with its demise. It ends by pointing to three consequences of the 1905 Revolution that were vital to the
formation of modern Yiddish culture: (1) the appearance of Jewish political
parties that tried to create a synthesis of the competing demands of nation
and class; (2) the coming of age of a new generation of Jewish leaders; and

(3) the new Jewish culture that was shaped by fractious and tendentious questions of language. This discussion provides a foundation for an exploration in chapter 2 of the contours of the Yiddish literary culture that materialized in the years 1903–17 and led to the formation of *Yidishe visnshaft*.

The impact of the 1905 Russian Revolution on the subsequent development of East European Jewry has been largely overlooked by scholars. While the destructive events of those years have been told in compelling detail by historians such as Shlomo Lambroza, Edward H. Judge, and Robert Weinberg, their many long-lasting effects only recently have become a topic of study.[2] On the whole, broad surveys of Russian-Jewish history typically abridge their discussions of this period, pausing only to linger on the suffering and despair brought on by the events while not reflecting on the hope and optimism that was also present.[3] Such studies often ignore how the pogroms also prompted tens of thousands of Jews to join self-defense organizations, unions, and revolutionary political groups, how the impact of the revolution led to an explosion of Jewish nationalist sentiment, and how it forced the Zionist movement to reorient its focus on the immediate, material needs of Jews within the empire.

One reason that the impact of the 1905 Revolution on the modernization of Russian Jewry is often downplayed by historians may be because it falls between the seemingly more dramatic 1881–82 pogroms that destroyed Jewish communities throughout the Russian empire and the 1917 Revolution that finally emancipated them. This neglect is misguided, however, for the years 1903–17 were the time when Jewish radical political ideologies previously advanced by an elite few became mass movements with tens of thousands of adherents. This is not to assert that 1905 was somehow a more critical turning point in Russian-Jewish history than were the years 1881–82 or 1917, or to diminish the importance of those two historical moments. Nevertheless, it is useful to understand the 1905 Revolution as the time when several of the emancipatory ideologies developing in the final quarter of nineteenth-century Russia became comprehensive political programs that would be put to the test in the Soviet Union and Poland after 1917. If the pogroms of 1881–82 dealt "a heavy blow to the hitherto prevailing faith in the onward march of liberalism as the natural solution to the Jewish question," as Frankel asserts, it was the revolution of 1905 that solidified the nationalist socialist agenda as the dominant emancipationist model of Russian Jewry for the first half of the twentieth century.[4]

Examining the impact of the 1905 Revolution on the Yiddish language not only provides a type of "missing link" between 1881–82 and 1917, but it also forces a reconsideration of the overall development of Yiddish culture and highlights the revolution's central role in the creation of *Yidishe visnshaft*. Yiddish did not "leap" from being the ideology of a select group of visionaries to the cultural basis of interwar Eastern European Jewry. Instead, its function and significance was transformed during the 1905 Revolution and the decade that followed, during which time there developed a bold new confidence in the ability of Yiddish to serve as a unifying principle upon which to assert a national identity.

The tension that finally exploded in January 1905 had been building for decades. Since the ascension of Alexander III (1881–1894) to the throne in March of 1881, the tsarist administration had been on the defensive: threatened by a small coterie of terrorists who had assassinated his father, challenged by an increasingly powerful liberal opposition who believed that the autocracy was a barrier to the empire's economic and political modernization, and kept in check by reactionaries who strove to undo the liberalizing changes already underway. As the nineteenth century came to a close, his successor, Nicholas II (1894–1917), appeared less a benevolent ruler sitting above the ideological fray than as one of the many forces vying for power, and he was at a loss whether to repress his opponents or to acquiesce to their demands. The regime had fallen out of favor with nearly every aspect of society: nobles saw their political authority, social privileges, and economic might diminished; artisans, peasants, and workers suffered the geographical displacement and economic pains of industrialization; students and the intelligentsia increasingly adhered to more Marxist positions; the growing middle class agitated for "Western-style" economic and political liberalization; and Russia's various ethnic minorities clamored for cultural and political freedoms.[5]

In comparison to its neighbors, the empire's situation was no better. The wars Russia had fought in the second half of the nineteenth century scarcely helped to modernize and industrialize the economy. In fact, they made a bad economic situation worse. Russia was faced with monetary shortages, painfully meager railway lines, and little capacity for mass industrialization. Despite its vast population and size—the empire of 129 million inhabitants stretched from the Carpathians to the Pacific, encompassing 8.6 million square miles—its diminished capacity for war greatly reduced its influence on the world stage and weakened its position in the rapid geopolitical reshuffling occurring between Germany, France, and Britain. Since Russia's loss in the Crimean War in 1856, its foreign policy was driven by a desire to live up to the glories of its imperial past but was constrained by its actual economic and military might. Its expansion farther into Asia, the building of the Trans-Siberian Railway, and the push to modernize its industry, railroads, and military in the last decade of the nineteenth century served only to stress the economy rather than to expand it. The 1904–5 war with Japan, one that Nicholas II had hoped to avoid, further demonstrated that the government's power was weakening and that its military was antiquated.[6]

The spark for the 1905 upheavals occurred on what has become known as "Bloody Sunday" (January 9, 1905), when police fired upon a crowd marching in a peaceful, gentle demonstration during which they hoped to present the tsar with a list of grievances. Reports of the number of dead and wounded vary wildly, but conservative estimates indicate that one hundred thirty were killed and nearly three hundred were wounded. More importantly, in the immediate aftermath, the number of dead was widely thought to have been in the thousands.[7] Unlike prior expressions of public discontent, the protest movement that rose in response was not confined to groups of radicalized students and intellectuals, but was infused with popular support from throughout the empire, including heavy participation from Jewish self-defense organizations that joined the strikes, and took part in street battles with police. From across the political spectrum, condemnation of the government was nearly universal. Hundreds of thousands of workers went on strike and bloody riots quickly followed. Ad hoc political organizations were formed by students who boycotted their classes and plotted with workers' organizations. Revolutionary figures who were soon to become household names, such as V. I. Lenin, Leon Trotsky (1879–1940), and Rosa Luxemburg (1871–1919), found their political footing during this time. A strikingly large number of those arrested, nearly one-third, were Jews, and it was widely believed that the level of Jewish participation was even greater.[8]

The Russian army, with much of its forces thousands of miles away in a fruitless war in the East, was not able to respond effectively, and the rebellion quickly gained in strength. It soon became clear to Nicholas II (with the counsel of his newly appointed prime minister Sergey Witte) that concessions were needed to halt the unrest. After nine months of havoc, the tsar reluctantly responded with liberalizing measures. On October 17, he issued a manifesto that granted basic freedoms of speech, assembly, and association, as well as reconvened the Duma. Further declarations abolished the preliminary censorship of publications and expanded suffrage. However, rather than placate his opponents, the October Manifesto emboldened them further and also sparked an angry reaction from those loyal to the tsar. The following days saw pogroms against Russia's Jews with nearly nine hundred killed and thousands wounded in at least six hundred and fifty pogroms.[9] The following year brought more violence and turmoil as the number of mutinies, assassinations, peasant uprisings, mass arrests, and repressive government actions increased. Attacks on Jews seemingly came from every sector of society, including the most destitute peasants, the loosely organized reactionary group known as the Black Hundreds, industrial workers, members of the middle class, and finally, from agencies within the government itself. Dubnow graphically portrayed the cycle of despair and hope in December 1905:

> We are standing on a volcano that has already swallowed tens of thousands of Jewish victims, and the crater is still smoking. . . . People are gripped by great confusion. . . . The great mass of refugees has taken the old path out of the Russian Egypt . . . to the promised land of America. . . . And now, as Russia, about to become a land of freedom, has not ceased to be a land of pogroms.[10]

The new constitution reestablished the Duma and implemented a two-house system, with the lower house to be entirely elected. At first, radical Jewish leaders encouraged their followers to boycott the elections on the grounds that voting restrictions left most Jewish workers in the Pale disenfranchised. In the end, however, twelve Jews were elected as deputies, because of the support for the elections by Jewish liberal leaders.[11] The Duma immediately took decisive actions that included calling for the abolishment of the upper house, and for a series of increased powers. This Duma was short-lived, however. The tsar dissolved it in July, just three months after it convened.

The second Duma, convened in February 1907, was even more radical than the first, and Jewish representation was reduced from twelve to four deputies. For the new election, Jewish revolutionary groups joined in the campaigns in earnest, hoping to propel the revolution from this front. Just four months later, however, an impatient tsar again dissolved the Duma, and issued a new set of electoral guidelines that diminished the might of the radical and liberal parties, and effectively put the legislative body under his control. A period of harsh reaction and reprisals began, and thousands of dissidents were executed or imprisoned. Consequently, the radical parties lost much of their strength and were neither able to capitalize on their limited advances nor turn the weakness of the tsar into a stepping-stone for the fundamental transformation of Russian society they envisioned. Far from implementing a solution to the systematic ills plaguing Russia—the inefficiency of the autocratic regime, the growing restlessness of its minority groups, its disastrous economic system—the "Ambiguous Revolution" offered but a decade's respite from a complete reordering of society.[12] As the historian Isaac Deutscher characterized it, "the year 1907 was the year of the Tsar's revenge."[13]

The 1905 Revolution delivered few tangible political freedoms to Russia's ethnic minorities, which had long been resisting the empire's attempts to deemphasize cultural distinctions and to combat burgeoning national movements. Nevertheless, for many minority groups, the 1905 upheavals reflected a high point in their emancipatory expectations and dreams of national liberation. Even before the time of Catherine the Great (1762–1796), Russia had attempted to unify the various ethnic and cultural groups under its control and to promote a "one-Russia" policy. According to Geoffrey Hosking, the plan of the tsarist regime was to forge them into a cohesive whole via the "supreme persona" of the tsar.[14] The policy sought to Russify the empire's minorities, "first by administrative integration, then by inculcating in each of them as far as possible the language, religion, and culture of Russia, leaving their own traditions as subsidiary, colorful ethnographic remnants rather than active social forces."[15] The strategy was dependent on highly malleable populaces, ready to forfeit their own group identities and to welcome Russia's. This was easier in earlier times when Russians made up a majority of the inhabitants of the empire and before national sentiments began to cohere among its smaller minority groups. By the end of the nineteenth century, however, with Russian expansionism stretched to its limits and nationalist movements at their peak, Russification was an impossible goal. Complicating matters further, the census of 1897 only confirmed what had been suspected for some time: at only 44 percent of the total population, ethnic Russians no longer dominated the empire.[16] This made the facade of "one Russia" all the more apparent, and from the point of view of the authorities, it made the need to crack down on divisive ethnic nationalisms all the greater.

In fact, despite efforts to unite Russia's populations under a policy of single rule, political realities dictated that its various minority groups were governed differently from one another. The level of self-governance of any particular region was typically a consequence of how and under what terms it came under Russia's dominion. Finland, for example, which joined the empire in the 1808–9 war against Sweden, was permitted a measure of self-governance unmatched anywhere else in the empire. There were separate laws for the Finns, who were allowed to hold elections, to run their own parliament, and to maintain their own military and civilian forces. At the end of the nineteenth century when Russia attempted to rein in some of these freedoms during the period of reaction, it was met by resistant Finns whose national sentiment had been allowed to develop with only slight imperial hindrance. Their steadfastness forced government authorities to soften their stance. In the wake of the 1905 Revolution, the tsar reformed the Finnish Diet, extended the franchise by a factor of ten, and granted Finnish women the right to vote.[17]

Poland, by contrast, was the target of some of the harshest policies of Russification. It was forcibly brought into the empire with the partitions of 1772, 1793, and 1795, which split the once-cohesive kingdom between Russia, Habsburg Austria, and Prussia. Poles in general were hostile to and resentful of their Russian rulers. Polish leaders and intellectuals most often looked west for their cultural influences and political ideologies, and were highly resistant to Russian political and cultural hegemony. While Alexander I (1801–1825) initially granted his Polish lands a broad measure of autonomy, he retained ultimate power for himself. The demonstrations and marches that followed over the next several decades culminated in a series of revolts and insurrections, the most notable of them occurring in 1830–31 and 1863. After the 1863 uprising, Russia abandoned its policy of limited autonomy for Poland. For the rest of the century, Russia committed the region to a program of severe Russification. Poland's governing institutions were forcibly incorporated into the imperial framework; church property was taken into state custody; the Russian language was required in all state business; classes in schools and universities were conducted in Russian; and its governmental affairs were now directed from St. Petersburg. Following the 1905 Revolution, Poland's last vestiges of sovereignty further diminished as even harsher measures on their cultural development restricted Polish national aspirations to a greater degree.[18]

Russia's treatment of its Ukrainian population is of particular interest to Jewish historians, not only because of the legacy of the pogroms that Jews periodically suffered at the hands of Ukrainians, but also because the Russian policies enacted against Ukrainians in the latter half of the nineteenth century often mirrored those taken against the Jews, albeit toward opposite ends.[19] Whereas policies against Jewish cultural development in the post-1881 period were designed to curtail Jewish participation in Russian affairs and to encourage their emigration abroad, in the case of the Ukrainians, measures were enacted to keep them fully within the Russian fold. Because Ukrainians numbered as many as 23 million (18 percent of the empire's total population), there was great incentive among Russian authorities to deny Ukrainians their claim as a nation deserving of minority rights. Suppressing their distinctiveness permitted ethnic Russians to maintain the farce of declaring themselves a statistical majority of the over-all population. Because the Ukrainian population was large enough to pose a threat to Russian cultural hegemony, the Ukraine was the site of some of the most repressive regulations in service of the tsar's goal to keep the "Little Russians" Russian, and to prevent them from developing an autono-mous national identity.

Ukrainian national consciousness began to cohere near the end of the first half of the nineteenth century, as a small group of intellectuals and authors began to champion their mythic, folkloric past.[20] By the late 1840s Russian authorities felt threatened enough by the budding move-ment to take action against Ukrainian cultural nationalists by shutting down their organizations and exiling the movement's leaders to Austrian Galicia. The Valuev Edict of 1863 (censuring the Ukrainian press) dealt a more severe blow to efforts at national consciousness, as did Alexander II's (1855–1881) order in 1875 to create a commission investigating the threat of increased Ukrainophilism, and the 1876 Ems ukase that prohibited pub-lishing or importing works in Ukrainian.[21] To justify their position that Ukrainians were ethnically a part of Greater Russia, authorities argued that the Ukrainian language was only a dialect of Russian. The commission enacted another round of severe legislation against Ukrainian publications and imposed the Cyrillic alphabet and Russian orthography on all printed materials. In 1876 the Ukrainian theater was banned, the press was closed, and a strict policy of Russification was enacted. The remaining leaders of the new movement fled across the border to Galicia, and did their best to keep national sentiments alive. Although Ukrainians did not openly rebel against these harsh measures as did the Poles, the ideology of Ukrainian national culture was bound up with desires for political independence.[22] It was only with the uprisings of 1905 that the Russian Academy classified Ukrainian as a distinct language, and as with Yiddish and Hebrew, the government relaxed restrictions on Ukrainian publishing.[23]

Considering the wide range of ethnicities and the near-total absence of real political power for any minority group in the empire, it is initially striking that the events of 1905 had such a particularly profound impact upon the Jewish community. In many respects, the situation of the Jews in Russia was similar to that of all other minorities: they had no recognized rights as an autonomous group, their cultural development was hindered by the government, and for much of their time under tsarist rule, they were subject to harsh polices of Russification. Despite these similarities, the situation of the Jews was distinct in many regards. Most notably, they were members of a religious group that was often the target of violence by the non-Jews around them, making them among the most vulnerable of populations. They were highly urban (more than 80 percent lived in cities and towns), had no contiguous territory to call their own, and had a difficult time disavowing the centuries-old charge that they were aliens wherever they lived.[24] In the modern period, this was often perceived as a threat to their host population's national aspirations. Jews were spread far and wide across the empire, despite an irregularly enforced requirement that they had to live in the area along Russia's western rim called the Pale of Settlement, where they never accounted for more than 12 percent of the region's population but were highly concentrated in cities. They had no tradition of working the land, many dressed in clothing different from their neighbors, and they spoke a language that was incomprehensible to non-Jews. So many Jews were disillusioned with both the regime overseeing them and—of equal importance—their neighbors alongside of them that an entire generation of intellectuals and activists was prompted to bring about a fundamental change in their status in the empire.

Until the last decades of the nineteenth century, Russian authorities were most often unconcerned with the small number of Jews in their midst, resulting in the government adopting erratic and often contradictory strategies for ruling them.[25] As Hans Rogger has noted, "Jewish policy wavered between encouraging assimilation by selective concessions, . . . to protect[ing] the nation from Jewish alleged exploitation and intrigue."[26] Policies ranged from inconsistent and often brutal attempts at incorporating them into the empire by "productivizing" them to efforts at isolating them to encourage their emigration. Jews were typically forbidden to own land, their internal governing structures were dismantled, and for a time their boys were sent off to special military units in the hope of converting them to the church and weakening the overall community. Until 1905, Jewish presses were heavily censored, nonreligious Yiddish- and Hebrew-language publishing and cultural institutions were most often banned, special taxes were imposed upon Jews, and their religious practices and communal institutions were restricted by the state. In short, although often ignored, when Jews were paid attention to, they were considered a nuisance to the state and an obstacle to its unification and dominance on the world stage. Heinz-Dietrich Löwe has pointed out that as Russia attempted to modernize itself at the end of the nineteenth century, Jews were targeted by the reactionary right as agents of the social and economic change that was undermining its power.[27] Efforts by Russian authorities to settle the "Jewish question" were caught up in the conflict between those who wished to look to the "Enlightened West" and those who wanted to develop a distinctly Slavic path of development. The inability to solve this tension often resulted in the cruelest of stances toward its Jews.

The pogroms of 1881–82 put an end to any wavering in Russian policy.[28] The assassination of Alexander II on March 1 by the revolutionary populist group Narodnaia Volia (People's Will) left the government in a state of shock and terrified at the prospect of further social unrest. Once assaults broke out six weeks later in the city of Elizavetgrad, they quickly spread throughout the Pale. By the end forty Jews were dead, hundreds of Jewish women were raped, and thousands were injured in a reported 259 pogroms. The pogromists, protesting against "Jewish exploitation" and supposed complicity with the terrorists, were acting on a rumor (shown later to be false) that the new tsar had given permission to attack Jews in retaliation for the assassination. This belief was supported by the inaction that characterized the local authorities' response to the outbreak of violence as well as by the widespread perception that the pogroms were occurring spontaneously across the empire.

While recent scholarship has disproved the oft-repeated charge that tsarist authorities actively sponsored the pogroms, the response of the government was to place most of the responsibility onto the Jews themselves and to blame their alleged exploitative business practices for the violence.[29] Under the direction of Minister of the Interior N. P. Ignatiev, the government enacted a new round of anti-Jewish legislation. Under the new "May Laws" of 1882, Jews were forbidden to conduct business on Sunday mornings and Christian holidays, to build new homes outside of cities and towns, and to buy land in the countryside. As John D. Klier and Shlomo Lambroza have pointed out, these laws gave tremendous latitude to local authorities, who often enforced them with great arbitrariness, leading to further Jewish insecurity.[30]

Along with the Jews' increasingly fragile legal status, their economic life dramatically declined in the last decades of the nineteenth century, and millions were driven into the newly identified urban working class or outright poverty.[31] Despite the presence of a large proportion of Jewish dealers in the liquor and alcohol trades, as well as a substantial number of Jewish factory owners, Jewish workers suffered particularly dire consequences from the growth of large manufacturing plants. They tended to work in smaller, less profitable manufacturing shops, such as food and clothing, and were unattractive to factory owners because their day of rest fell on Saturday rather than Sunday. As the nineteenth century came to a close, increasing numbers of Jews were living at a subsistence level. By 1898, nearly one out of five Jewish families was looking to welfare organizations for help.[32]

The widespread conviction that the empire had once and for all decided to reject its Jews and their severe economic situation forced Jews to consider a new set of options on how best to respond. While some (especially those permitted to live outside of the Pale) redoubled their efforts to promote Jewish integration into Russian society, the first choice for many was to leave the empire altogether.[33] From 1881 to 1914, well over 2 million Jews emigrated, mostly to the United States, but also to England, France, Germany, Palestine, and Argentina. Furthermore, during this period there was an upsurge in nationalistic movements with organizations such as the Am Olam (The Eternal Nation), Hibbat Zion (Lovers of Zion), and the Bilu (an acronym based on a verse from Isaiah, *Beit Ya'akov Lekhu Ve-nelkha*," (Let the house of Jacob go). Members aligned with these groups eventually formed much of the core of the Zionist Congresses that began in 1897. Along with increased participation of Jewish youth in the Russian and Polish Social Democratic movements, this time also marked the beginning of Russian-Jewish socialist organizations such as the Vilna Group, the precursor to the Jewish Labor Bund. Founded in Vilna in 1897, the Bund claimed the exclusive right to agitate among Jewish workers.[34] By mid-1903, it was the largest mass movement in Russia, claiming a membership over thirty thousand.[35]

If most Russian scholars point to the events of Bloody Sunday as the beginning of a chain of events that culminated in the 1905 upheavals, the revolutionary tide began to turn for the Jews on Easter Sunday in 1903 in the city of Kishinev. The capital city of the Moldavian province of Bessarabia and home to fifty thousand Jews (nearly half of the city's population), Kishinev had been primed for an anti-Jewish assault by its popular tabloid newspaper, *Bessarabets*, which published provocative anti-Jewish essays for months preceding the attack.[36] Articles called for sacking Jewish workers from government jobs, demanded that they convert to Christianity, and featured headlines such as DEATH TO THE JEWS! and CRUSADE AGAINST THE HATED RACE! On the heels of this campaign came an accusation of the blood libel, the charge that Jews secretly murder Christian children and use their blood to make matzah, unleavened Passover bread.

The press campaign, the blood libel, and rumors that Tsar Nicholas II had given his permission to begin assaults on Jews combined to create an atmosphere ripe for explosion. The spark finally came on Easter Sunday (April 19) in Chuflinskii Square in the southeastern part of the city when a large number of people gathered after mass and several of them harassed the few Jews who happened to be present, "shouting, as if it were a joke, 'Beat the Yids!'"[37] People began to throw rocks at Jewish homes and soon, many smaller groups (as many as two dozen) broke off from the square, entered Jewish neighborhoods, and proceeded to vandalize, loot, and scavenge. On the second and third days of the pogrom, the situation grew direr as crowds moved through Jewish neighborhoods and assaulted the residents, some of whom had begun to organize in self-defense. Many Jews were beaten, others were raped, and dozens were murdered. The brutalities included a boy's tongue being cut out, another being blinded, nails being driven into the heads of live victims, and some women having their breasts cut off. The level of violence was so extreme that, in the end, fifty-one people were dead (all but two of them were Jews), over four hundred people were wounded, and nearly one-third of all buildings in the city sustained damage.[38]

World opinion was unanimous in its condemnation, and the Kishinev pogroms quickly came to symbolize Jewish persecution in Russia. Most of the protests targeted the Russian government, which was caught off guard both by the pogroms and the ferocity of global reaction. Press reports from around the world attacked the long legacy of anti-Jewish hatred in Russia and accused authorities of not intervening until the rioters had inflicted most of their damage. Others condemned the government for allowing the press to stir up anti-Jewish hatred and for inciting the violence itself. The government's response ranged from deflecting blame for the attacks onto the Jews themselves to enacting a series of cosmetic reforms designed to placate international opinion.

In the wake of the deadliest century in human history and the near total elimination of Jews from Europe, the events of 1903 may seem comparatively mild. However, for its time, Kishinev was the site of the bloodiest attacks against Jews in modern history. The pogrom quickly assumed a position of monumental importance to Jewish groups around the world and prompted waves of emigration abroad.[39] One scholar has even argued that Kishinev became the "paradigm" by which the world viewed Russia's treatment of the Jews and by which many Jews viewed their own impotence.[40] For the historian Dubnow, the violence that began in 1881 and continued until Kishinev was a lesson to the Jewish people of the need for self-sufficiency because of their isolation in the world. He wrote in May 1903:

Jewish hearts still ache from the pain of the frightful pogroms that passed over us and our eyes are still dim from a profusion of tears; but at the same time a new stream of energy calling for action has become evident. There is a passionate current of national spirit such as stood us in good stead generation after generation in moments of severe crisis. The latest blow we received found us better prepared psychologically than we were during the pogroms of 1881. What can we still expect after twenty-two years in which "each and every day killed a hope and a dream?" . . . The past decades have taught us that our fate depends not on our environment but on ourselves, on our will and our national effort. The new pogroms have engraved the watchword "self-help" in flaming letters on the Jewish nation. It is as if a powerful electric charge had passed through the body of our humiliated people.[41]

The "self-help" manifested itself in a variety of ways, including the creation of armed Jewish defense organizations, emigrant societies, banking associations, worker cooperatives, educational networks, trade schools, presses, and, as will be shown, a new stance toward their spoken language.[42]

The one point around which all Jews were united was profound shock at the ferocity and magnitude of the killings, although each group tended to understand the violence in light of its own particular stance on the "Jewish question." For liberals who generally favored a high level of Jewish integration into Russian culture and politics on an individual basis, the attacks prompted them to organize in defense of Jewish interests and to speak on behalf of Jews on the whole.[43] They took the lead in disseminating information about the pogroms and about the overall declining situation of Jews in an attempt to put foreign pressure on the Russian government to protect its Jewish subjects. At the same time, they provided the legal defense for those Jews who were prosecuted as instigators of the pogroms. This was followed by similar calls by Dubnow, the Hebrew essayist Ahad Ha'am (pen name of Asher Ginzburg, 1856–1927), the poet Chaim Nachman Bialik (1873–1934), and others.

The Jewish Labor Bund's responses to the attacks in Kishinev and especially to others that occurred in the city of Gomel six months later marked the high point in their campaign for Jewish self-defense and was one of the first times in the modern period that organized groups of Jews took up arms against their attackers. The Bund's membership swelled, making it the largest of all revolutionary organizations in the empire.[44] For over half a decade the Bund had been organizing Jewish workers and had earned wide respect from Jews across the Pale of Settlement, especially as it began to agitate on behalf of Jewish national rights. As a result of the Bund's dominant role in the Jewish self-defense movement, the breadth of its organizational skills, and its members' willingness to battle the police and army, it became the model of organization a new set of Jewish political groups tried to emulate.

By contrast, the mainstream Zionists, who had long been insisting on the futility of Jewish diasporic existence in their efforts to resettle Jews elsewhere, paradoxically fared much worse in the immediate post-Kishinev period.[45] From its founding, the movement had focused nearly all of its attention on the issue of resettlement and was thus ill prepared to deal with the immediacy of the crisis at home. Their leader, Theodor Herzl (1860–1904), who would die just a year later, would soon become enmeshed in the Uganda imbroglio (when he proposed that East Africa be considered as the site for a Jewish state) and was not in a position to provide the material assistance needed to help Jews on the ground.[46] His meetings in August 1903 with Count Witte and Interior Minister V. K. von Plehve (assassinated in 1904 by the Jewish revolutionary and police agent Evno Azef) amounted to little—other than generating a great deal of criticism among many of Herzl's young supporters for negotiating with the enemy.[47]

The 1903 pogroms exacerbated a series of tensions already present within the Zionist movement as a younger generation, inspired by revolutionary and socialist ideologies, agitated for a leftward shift. Their ideological leader was Nachman Syrkin (1868–1924), who sought a synthesis between socialist and Zionist ideals to avoid reproducing class divisions in a future Jewish state.[48] Before the Kishinev pogrom, Syrkin was a relatively minor figure within the overall Zionist movement. In its immediate aftermath, however, he became one of its most powerful leaders as he inspired Jewish youths with his calls to transform Zionism into a liberation movement that would defend Jewish communities and find a territorial solution to their physical and economic woes.[49]

A host of Jewish student radical groups that had been active in the first years of the twentieth century also began to organize on a larger scale in the wake of the Kishinev pogroms. Bearing names such as Poalei Zion and Kadima (Forward) a generation of youths agitated for revolutionary changes within the larger Zionist movement. As the activist Moshe Zilberfarb (1876–1934) recounted:

> The Kishinev pogrom (1903), which came like a thunderbolt on a hot day, made many of us aware. Indeed, it tore open our eyes and forced us to look around at what was happening in the world. Those of us who had maintained that the Poalei Zion must not take up the revolutionary struggle against the autocracy in order that it not waste nationalist energy, which must be collected and conserved on behalf of the demands of the national ideal, got a lecture from the Kishinev pogrom that national

energy can in no way be "collected and conserved" while a people with a
bent back receive bloody blows from the pogromist-regime.[50]

During Passover 1903 (while the Kishinev pogrom was occurring) a
group of activists including Zilberfarb, the future failed assassin Pinkhes
Dashevsky (1879–1934), and the future Yiddish linguist and architect of
the YIVO Nokhem Shtif gathered in the city of Rovno to organize a mass
meeting of fellow left-wing Zionists. The result was the creation of the Vozrozhdenie (Rebirth) group in September 1903. This group, which counted
among its members several of the future founders of *Yidishe visnshaft,*
including Shtif, the future demographer Jacob Lestschinsky (1876–1966),
Shmuel Niger, later known for his Yiddish literary critic work, and Zelig
Kalmanovitsh (1885–1944), who went on to become a leading philologist/
literary historian, hoped to create an alternative for Jewish activists frustrated with the Zionists' lack of a response to the rising Jewish hatred in
Russia, the inattention of the Bund to the cause of Jewish national autonomy, and the Russian socialists' demand for assimilation.[51] While Vozrozhdenie activists advanced the long-term goal of resettlement in a Jewish
territory, their short-term solution to the Jewish problem was to promote
Jewish cultural autonomy and the creation of a Jewish parliament within
Russia. They argued for the right of Russia's ethnic minorities to control
their own national affairs, schools, communal organizations, newspapers,
publishing houses, and separate national assemblies—and to do so in their
own national languages, and by whatever means possible. Although the
Vozrozhdenie group lasted only a brief period, it reflected the revolutionary
disposition of a generation anxious for change, one that drew as much from
the nationalism of Zionists in their calls for Jewish political and cultural
autonomy as it did the Marxism of the Bund and the Russian Social-Dem-
ocratic Workers' Party (RSDWP) in its calls for a socialist society. Furthermore, the group helped to lay the groundwork for a set of new political
parties to be launched once the 1905 Revolution was fully underway.

Despite the unprecedented violence and limited achievements of the 1905
Revolution, three consequences were crucial to the subsequent development

of Yiddish culture and *Yidishe visnshaft:* (1) the formation of new Jewish political parties that positioned themselves ideologically between the Zionists and the Bundists by synthesizing nationalist and socialist thought; (2) the coming of age of a new generation of Jewish leaders who made nationalist socialism the dominant ideological force among Russian-Jewish activists; and (3) a commitment by many within this generation to continue developing Jewish national culture in the Yiddish language once political opportunities to further the revolution were blocked.

Reflecting criticisms that the Bund was slow to incorporate a strong national component to its platform, the Zionists slow to confront the material needs of Russian-Jewish workers, and the Jewish liberal parties timid on the issue of the tsar's overthrow, several new parties arose during the 1905 Revolution to redefine Jewish politics.[52] With very few exceptions, the first practitioners of *Yidishe visnshaft* were aligned for a time with these new parties that sought to position themselves as incorporating the revolutionary message into their vision of the Jewish nation.[53]

The first party to position itself between the Bund and the Zionists was the Zionist Socialist Worker's Party, known by its Russian initials S.S.[54] Its members were to an extent "disciples" of Syrkin (who had been close to the Vozrozhdenie group) but were more dogmatic in their Marxism. Formed in Odessa in February 1905, the S.S. argued that Jews needed their own independent territory to develop the necessary class consciousness to create a Jewish proletariat and to overthrow the capitalist system. The S.S. deemed misguided the Bund's platform that called for Jewish cultural rights and instead limited their demands to calling for equal rights for Jews and their languages. Likewise, S.S. members differed with other Zionists on the question of Jewish colonization of Palestine. They argued that what was needed for Jews was territorial concentration wherever viable—and saw the general Zionists' attachment to Palestine as a frivolous form of Romantic nationalism.[55]

The second of these parties—and the most enduring—was the Jewish Social Democratic Workers' Party—Poalei Zion, whose primary theorist and leader was Borochov.[56] In early 1906, the Poalei Zion broke off from the mainstream Zionists out of disenchantment with the movement's inattention to the immediate concerns of Russian Jews and its preoccupation with global diplomacy as a solution to the status of Jews. Like the S.S., the Poalei Zion adopted a Marxist analysis of the Jewish role in the 1905 Revolution, but in contrast to it, its members supported Jewish settlement in Palestine.

The third party to situate themselves between the Bund and the Zionists was the non-Marxist Jewish Socialist Workers' Party, known as the SERP (or the Seymist party).[57] Founded in April 1906, the SERP (and to a lesser degree the S.S.) had grown out of the Vozrozhdenie group and was concerned with the cultivation and preservation of Jewish life in the Diaspora. Its members were inspired in part by the Diasporist Nationalist leader Chaim Zhitlowsky (1865–1943) and saw political and cultural autonomy as the highest goal for Russia's minorities. They argued for the convening of a parliament (a *seym*) for Jews (with the power to tax and to legislate over Jewish affairs) as well as the right to develop their national cultural institutions in Jewish languages. As Jack Jacobs relates, if the S.S. thought the Bund's goals too unrealistic, the SERP thought them "too timid," and demanded that not only cultural autonomy must be granted to Jews but political autonomy as well.[58]

Although these organizations had to conduct their work largely underground, they quickly assumed positions of great stature among Jewish workers. By 1906, their combined official membership was more than 50,000.[59] They were forced to walk a difficult line between agitating for a class struggle that united them with workers from other nations in the empire and simultaneously trying to defend their fellow Jews against pogromists from those very same groups. With the dissolution of the second Duma, however, the fervor for revolution waned and over the next decade, radical political activity—both among Jews and throughout all of Russia—was sharply curtailed. For Jews, "the high point of their emancipatory faith" had reached its zenith in Russia and would never return.[60] Faced with the choice of engaging in nonpolitical cultural work or emigrating abroad, many leaders fled the empire and the membership of the Poalei Zion dropped to 1.2 percent.[61] By 1908, the SERP and S.S. parties had largely disbanded and their members began to look for new opportunities to continue promoting Jewish national culture.[62]

From the distance of a century, the differences between these parties that existed between the Zionists and the Bund appear slight, and the existence of two of them (the S.S. and SERP) too brief to have had any sort of impact on subsequent developments. However, the battles between them (and at times within them) were fiercely fought as each hoped to supplant the authority of the Bund and the Zionists to chart the future of Russian Jews. The influence of these parties during the 1905 Revolution was substantial as they forced the Zionists and Bundists to take one another's positions more seriously, but most important to the history of *Yidishe visnshaft* was that they were also the home to many of the future thinkers, activists, artists, and scholars who would shape Yiddish culture for the next generation.

While it is outside the scope of this study to relate a full accounting of the development and activities of these parties, it is valuable to understand that despite their differences on the definition of Jewish liberation and the means by which to achieve it, the S.S., SERP, and Poalei Zion shared many ideological assumptions and held similar diagnoses of the problems facing the Jews. They rejected the Haskalah and other liberal efforts to integrate Jews into Russian society. Its members argued that the situation of the Jews was abnormal and grew out of Jews' landlessness and political powerlessness. They committed themselves to the overthrow of the autocracy in the hopes of achieving the collective emancipation of the Jews. Although they asserted the primacy and authenticity of the Jewish nation, they linked their national struggle with the struggle to liberate all workers. Finally, they insisted upon the right to advance Jewish national languages in all realms of life.

Along with nationalist socialist Jewish parties, the 1905 Revolutionary era also brought a new generation of leaders to the forefront of Jewish society. The generation of 1905 popularized and radicalized many of the theories advanced by the prior generation and turned them into programs for action. Frankel describes them as

> very young, numerous, possessed of precocious political and organizational experience, confident in itself and its methods, trained by the Marxist method to think in terms of world-historical categories and change, ready to lead whenever the opportunity came.[63]

What separated the 1905 generation of Russian Jews from previous generations was, most of all, a desire for action. As youths, they were less concerned with nurturing their ties to the past than with fleeing the *khey-der*—the famously oppressive religious elementary schools where children were taught the basics of the Torah—for the utopian worlds promised by socialism and nationalism. When they went off to study, it was not to *yeshiva* to master Talmud and Torah, but rather to universities abroad to train (if only for short while) in philosophy, linguistics, sociology, demography, folklore, and history to continue with the national struggle. They formed self-defense units to counter anti-Jewish attacks. This generation was the ideological core of the second aliyah to Palestine and dedicated itself to creating a world through Hebrew labor. They participated in the Marxist parties that hoped to overthrow the tsar and usher in a workers' paradise. They advocated regime change—at times through violence and terror if necessary. Most important to the development of Yiddish culture, this generation included those who did not accept the widely perceived limits of Yiddish and ultimately expanded its uses to all realms of thought and expression.

The generation of 1905 generally did not include great Jewish theoreticians of the stature of Dubnow, Ahad Ha'am, Syrkin, Peretz, or Zhitlowsky. Rather, it was made up of activists who drew their ideas from those who preceded them and injected them with a revolutionary ethos. In their late teens and twenties, and often intensely engaged in the upheavals of 1905, these new leaders included Bundist and Zionist leaders such as Vladimir Medem (1879–1923), Esther Frumkin (1880–1943), Vladimir Jabotinsky, Borochov, Yitzhak Ben-Zvi (1884–1963), and David Ben-Gurion (1886–1973). Rosa Luxemburg, Leon Trotsky, and Adolph Joffe (1883–1927) were among those "non-Jewish Jews" who became major figures in revolutionary politics.[64] Others such as Avrom Reisen (1876–1953), A. Vayter (1878/79–1919), Sholem Asch (1880–1957), Shmuel Niger, Bergelson, and Joseph Opatoshu (1886–1954) were responsible for much of the burgeoning modern Yiddish literary culture, while Bialik, Saul Tchernichowsky (1875–1943), Yosef Haim Brenner (1881–1921), Shmuel Yosef Agnon (1887–1970), and Zalmen Shneour (1887–1959) modernized Hebrew literature. Finally, and most important in terms of this study, this generation also includes those who brought Yiddish and Hebrew to new heights of mature scholarship, such as Jacob Lestschinsky, Noyekh Prilutski, Elias

Tcherikower (1881–1943), Ben-Zion Dinaburg (1884–1973), and Joseph Klausner (1874–1958), in addition to Borochov, Niger, and Shtif.

The relationship of the 1905 generation to the previous one was fraught with complications. On the one hand, during the tumultuous years of 1903–7, many young radicals saw figures like Dubnow and Ahad Ha'am as relics of an increasingly outmoded moderate stance as the 1905 Revolution gained momentum. The members of the Zionist socialist parties quarreled bitterly with the liberal Union for the Attainment of Full Equality for the Jewish People, arguing that it was betraying Jewish national interests by aligning with the liberal Kadet party. By contrast, members of the "transitional generation" tended to view the rank and file of the radical parties as misguided youth who were exchanging their Jewish identities for revolutionary ones and ignoring the real dangers to the Jewish community that would undoubtedly accompany any political upheavals.[65]

"The Incident" involving Hebrew writer Yosef Haim Brenner is an example of this generational tension. As Matthew Hoffman recently recounted, Brenner caused a scandal in the Zionist world when he published his 1910 essay, "Journalism and Literature," in the Hapoel Ha-Tsair (Young Workers Party) paper and concluded that the trend of Russian Jews converting to Christianity was not a problem because it was prompted by legal and material concerns and had no impact on their national affiliation.[66] Furthermore, Brenner asserted the right of each individual Jew to find spiritual inspiration from any source. He expressed his desire "to work and create Jewishly, to speak the Jewish language, to receive spiritual nourishment from our literature, to toil for our free national culture, to defend our national honor and to wage the struggle for our existence."[67] He argued that one's individual religious belief played no role in one's national affiliation or fealty, especially in a world that was rapidly secularizing. Appalled by such recklessness, Ahad Ha'am led the attack, fearing Brenner's stance would be the undoing of the cultural Zionist project he hoped would be centered in Palestine. Ahad Ha'am quickly arranged for a portion of the newspaper's funding to be suspended and tried to align the executive committee of the Hovevei Zion against Brenner.[68] Those who came to Brenner's defense did so less out of agreement with his ideas, but rather in defense of his freedom of expression. However, the battle quickly took the form of a struggle between generations, with the Hovevei Zion widely viewed as trying to control the ideological development of a younger generation by preventing radical expressions of Zionism from taking root among the younger second Aliyah. As Steven Zipperstein writes:

> most of Ahad Ha'am's opponents, even those of Brenner's ilk, remained at least vaguely indebted to him, as was admitted frequently in the debate, ironically for having first taught them the very terms with which they attacked him. Their plaint was thus fueled by a sense of disappointment, by the feeling that someone who had once been respected by them had let them down—someone who was perhaps dated but who had played some role at one time in their intellectual growth.[69]

Along with the formation of the new political parties and the rise of the new generation to power, the third outcome of the 1905 Revolution that was instrumental in setting the context for *Yidishe visnshaft* was the acceleration of "organic work" in the immediate postrevolution era, in particular the fostering of Jewish national culture and institutions in the Yiddish and Hebrew languages.[70] While many leaders of the Jewish revolutionary movement fled the empire to continue their work abroad, others remained and redirected their efforts toward the task of nation-building in the absence of legal autonomy through projects, such as collecting Jewish folklore, organizing educational systems, launching presses, periodicals, and establishing a broad range of self-help organizations. The shift in emphasis from revolutionary activity to cultural productivity followed the model of other nineteenth-century national groups whose attempts at political autonomy were similarly arrested.[71] Despite critics who viewed the turn away from overt revolutionary activity as a betrayal of Jewish working class or national struggles, the seemingly sudden change was less a rupture than it was a shift in emphasis. As Ivan T. Berend has shown, the promotion of national cultures was fundamental to the project of Romantic nationalism across eastern Europe, "Romanticism became a paramount nation-building movement in the East: a newly created literary language fueled romantic arts, poetry, and drama, which joined forces with music, architecture, and history writing in the struggle for nationhood."[72] The labor leader Raphael Abramowitz (1880–1963) described the post-1905 shift to culture as a consequence of the defeated emancipatory hopes and the violence against the Jews:

> Among Jewish intellectuals there arose a particular phenomenon: a tremendous strengthening of Jewish nationalism. This wasn't only the natural strengthening of national sentiments that is a constant accompaniment to great social movements, this was a special nationalism that arose as a response to the pogroms of 1905–6 and from the disappointment of the awakened national expectations that were a result of the defeat of the revolution.[73]

The increased attention given to cultural productions was in many respects a continuation of the larger transformation in Russian-Jewish society that began in the years leading up to the revolution, and one must be careful not overstate the degree to which politics ended and cultural activity began. In fact, much cultural work took place in both Yiddish and Hebrew among the Jews before (and during) the 1905 Revolution and a significant amount of political work occurred after its demise.[74] Nevertheless, a new appreciation for the utility and possibilities of Jewish culture began to surface in the waning days of the revolution as the movement toward independence and national development was increasingly conducted via the production of Yiddish and Hebrew newspapers, journals, theaters, and ultimately, scholarship. While nationalist in scope, the new culture was defined by its advocates' attempts to distance themselves from traditional forms of Judaism that stressed either religiosity or Russification and instead focused on the development of new Yiddish and Hebrew cultures that were European in form.

With many of the bans on Yiddish and Hebrew productions either lifted or relaxed, the new national culture permeated all aspects of Russian-Jewish life. Within a few years, hundreds of Yiddish newspapers, and a much smaller number of Hebrew ones, appeared in Jewish communities across the Pale of Settlement.[75] New publishing houses and hundreds of new Yiddish literary and journalistic ventures were launched while new theater and musical companies such as Avrom Kaminsky's (1867–1918) Warsaw-based troupe, the St. Petersburg Jewish Drama Circle, and the Lodz-based Harfe were started.[76] The Society for the Spread of Enlightenment took up the task of modernizing Jewish education, the Central Jewish Literary Society was founded to promote Jewish cultural literacy, the University for All tried to provide university training in a broad range of the social sciences, and Yiddishists agitated on a broad scale for the use of Yiddish in state schools.[77] Groups of Yiddishists and Hebraists launched folkloric expeditions to gather "raw" ethnographic material such as folktales, songs, jokes, and aphorisms.[78] Likewise, a new generation of writers began to dominate the Yiddish and Hebrew literary scenes. Authors such as Uri Nissan Gnessin (1879–1913), Brenner, Opatoshu, Bergelson, Asch, and David Fogel (1891–1944) increasingly moved away from both traditional and *maskilic* forms of literature, and instead incorporated contemporary European literary styles into their texts in the hopes of recasting Jewish literature as authentically modern.[79]

A final consequence of the turn toward culture was a partial depolarizing of the often extreme political differences that were present during the revolution. The radical parties were either disbanded or in severe distress, and liberals saw much of their integrationist hopes deflated. The lack of available political avenues meant that both radicals and liberals moved closer to one another—to the point of cooperating on several key publishing and educational projects.[80] In place of these struggles, however, the issue of language became the new battleground for resolving conflicts over the future of Russian Jewry. If a hallmark of pre-twentieth-century Russian Jewry was its multilingualism, an increasing number of activists promoted a new monolingualism, as Yiddishists and Hebraists fought over which language was more appropriate to convey Jewish national culture.[81] Each of the new initiatives—school curricula, publishing ventures, folkloristic expeditions, language and writers' conferences (for Yiddish in 1908 and Hebrew in 1913)—was the site of bitter struggles over which language, the ancient Hebrew or the contemporary Yiddish, would carry the nation forward.[82]

Despite its many failures, the 1905 Russian Revolution played a dramatic and transformational role among Russian Jews. The combination of revolutionary optimism and crushing violence spurred a new generation of Jewish leaders to advance a range of radical solutions to the Jewish question by finding a balance between nationalism and socialism. While political opportunities for emancipation were effectively sealed off for Jews after 1907, their desire for revolutionary change led many to redirect their energies to the development of a variety of new cultural expressions based on the Yiddish and Hebrew languages. While drawing heavily from European literary styles in their hopes of modernizing the generation that came of age with the 1905 Revolution, Jewish leaders began to establish the foundation for a new nation that would take seriously its relationship to its history, culture, and place within modern society. As chapter 2 discusses, the immediate postrevolutionary era would see the creation of new Yiddish literary and scholarly ventures that reflected the growing sophistication and modernization of Russian Jewry and ultimately led to the creation of a new science dedicated to their language's development.

2 From Jargon to *Visnshaft*

I don't know how others number the years. But I count them from 1905.
—Dovid Einhorn (1886–1973)[1]

Concurrent with the political changes in Russian-Jewish society during the 1905 Revolutionary period came a similarly profound shift in the status, function, perception, and significance of the Yiddish language. Although a centuries-old sophisticated and multifarious literary tradition in Yiddish already existed, in the second half of the nineteenth century in Russia the language was widely perceived as a folk idiom incapable of conveying sophisticated thoughts. Its cultural forms (such as literature, theater, and the press) were sharply restricted by authorities, and it was only reluctantly engaged by Jewish intellectuals to disseminate Haskalah and revolutionary literature among Jews not literate in languages that were thought to be more appropriate, such as Russian or German. Amid the war and conflicts that defined the early years of the twentieth century, the use of Yiddish among Jews of the Pale of Settlement expanded far beyond these nineteenth-century instrumental functions and became a viable means to convey messages of nationalism, revolution, modern culture, and science. In the first decade of the twentieth century, an ideology known as Yiddishism was championed by activists who saw its potential as the basis for a dynamic Jewish national culture that would elevate Russian Jewry to the status of other European nations. Sophisticated forms of Yiddish modernist literature, literary and art criticism, and journalism quickly came to dominate Russian-Jewish intellectual society. These changes soon led to the first attempts to use Yiddish as a medium of scholarly discourse, with the goal of facilitating its reform, standardization, and enrichment, and promoting its intellectual stature.

Similar to the way that scholarship on Russian-Jewish history has tended to downplay the significance of the 1905 Revolution, studies of modern Yiddish literature and culture often have not recognized its rapid expansion during this period. By contrast, much attention has been paid to its so-called "Classic" era in the final decades of the nineteenth century, when figures such as Abramovitsh, Peretz, and Sholem Aleichem first engaged it as a vehicle for modernist literature. Significant attention has been paid to the first "architects" of the linguistic nationalistic movement of Yiddishism, such as Chaim Zhitlowsky, Nathan Birnbaum (1864–1937), and Peretz. Similarly, much effort has been dedicated to the period between the two world wars. During this time in Poland and the Soviet Union (as well as in the United States), Yiddishism came into its own as a cultural movement, replete with vibrant Yiddish school systems, presses, theaters, and institutions. This era also saw the establishment of three significant centers of Yiddish research in the cities of Vilna, Kiev, and Minsk.

By contrast, the generation of writers, activists, and ideologues that link them to one another, only recently has become a topic of study.[2] This neglect has contributed to a distorted picture of Yiddish's development, for the first two decades of the twentieth century were the time when perceptions of Yiddish shifted from it being thought of as a limited jargon to serving as the foundation of an ideology of Jewish liberation and the basis of a new scholarly discipline. The years 1903 to 1917 in particular witnessed an explosion of Yiddish cultural activity in Russia, first motivated by the revolutionary optimism that ignited the emancipatory expectations of a generation of youth, and then by the new Jewish national pride that had captivated them.

Yidishe visnshaft came into being through a series of halting, interrupted, and abridged steps that eventually culminated in its institutional development. Most of the early forums for Yiddish critical studies, including party organs, literary journals, publishing houses, and a language conference, could not be sustained beyond a brief period. Its first practitioners had to maneuver around obstacles that threatened to prevent the budding discipline's further development, including censorship, the demands of the marketplace, limited economic resources, an uneducated readership, divided political loyalties, and attacks by ideological opponents. The first works of *Yidishe visnshaft* were to a great extent defined by efforts to surmount these barriers, thereby accounting for the defensive, apologetic posture present in much of the early scholarship.

The creation of secular Yiddish literature and a press that supported it was one of the largely unintended consequences of the efforts by Russian-Jewish *maskilim* to Russify their brethren in the second half of the nineteenth century. From approximately the eleventh century until the mid-twentieth, the vernacular of most Ashkenazic Jews was Yiddish (although it was not named as such until the late nineteenth)—a mixture of Middle-High German and Hebrew/Aramaic with a strong Slavic component among its East European speakers.[3] In premodern times, Ashkenazic Jews tended to be multilingual, with Yiddish serving both as the language of day-to-day communication and for texts ranging from the erudite to the popular.[4] Use of Hebrew by Jews was generally limited to study and prayer (as well as for some formal writing) while fluency in the language (or languages) of the surrounding population was often determined by individual Jews' degree of contact with people outside of their community.[5] Like other Jewish vernaculars of the Diaspora (Judeo-Arabic, Ladino, Judeo-Persian, etc.), Yiddish was not considered by its speakers to be sacred like Hebrew (the language of scripture) and Aramaic (the language of the Talmud). Rather, Yiddish was viewed as a derivative of German, and not as a language unto itself.[6]

In the second half of the eighteenth century, Yiddish became a topic of ideological debate among Western and Central European Jews who saw it as one of the many aspects of their condition (along with appearance, occupations, and forms of religious worship) that was in need of substantial reform. As David Sorkin has noted, relinquishing Yiddish was viewed as an indispensable step for the enlightenment of Jews.[7] Although the founder of the Haskalah, Moses Mendelssohn (1729–1786) regularly employed Yiddish as a language of conversation as well as correspondence, his followers quickly identified it as a corrupt jargon that symbolized the degenerate state of German Jewry.[8] In its place, advocates for Jewish reform encouraged the use of German as both the day-to-day language of Jews and "for general philosophy and for those works on Judaism which had a decidedly apologetic purpose."[9] Distancing themselves from Yiddish, *maskilim* instead looked to Hebrew in the hope of creating a new progressive Jewish culture, which led to the founding of a number of Hebrew periodicals and the first attempts in the modern period to transform the language via a return to biblical forms. Although efforts to "de-rabbinize" Hebrew had mixed results, attempts to dissuade Western and German European Jews from speaking Yiddish were overwhelmingly successful, and its use rapidly declined.[10] Despite the tendency of *maskilim* to disparage Yiddish, they also occasionally recognized its utility, and turned to it at times as a means of spreading the Enlightenment among their fellow Jews. In late eighteenth-century Amsterdam, for example, a series of Yiddish *Diskursn* (polemical pamphlets written in the manner of satirical dialogues) were published by both the new and old Jewish communal leaders in a battle over Enlightenment demands of reform and progress in the community.[11]

As the Haskalah moved eastward in the early nineteenth century, Russian *maskilim* hoped to emulate this model of language reform. However, Jewish enlighteners in Russia had a much less receptive audience for their message. Try as they might to mimic the experience in Germany, the situation of the Jews in Russia was remarkably dissimilar and presented many obstacles for an easy linguistic transformation. Most notably, the demographic and geographic situation of Russian Jews was much different than that of their brethren to the west. Jews in Russia lived across the Pale of Settlement (a vast area roughly the size of France) on Russia's western rim and were concentrated in cities and towns among many different ethnic and linguistic groups. The sheer number of Russian Jews made the prospect of assimilation all the more daunting.[12] The populist Hasidic movement had already captured the loyalty of many Russian Jews with a message of spiritual regeneration and religious exuberance. Eradicating Yiddish was even more difficult because the initial attempts at promoting Enlightenment were conducted during the reign of Tsar Nicholas I (1825–1855); therefore, efforts to dissuade Jews from using Yiddish were widely perceived as part of his brutal efforts at forced Russification.

Nevertheless, from the outset, the agenda of the Russian Haskalah included a strong opposition toward Yiddish. As Isaac Ber Levinsohn (1788–1860), proclaimed in his *Teudah be-Yisrael* (Testimony in Israel,

1828), "In this land, why use the Yiddish language? Either the pure German tongue or the Russian language, for that is the language of the state."[13] Like their German-Jewish predecessors, Russian-Jewish *maskilim* tried to fashion modern forms of Hebrew, but most often only produced highly didactic, formal prose that was largely inaccessible to its intended audience. With great reluctance, many reformers recognized that Hebrew could not be the vehicle for the Enlightenment because their message was going unheard. Russian too was an impractical choice—Jews did not generally live among ethnic Russians and therefore had little engagement with the language. In time, some *maskilim* reluctantly began to question whether Yiddish had to be at least the temporary vehicle for the enlightenment of Russian Jewry.[14] Even as they despised the "jargon," and despite the resistance of many of their adherents, a small number of *maskilim* in Russia began to reevaluate their objections to Yiddish in light of its potentially practical benefits. By engaging Yiddish, and contrary to their efforts to defeat the language, they expanded its uses and prepared the ground for its modern forms. Within a generation, a tradition of "enlightened" Yiddish writing developed from which later authors who were more sympathetic to the language, could draw.

The first modern Yiddish periodical, *Kol mevaser* (Heralding Voice, 1862–73) provides a useful illustration of this phenomenon. Although the first Yiddish newspaper dates back to Holland in the late seventeenth century with the *Dinstagishe un fraytagishe kurant* (Thursday and Friday Courant, 1686–87) and Yiddish periodicals continued to appear sporadically for the next two centuries, Alexander Tsederbaum (1816–1893) was the first successful publisher of Yiddish journalism in the Russian empire. Both a *maskil* and a pragmatic businessman with a strong sense of the demands of the marketplace, Tsederbaum initially turned to Hebrew out of ideology, and later to Yiddish out of necessity.[15]

Born in the Haskalah stronghold of Zamosc, Poland, Tsederbaum moved in 1840 to Odessa, a city with a rapidly modernizing Jewish elite and which was for a time, the center of Russian-Jewish intellectual life.[16] In 1860, the reform-minded Tsederbaum received permission from the Tsarist authorities to begin printing *Ha-Melitz* (The Advocate, 1860–1904), the first Hebrew weekly in Russia. *Ha-Melitz* was founded on the Haskalah premise that it was necessary to revive the Jewish people through the modernization of the Hebrew language and the introduction of Western ideas and ways to Russian Jews. Tsederbaum and other Russian-Jewish *maskilim* like him believed Russian Jewry was trapped in medieval superstitions and religiously backward orthodoxies. They were concerned that Eastern European Jews had not yet recognized the cultural and intellectual virtues of the West and were still living chiefly as they had for the past several centuries without change or improvement. Like *maskilim* of generations before them, they cultivated the Hebrew language out of a belief that it was the ancestral language of Judaism and therefore, the ideal vehicle through which to reform the Jews. Their native tongue, Yiddish, was to them no more than a corrupted form of German, and served, in the words of one later commentator, as "a type of yellow badge, a symbol of the dark exile, of an enslaved life."[17] To assist Jews with the new Hebrew forms, each issue contained essays on basic Hebrew grammar, etymology, and pronunciation. Further, in an attempt to introduce Jews to discoveries in the larger world, there appeared a steady stream of essays on the physical sciences, astronomy, and anatomy. The Hebrew writers Y. Eichenbaum (1796–1861), H. Z. Slonimsky (1810–1904), Avrom-Ber Gotlober (1811–1899), Judah Leib Gordon (1830–1892), and Abramovitsh were among the contributors.

Despite some initial success, *Ha-Melitz* remained largely inaccessible to its intended readership. The Hebrew language was not yet developed substantially enough to convey adequately the enlightened message its authors intended. Even more of a factor was that Hebrew literacy among Jews did not increase sufficiently to attract a wide audience. "Enlightened" and acculturated Jews were turning to Russian, while the vast bulk of "unenlightened" Jews kept to Yiddish. Educated religious Jews who had enough fluency in Hebrew to comprehend the paper most often refused to read it because of its modern ideas and attacks on orthodoxy. In response to this dilemma, within two years of the founding of *Ha-Melitz*, Tsederbaum decided to publish a Yiddish supplement to the Hebrew, and *Kol mevaser* was launched.

The Yiddish language *Kol mevaser* quickly became the more successful of the two publications, both for its linguistic accessibility and for its more popular format. *Kol mevaser* was similar to *Ha-Melitz* in that it contained a news section, letters from readers, essays, and editorials. However, *Kol mevaser* was not a Yiddish translation of the Hebrew weekly, but was directed toward a less educated readership, one the editors assumed was in greater need of rudimentary knowledge. *Kol mevaser* was highly didactic and filled with essays that brought its Jewish readers information about the outside world, as well as contained articles on science, mathematics, and polemics criticizing the backwardness of Russian Jewry. Like many of the contributors to his Yiddish journal, Tsederbaum assumed that as Jews became more adept in the ways of the modern world, they would recognize the need to abandon their Yiddish and take up more sophisticated languages such as Hebrew or Russian.[18] Instead, it was Yiddish that became modernized and legitimized in part through his effort. Lacking any orthographic or grammatical standardization of the language, Kol mevaser's contributors continually labored to craft a language that could express the forms, meanings, and moods that were present in Russian and German literature. Over the course of more than a dozen years, writers such as Abramovitsh, Avrom Goldfaden (1840–1908), and Mordecai Spektor began to transform Yiddish into a language in which sophisticated literary forms could be conveyed, while many contributors, journalists, and readers reported and commented on the important news of the day. As Emanuel S. Goldsmith points out, over the twelve years of its existence, *Kol mevaser* helped to create a broad reading public for Yiddish, began the process of its orthographic and grammatical standardization, and introduced Jews (male and female) to the possibility of a modern Yiddish literature.[19]

A similar phenomenon occurred decades later in the early years of the Jewish labor movement. Like the creation of modern Yiddish literature—which in large measure grew out of a reluctant, frustrated Haskalah—the 1890s expansion of Yiddish into the realm of political propaganda also began more out of necessity than conviction.[20] Having conducted much of their initial work in Russian, the idea of using Yiddish as a suitable vessel for political propaganda was at first inconceivable to many Russian-Jewish socialists. Early Jewish labor leaders such as Arkadii Kremer (1865–1935), Vladimir Medem, and Julius Martov (1873–1920) (a grandson of Tsederbaum) conducted their work almost exclusively in Russian—aiming at educating small circles of workers in secret. It did not take long, however, for them to recognize that the language of the new politics had to be Yiddish if they were to reach a mass audience of Jewish workers. By 1901, the largest Jewish labor organization, the Bund, acknowledged the efficacy of Yiddish and the growing national sentiments of Jewish workers.[21] This resulted in the wide-scale production of Bund-sponsored Yiddish language materials such as newspapers, pedagogic materials, theaters, and belles letters, and prompted similar Yiddish works by the Jewish section of the Polish Socialist Party.[22] As Goldsmith notes, by the onset of the 1905 Revolution, the Bund had already published (mostly illegal) 73 Yiddish pamphlets, in addition to newspapers.[23] Despite its leaders' initial hesitation about the efficacy of Yiddish and the utility of promoting Jewish culture, the Bund became responsible over the next four decades for much of the Yiddish theater, school-systems, and press.[24]

The last two decades of the nineteenth century also saw a dramatic rise in the number of influential forums for the new Yiddish literature. For example, Tsederbaum, who by 1881 had been gradually giving up his faith in the Haskalah and aligning himself with Jewish national causes, decided to launch a new Yiddish language venture, the *Dos yidishes folksblat* (The Jewish People's Paper, 1881–90). This paper was responsible for publishing some of the most sophisticated Yiddish writers of the day, such as Sholem Aleichem, Yankev Dinezon, Dovid Frishman (1860–1922), Shimen Frug, and Yankev-Mordkhe Volfzon (1867–1929). In the highly charged climate after 1881–82, increasing numbers of Yiddish works appeared, often to the dismay of other cultural activists who argued on behalf of a literary renaissance in Hebrew. Sholem Aleichem published the *Di yidishe folks-bibliotek* (The Jewish People's Library, 1888–89) to publicize much of the new Yiddish literature. The Yiddish writer and editor Mordecai Spektor (1858–1925) published the journal *Der hoyz-fraynd* (The House-Friend, 1888–96) and Peretz edited the occasional *Yontef bletlekh* (Holiday Leaflets, 1894–96), which contained the best of new Yiddish writing. In 1899, the short-lived literary journal *Der yid* (The Jew, 1899–1902) began to provide readers with regular access to the best of the new Yiddish writing. Edited in Warsaw, but published across the Russian border in Cracow (then part of the Austro-Hungarian empire) to get around the imperial ban on Yiddish periodicals, *Der yid* was an important precursor to the Russian-Yiddish press because it not only provided a regular forum for writers such as Abramovitsh, Sholem Aleichem, and Peretz, but also because it was the early home for figures such as Frug, Avrom Reisen, Bialik, and Asch.[25]

By the early twentieth century, the growing Yiddish press, the Jewish labor movement, and nationalist sentiments became fused together by cultural and political activists and writers into an ideology of linguistic nationalism that in time came to be named Yiddishism. As conceived by Zhitlowsky, Birnbaum, and Peretz, Yiddish had the potential to serve both as an alternative to the assimilatory tendencies within the Haskalah and as the cultural identity of Jewish workers.[26] Although this discussion is not the place for a full recounting of the development of Yiddishism, it is useful to focus on two of its most important early ideologues—Peretz and Zhitlowsky—as a means of understanding its complexities, and their influence on the first generation of modern Yiddish scholars. In a recent discussion, David E. Fishman suggests that these two figures represent contrasting ideological streams within the growing movement of Yiddishism, with Peretz advancing its neoromantic possibilities and Zhitlowsky its revolutionary potential.[27] Their efforts to reimagine Yiddish as the basis for a national movement helped to lay the foundation for the broader movement that appeared in the wake of the 1905 Revolution.

I. L. Peretz was born in Zamosc, Poland (the same city as Tsederbaum) in 1852, and no other figure ruled over modern Yiddish literary culture as he did. Although he began writing in Hebrew and Polish, he soon became, if not the best of modern Yiddish writers, certainly its most influential.[28] As a dedicated Bundist during the early years of the movement, he wrote for an urbanized audience one generation removed from traditional observance and strove to connect his readers back to the world they had forsaken, while simultaneously propelling them further into the modern one. Reflecting after World War II on Peretz's career and dominance, literary critic Shmuel Niger credited him as the most important figure in all of Yiddish literature:

> Peretz was the future. Everyday of his life was dedicated to one day—tomorrow. *To strive*—this was his life. *To seek*—this was his goal . . . not only

knowledge but understanding. . . . Born in an enlightened age, he undertook all phases of the new Yiddish culture. He is the literary movement.[29]

Peretz championed Yiddish cultural activities and became a hero to much of the ever-growing Jewish working class in Russia and abroad. Although he was not an opponent of Hebrew and indeed wrote in the language, he led initiatives to create Yiddish drama and music groups, contributed to a Yiddish open university, and published his own literary magazine. More than this however, Peretz directed an entire generation of Yiddish writers. From his salon in Warsaw, Peretz was known as a maker and breaker of careers, and it was through his influence that many young authors brought a modernist sensibility to their works. As critics over several generations have argued, Peretz stood at the center of the Jewish cultural renaissance in Eastern Europe.[30]

The romantic attribution to Peretz stems from his embrace of a mystical, glorified Jewish past that became a leitmotif of his later fiction. As he grew older and his distance from the orthodox world grew greater, Peretz's earlier harsh stance toward Jewish tradition softened. After a three-month imprisonment in 1899, (which he served with Mordechai Spektor for socialist activity), Peretz began to depict the Russian-Jewish past in a way that was at odds with the one that many of his readers had fled. In contrast to the oppressive *kheyder,* the suffocating orthodoxy, and the strangling poverty upon which he dwelt in much of his early writing, the older Peretz began to refashion the *shtetl* as a mystical, holy, and sanctified world. Stories such as "Between Two Mountains," "Three Gifts," and "Even Higher" describe the Hasidic way of life as one of simplicity and folksiness, and recast it as a noble universe, albeit fraught with tremendous danger.[31]

If Peretz's romantic view of Yiddish helped to modernize its literature, Chaim Zhitlowsky's revolutionary vision for Yiddish prompted many of the generation of 1905 to take up the cause on its behalf. From his bases in Switzerland (where he lived from 1887 until the 1905 Revolution), Russia (during the revolution), and the United States, (from 1909 until his death in 1943), Zhitlowsky worked as a philosopher, teacher, journalist, literary critic, and public speaker. Rather than serve any one particular ideology throughout his life, Zhitlowsky supported a variety of national causes in

an effort to chart a revolutionary path for Russian Jews that would preserve their existence in the Diaspora, remain faithful to socialist ideals, and
maintain the centrality of their communal language. As his protégé and
future architect of the YIVO, Nokhem Shtif, said of him in 1913:

> 15 years ago he explained that Yiddish is and must increasingly be the
> central part of our culture; that there must be and will be created a rich
> literature in Yiddish—one as beautiful as science—and around it learning
> and democracy will be united.[32]

Zhitlowsky shepherded many members of the 1905 generation through an
ideological thicket to their national identities. He inspired this generation,
Shtif wrote, with "a positive Jewish program of national autonomy" and
declared that:

> Jews, as a collective, are equal to other nations, have their own culture,
> their own language, and have the right and obligation to develop them-
> selves in their schools, in their families, in the public realm, and to create
> a healthy modern nation in the Diaspora.[33]

Raised in a Yiddish-speaking home in Vitebsk (now in Belarus), Zhitlowsky was provided with a modern education in Russian and received
traditional training in Hebrew. Although inspired by the antiassimila-
tion stance of early Jewish national groups such as the Hibbat Zion that
formed in the wake of the 1881–82 pogroms, he initially found himself
more attracted to the cause of Russian socialism. Under the influence of
his childhood friend, Sh. An-sky (1863–1920), Zhitlowsky, a socialist revolutionary, became for a time a supporter of the Narodnaia Volia, and like
many similarly aligned Jews, he adopted a Russian name for himself (Yefim
Ossipovich).[34] However, he soon became disillusioned with the populists'
assimilationist demands and began to participate in Jewish national organizations. In time, Zhitlowsky came to advance an ideology that he referred
to as Diaspora Nationalism.

Diaspora Nationalism combined a commitment to a renewed, modernized Jewish diasporic existence with socialist values that protected the
rights of all workers. Zhitlowsky laid out his agenda in compelling essays
at the turn of the century like "A yid tsu yidn" (A Jew to Jews), "Tsienizm

oder sotsializm" (Zionism or Socialism), and "Farvos dafke yidish?" (Why indeed Yiddish?).[35] He supported the early Yiddish cultural group Tsaytgayst that was established in response to the first Zionist Congress of August 1897, and agitated for Yiddish as the national language of the Jewish people.[36] In Bern in the 1890s, Zhitlowsky and a circle called the Group of Jewish Socialists Abroad began to translate socialist texts into Yiddish for Jewish workers in the empire. It was to this circle that the Bund's leaders first turned for help when it began to conduct its propaganda in Yiddish.

During his long life, Zhitlowsky played a role in nearly every major secular Jewish movement including Zionism, Bundism, Territorialism, and Stalinism. In 1903, Zhitlowsky joined with the young Jewish left-wing nationalists who formed the Vozrozhdenie group. With the reconvening of the Russian Duma in 1906, Zhitlowsky was a candidate for the SERP but was prevented from taking his seat because of his earlier revolutionary activity.[37] Watching the Duma steadily weakened by the government, Zhitlowsky relinquished his dream of creating a Jewish autonomous zone in Russia and turned his attention to the rapidly growing Russian-Jewish émigré community in the United States. In 1908, he returned to Europe from New York to participate in the Yiddish language conference held in the city of Czernowitz, in the Austro-Hungarian empire. At this conference, Zhitlowsky sided with the radical Yiddishists who asserted that Yiddish should be considered the sole national language of the Jewish people. By contrast, the romanticist Peretz was one who brokered the compromise that declared both Hebrew and Yiddish Jewish national languages.

Zhitlowsky gave voice to the ideal that Yiddish could serve as the foundation for a rejuvenated Jewish nation. Not only did it already serve as the language of the people, it was also a potentially effective defense against Jewish assimilation. By preserving their national language, he argued, Russian Jews could act as a cohesive nation. At stake was, "the highest and the most important thing in the world: the enlightenment of the folk, of the masses, of the improvement of their thought and their feelings."[38]

The efforts by figures such as Peretz and Zhitlowsky to create a Jewish nationalism grounded in the Yiddish language and its culture resonated deeply with Jewish political activists who came of age with the 1905 Revolution. To many young revolutionaries, Yiddish was more than a practical instrument through which to further their revolutionary nationalist aspirations. Rather, it was the highest expression of the Jewish people and contained the potential to transform their existence within the Russian empire.

Despite these aspirations, the obstacles facing advocates for Yiddish were daunting. At the turn of the twentieth century, there still existed no regular Yiddish newspapers, literary journals, theater companies, or modern Yiddish schools in the empire.[39] The appearance in January 1903 of *Der fraynd* (The Friend), the first Yiddish daily newspaper in Russia, marks an important moment in the transformation of Yiddish from its nineteenth-century role as a vehicle for the dissemination of enlightenment and revolutionary messages to the basis of a national liberation movement. As Sarah Abrevaya Stein relates in her study, the newspaper and its supplements not only provided a forum (and access to a mass reading audience) for well-known writers such as Abramovitsh, Sholem Aleichem, and Peretz, but also featured several of the best of the new generation of Yiddish writers and critics such as Asch, Hirsch Dovid Nomberg (1876–1927), Niger, and Shtif.[40] Reflecting the fact that questions of Jewish language, national definition, and relationship to the Russian empire were not as fraught or divisive as they would soon become in the post-1905 period, *Der fraynd* at its outset was proudly secular, moderately Zionist, and pro-Yiddish.

Der fraynd was launched in Russia's capitol, St. Petersburg, with the permission of tsarist authorities, who hoped that the newspaper would assist in efforts toward Jewish Russification.[41] Located in western Russia, (outside of the Pale of Settlement), St. Petersburg was a foreign place to most Jews. However, beginning with a relaxation in the rules governing Jewish settlement in the 1860s, tens of thousands began to settle in the interior of Russia and acculturate into the intellectual life of Russian society. By the time of the 1881–82 pogroms, St. Petersburg had, at least temporarily, replaced the once-thriving hub of Odessa as the center of Jewish cultural life as Jews sought university training, government positions, and economic opportunity.[42]

The choice of St. Petersburg for *Der fraynd* was a curious one. Notwithstanding its distance from the masses of Yiddish readers, that it was published in a language whose use was rapidly declining among the city's acculturating Jews, and that the city was identified with the by-then antiquated Haskalah, there were solid reasons for locating the paper there. The most important was that St. Petersburg was the center of political power in Russia; therefore, it was in the interests of both the newspaper (among whose goals were to increase Jewish visibility in the capitol and to demonstrate Jewish loyalty to the government) and the authorities (who wished to keep a close eye on the paper's contents). At the turn of the century, relations between St. Petersburg's Jews and the authorities were more relaxed, and consequently, the new Minister of the Interior, Vyacheslav Pleve, allowed *Der fraynd* to appear on a test basis.[43]

In its first years, *Der fraynd* was successful far beyond its editors' expectations. With its serious stance toward Yiddish (which it called "jargon" in its early years) *Der fraynd*'s eagerness to promote secular literature, and its regular diet of news, it quickly attained near-mythic status in some quarters of the Pale. For those readers who were straining against the confines of a traditional Jewish way of life, *Der fraynd* was the vehicle that brought the modern world to them. At the same time, the newspaper helped its readers begin to imagine themselves constituting a unified nation with a shared political and cultural lingua franca. As one observer noted, its editors enforced grammatical and linguistic standards and were the first to create a "newspaper language" out of Yiddish, replete with "new words, new concepts, [and] new technical expressions."[44] At its peak, *Der fraynd* had 90,000 to 100,000 subscribers, and the number of actual readers was many more times that.[45] In an epitaph for the newspaper, the scholar, journalist, and one-time editor of the paper Khayim-dov Horovits (1865–1927) credited *Der fraynd* with marking a new age in Yiddish and Jewish cultural life, and noted its effect on the Yiddish language, "In the '*Fraynd*,' the Yiddish language was honed, polished, and perfected as far as such a thing could be."[46]

Despite *Der fraynd*'s dominance in the first years of the twentieth century, the very values that made it a successful publishing venture—its ability to strike a balance between Haskalah and Zionist ideals, its political ecumenicalism, and its location outside of the Pale of Settlement—made the paper ultimately a poor vehicle to transmit the new Yiddish culture that was becoming increasingly intertwined with the revolutionary movement growing in the Pale. The editors made many attempts to accommodate the rapidly changing situation, such as dropping its commitment to Zionism and relocating the paper's headquarters to Warsaw. However, the paper could not compete when it lost its monopoly once prohibitions against Yiddish publishing were lifted and other newspapers appeared on the scene. A less sophisticated but politically bolder press, like *Der veg* (The Way, Warsaw), *Der veker* (The Alarm, Vilna), and *Di tsayt* (The Times, Vilna) soon rose to the fore, reflecting a new confidence among Jews of the Pale that they were capable of carrying the weight of their culture.[47] Having effected a significant change among Russian Jewry, *Der fraynd* ceased publishing in 1913 and quickly became a relic of a prior age. As Stein concludes:

> Though *Der fraynd* was cursed by disagreements between its contributors and editors, though it failed to articulate a coherent political agenda, though it would soon be outmoded (and out circulated by its successors), this paper nonetheless ushered in a new era in Eastern European Jewish culture, an era defined by the production and consumption of news in Yiddish.[48]

The new militant Yiddish press that supplanted *Der fraynd* was one of the consequences of the relaxation of press censorship in late 1905. With names such as *Der arbeter* (The Worker), *Sotsial democrat* (Social Democrat), *Di yidishe tsukunft* (The Jewish Future), *Di yidishe yugend* (The Jewish Youth), and *Di naye velt* (The New World), these often highly partisan venues reflected the militancy of a dawning age, were dedicated to the revolutionary overthrow of the tsar, and were staunchly pro-Yiddish. Most crucial to the history of *Yidishe visnshaft*, the pages of the political newspapers, journals, and tracts that circulated around the Pale of Settlement were home to many of those figures who would later become its first practitioners. It was here that they first took up efforts to expand the importance and function of Yiddish, to use it as a medium for Jewish self-expression, and to assert themselves as leaders of a new class of Jewish intellectuals.

Many of the intellectuals who ultimately began the movement to transform Yiddish into a language of scholarship are found within the organs of the political groups that sought to synthesize the ideologies of socialism and nationalism—the Vozrozhdenie, S.S., the SERP, and the Poalei Zion. Two weekly journals in particular—the S.S.'s *Der nayer veg* (The New Way) and the SERP's *Di folksshtime* (People's Voice)—contained some of the first attempts to apply critical scholarly methods to the study of the Yiddish language, literature, and the material conditions of Russian Jewry *in* the Yiddish language, and were important precursors to the scholarly work that would appear in the post–1905 revolutionary period.[49] Although neither party organ lasted past the end of the 1905 Revolution, they served as a proving ground for many of those who would later found the Yiddish journals that expanded the language farther into the realm of *visnshaft*.

The connection between revolutionary politics and Jewish national culture was present from the very beginning of *Der nayer veg* and *Di folksshtime,* in part because their editors, writers, and party faithful argued that as a consequence of its landlessness, the Jewish nation was woefully underdeveloped and needed to create a sufficiently strong culture in order to fend off assimilation. *Der nayer veg* and *Di folksshtime* were some of the first forums for avant-garde Yiddish literary productions as well as some of the first critical studies of Jewish economic, folkloric, and cultural life. As the editors of the S.S. journal declared in its opening manifesto, "Our Tasks," adapting Russian Social Democracy to the particular case of the Jewish people necessitated the creation of cultural institutions that would promote the ideals of nationalist socialism. Among its demands was the right to direct Jewish culture and education:

> We will fight for the demands of the entire Russian Social Democracy and adapt it to the condition of Jewish life, which we will deepen and expand. We will demand that Jewish folk-education be handed over to the authority of the Jewish national body in the form of a free school society.

For a time that was often marked by ideological partisanship, the range of these short-lived journals was vast and anticipated future developments in Yiddish letters. The pages of *Der nayer veg* included literary criticism by Niger, fiction by established writers such as Peretz and Frishman, as well as younger writers like Asch and Einhorn, a feuilleton by Peretz Hirshbeyn, and an economic analysis of Russian workers by Lestschinsky. These contributions appeared comfortably alongside party news, reports of political developments abroad, analyses of political events, defenses of party platforms, and attacks on rivals. Likewise, the pages of the SERP's *Di folksshtime* were home to a broad range of contributions to the new Yiddish culture and included works by Zhitlowsky linking socialism and the new Yiddish literature, attacks on assimilation of the Jewish bourgeoisie by Nokhem Shtif, short stories by Avrom Reisen and Nomberg, and literary criticism by Bal-Makhshoves (pen name of Yisroel Eliashev, 1873–1924).

The efforts of the S.S. activist Jacob Lestschinsky to employ Yiddish for sociological and demographic research provide a useful illustration of how these revolutionary parties and presses supported the development of a Yiddish scholarly idiom. Lestschinsky—who would become the demographer and statistician of Russian Jewry par excellence—was a regular contributor to the S.S. weekly that published his essays on the rapidly changing economic conditions of Jewish workers. Born in 1876 into a religious family, by the age of eighteen Lestschinsky had become captivated with the Haskalah and then quickly fell under the Hebraist sway of Ahad Ha'am's cultural Zionism. After a brief stay in Odessa (in 1896) where he immersed himself in modern Hebrew letters, Lestschinsky sought out more formal training and began to study the Russian gymnasium curriculum. By 1901, he had made his way to the University of Bern, (as Shtif and Niger later did), where he joined with the political circles of students gathered there, shifted his allegiance to Yiddish, and returned to Russia a committed revolutionary. After working in labor-Zionist circles in Odessa, Warsaw, and Vilna, and after several brief stays in prison for this activity, Lestschinsky joined with other like-minded revolutionaries to form the S.S. party.[50]

From an early age, Lestschinsky was interested in documenting the economic transformation of Eastern European Jewry. In the years before the 1905 Revolution and the new Yiddish press, Lestschinsky published two important sociological studies. The first was in 1903, when Lestschinsky wrote a study of the process of proletarianization in one *shtetl* (his hometown of Horodyshche, Ukraine), where he and a group of like-minded Zionist intellectuals surveyed the rapidly declining material conditions of the residents. Published in the Hebrew-language *Ha-Shiloah*, his study, "Statistika shel ayara akhat" (Statistics of One *Shtetl*) offered a depressing portrait of the economic decline of a prosperous Jewish community as rapid industrialization forced its once-proud shopkeepers and artisans into poverty and emigration to urban areas in search of work.[51] Lestschinsky's motivation to turn his attention to the production of scholarship in a specifically Jewish language may have come from the editor of the Hebrew language periodical *Ha-Shiloah*. Upon assuming editorship of the journal in 1903 from its founder Ahad Ha'am, the linguist Joseph Klausner decided to make an editorial break with the journal's focus on the promotion of Hebrew literature and toward the development of Hebrew scholarship. In his opening editorial manifesto, Klausner called for the introduction of a new "Hebrew science" (*mada' 'ivri*) that would apply critical scholarly methods to Hebrew letters in the name of its cultivation and enrichment.[52] A year later, reflecting his increasing commitment to Yiddish, Lestschinsky contributed a lengthy study entitled "Di yidishe emigranten in london" to Peretz's miscellany *Di yidishe bibliotek,* in which he described the conditions of Jewish immigrants in London. Lestschinsky introduced readers to the "sweat system" that dominated the lives of Jewish laborers in London and other major cities, and which forced them to toil in small workshops for 18 to 20 hours per day.[53]

During his time with the S.S., Lestschinsky published a number of scientific surveys documenting the changing conditions of East European Jewry. One of his earliest works, a 1906 multipart essay in *Der nayer veg,* "Der yidisher arbeter" (The Jewish Worker) formed the introduction to a much longer work that was published later that year, *Der yidisher arbeter (in rusland)* (The Jewish Worker in Russia).[54] This volume marked the first comprehensive study of the subject in any language, and is among the first scholarly monographs to be composed in modern Yiddish. Replete with heavy Marxist determinism, *Der yidisher arbeter (in rusland)* represents an important milestone in the development of Yiddish, not only because of its detailed and documented approach, but also for the way it utilized Yiddish as the medium for scientific research, strongly foreshadowing the work of interwar scholars. To make his argument supporting Jewish territorial concentration accessible to the Yiddish reading public, Lestschinsky combined scientific methods with familiar Yiddish literary themes. For example, when describing the "tragic" state of the Jewish worker, Lestschinsky referred to a figure from a contemporary Sholem Aleichem story, "A gringer tones"

(An Easy Fast).[55] Upon losing his job and facing severe impoverishment, the hero of Sholem Aleichem's story, Khayim Khaykin, slowly starves himself to death, all the while explaining to his children that he is simply observing obscure religious fast days.[56]

Along with the choice to use Yiddish and Yiddish cultural references, what separated Lestschinsky's study from other attempts to account for the discrepancy between Marxist theory and the underdevelopment of Jewish labor was his scientific approach to the subject. *Der yidisher arbeter (in rusland)* was not only an appeal in Yiddish to Jewish workers to join the revolutionary movement; it was also a full-length statistical examination of the delayed "proletarianization" process of Jewish workers. Complete with rich documentation, fold-out graphs, tables, and charts, Lestschinsky's text examined all facets of Jewish economic life and compared the situation of Jewish workers in Russia to those in England and to other workers in the Pale. It drew from a broad array of sources including Russian census data, voting rolls, economic statistics, union records, Russian scholarship, and his own primary research to paint a portrait of the Jews' status in the industrial life of the empire, and to point toward new possibilities:

> We believe that while reality should not be so horrible, and that real life should not appear so tragic, only through the "unterrible" discovery of all of its dark sides, only by researching into its dark forms can we illuminate the way to a new future, can we mark the direction of the way that must be sought.[57]

Reconciling Marxist theories with the actual plight of Jewish workers was no easy task because Lestschinsky was forced to account for the stark differences between the presumably delayed process of economic transformation of Jews and the "normal" processes undergone by other workers in the empire. His goals in *Der yidisher arbeter (in rusland)* included demonstrating that the status of Jews was unique in that they did not follow precisely the strict Marxist process of proletarianization and explaining why Jewish workers lagged politically and economically behind workers from other national groups. By investigating the number of workers represented in a range of industries (such as food production, wood, textiles, ceramics, paper, metal, chemical, tobacco, brick making, and alcohol), his study argued that their stunted development was a consequence of several intersecting factors: the Jews' dispersion across the Pale, their high rate of emigration, their exclusion from large factories, and their overrepresentation in the petite bourgeoisie prior to industrialization.

The efforts of activist-scholars like Lestschinsky indicate how the new revolutionary Yiddish press expanded the possibilities within the language and helped pave the way for its development as a scholarly medium. If prior to the 1905 Revolution, its functions were circumscribed in large part by law, ideology, and the often negative perception of the language by its own speakers, by the time of the revolution's fall, it was poised to become the dominant cultural medium of Jewish national culture.

With the crushing of the revolution in 1907, and the waves of repression and mass arrests that followed, the possibility of spreading political propaganda was sharply curtailed. At the same time, Yiddish and Hebrew publishing was generally still permitted by the government, albeit under tight censorship that forbade political or economic agitation. Although Jewish activists were forced to cease advocating for radical changes in the empire, many redirected their efforts toward the creation of Jewish cultural productions (such as the new Yiddish and Hebrew press, theater, school systems, and various self-help organizations). As a result, the decade between the two Russian revolutions was a time of great expansion in the Yiddish press as newspapers, journals, and publishing houses sprang up throughout the Pale, reflecting the broad diversity of Jewish life. Unlike the Yiddish press during the 1905 Revolution, the new postrevolutionary periodicals were largely independent efforts and not organs of political parties. Lacking an institutional base (as well as a reliable readership who could afford a subscription), these new ventures appeared and disappeared with great frequency. Many lasted just a few issues while others remained for years, yet a periodical's longevity should not be confused with its importance, as several of the shortest-lived exerted the most influence. With their increasing ideological independent status (although they were now more dependant on the vagaries of the marketplace), the new Yiddish press contained a wider intellectual and aesthetic range of material than that of the revolutionary years.

Once politics were no longer a viable realm to debate the future direction of Russian Jewry, new divisions quickly appeared over questions of culture and language. In 1908, there occurred two attempts to assert the supremacy of Yiddish and to define the relationship between Jewish politics and culture, both of which contributed to a dramatic expansion of Yiddish into the realms of *visnshaft:* the journal *Di literarishe monatsshriftn* (Literary Monthly) and a late summer conference on behalf of Yiddish. *Di literarishe monatsshriftn* tried to force a rupture between politics and culture by creating a vehicle for the Yiddish national renaissance that would disavow overt political agendas and the gathering six months later in Czernowitz, Bukovina became a battleground over whether to elevate the significance of Yiddish to the level of serving as the prime repository of Jewish national culture. Although both efforts were only limited successes, they represent important, if complicated, moments in the increasing sophistication of Yiddish in that they were attempts to create new associations with a language that up until then, was still considered in most quarters as a jargon incapable of mature forms of expression. The decidedly mixed reception of both events likewise points to the fact that the political, economic, linguistic, and geographic divisions within Russian Jewry precluded any consensus on the language's place within the much sought after national revival.

The first shot fired in the battle to realign Yiddish literature and cultural criticism was the literary journal *Di literarishe monatsshriftn*. When it first appeared in February 1908, *Di literarishe monatsshriftn* was hailed by many as beginning a new era both within Yiddish literature and for the Jewish people as a whole.[58] Edited by three former party activists—Niger (S.S.), A. Vayter (Bund), and Shmarye Gorelik (1877–1943; Zionist)—the monthly tried to pry Yiddish literature away from its potent association with Jewish revolutionary movements and to locate it instead in the realm of pure aesthetics. Eschewing commonly held assumptions about the intrinsic limitations of the language, the journal's founders hoped to create a forum that would showcase Yiddish literature's most modern and sophisticated talents and advance the development of a Jewish national culture, removed from any particular political platform.

Di literarishe monatsshriftn was one of many Yiddish weeklies, monthlies, and miscellanies strictly dedicated to literature that appeared in the immediate aftermath of the 1905 Revolution. All of them lasted but a handful of issues. For example, 1908 saw the appearance of Avrom Reisen's *Kunst un lebn* (Art and Life), which featured contributions by Yosef Haim Brenner, Bal-Makhshoves, and Yitskhok Shiper (1884–1943), dedicated a large discussion to the ill-fated Czernowitz conference and reproduced a racy sketch by the German Symbolist Franz von Stuck. Several others, such as *Di velt* (The World), *Di naye tsayt* (The New Age), *Hilf* (Relief), *Fraye erd* (Free earth), *Goldene funken* (Golden Sparks), and *Der yunger gayst* (The Young Spirit) also attempted to bring sophisticated literature, criticism, and translations from European authors to a wide audience. Throughout 1910–11, Avrom Reisen published a weekly entitled *Eyropeyishe literatur* (European Literature), which was filled with translations of Europe's finest writers, including Goethe, Hamsun, Balzac, and Byron, occasional authors from the United States such as Twain and Poe, and original Yiddish works as well, including contributions by Peretz, Einhorn, and Reisen himself.[59]

Despite the large number of new Yiddish literary periodicals, several factors distinguished *Di literarishe monatsshriftn*: its deliberate, intentional exchange of politics for culture, the high quality of modernist works that it published, and the powerful reaction it prompted in many quarters. As Kenneth Moss argues, the journal broke with two competing forces in the larger Jewish community by arguing that a rejuvenated Jewish identity should be based neither on traditional religious values nor on revolutionary ones. In their place, the editors turned to European literary movements such as Decadence and Symbolism in the belief that—when created in a Yiddish "key"—they could foster a renaissance of Jewish culture and impart a new self-confidence among Jews. As Moss states, by deliberately placing abstract culture over practical politics, the editors envisioned that this new form of Jewish national identity "would be expressed and reconstructed through the distinctive forms of modern European high culture: literature, art, theater, and attendant institutions such as the press and the modern school."[60]

In the introduction to the first number, the editors stated their intention to create a forum that would elevate Yiddish letters to the level of other European literatures.[61] For too long, they argued, Jewish intellectuals catered to the cultural interests of other national languages because they could not conceive of a high culture written in their native tongue: "In the eyes of the orthodox-national intellectuals, Yiddish (jargon) literature is not a national literature, and the Yiddish folk-language—a Diaspora-shmate."[62] To counter this attitude, they positioned their journal at the vanguard of the growing national awakening: "The conviction is growing that the Jewish folk has the same rights as all other people to create their own culture, to express its national self in original forms, and to bind its own unique page into the great book of the world."[63]

As a forum for sophisticated Yiddish literary works, the four issues of *Di literarishe monatsshriftn* contained contributions by both well-known and up and coming writers, including Peretz, Einhorn, Asch, Nomberg, and Der Nister (pen name of Pinkhes Kahanovitsh, 1884–1950), whose contributions steered away from simplistic folksy representations of Russian-Jewish life and considered its darker psychological aspects. At the same time, the journal featured an essay by Gorelik on the Norwegian writer Knut Hamsun, four essays by Niger on the new Yiddish literature, an essay by Vayter on the new Yiddish theater, a translation of Kipling, and a study of the new "Yiddish renaissance" by Shiper.

The response to *Di literarishe monatsshriftn* was equal parts laudatory and vitriolic. On the one hand, the journal was hailed by many as marking the renaissance the editors had envisioned. The Warsaw literary circle of Peretz rallied around the journal and contributed heavily to it, as did Asch, Nomberg, and I. M. Weissenberg (1881–1938). However, it was rejected by political activists like the Bund's Mark Liber (1879–1937) and the writer Sh. An-sky, who refused to accept the decoupling of politics from the efforts to create a national culture. It was criticized as well by Klausner, the editor of *Ha-Shiloah,* and others like him who introduced similar changes, albeit in the Hebrew language. Others such as Shtif, Avrom Reisen, and particularly Brenner sharply questioned whether aesthetics alone was sufficient to rebuild an entire national culture.[64]

Although widely hailed as signaling a new period in the history of Yiddish letters and despite the initial positive response from many quarters, *Di literarishe monatsshriftn* could not be sustained beyond the first four issues.[65] The high hopes and expectations of the journal's founders would not be realized until the decade after World War I. The absence of any clear political agenda in such highly charged times added to its demise. Furthermore, as Moss demonstrates, the aesthetic tendencies of Decadence and Symbolism the journal hoped to foster could not be so easily tethered to nationalist causes because they contained their own set of assumptions and demands that were often contrary to the utilitarian needs of nationalism. Finally, and perhaps most definitively, financial considerations also doomed the journal, notwithstanding the sensation it caused when it first appeared.

Six months after the launch of *Di literarishe monatsshriftn,* the first major organized attempt to assert Yiddish as a bona fide language of the Jewish people occurred in the city of Czernowitz. In the vision of its chief organizer, Nathan Birnbaum, the gathering would bring together the most creative and influential figures in Yiddish letters to announce to the world the centrality of Yiddish in the Jewish renaissance and to assert its place among European languages. Although Czernowitz's location in the Austro-Hungarian empire prohibited many from attending the conference, several of the most prominent Yiddish activists of the day were there, including the "elders" Birnbaum, Zhitlowsky, and Peretz, as well as many from the younger generation, such as Frumkin, Asch, Avrom Reisen, and Prilutski to discuss the future of Yiddish.[66] While Birnbaum, who had only a rudimentary knowledge of the language, wanted to promote an agenda of standardizing the orthography and grammar of Yiddish, the conference instead became mired in whether or not Yiddish should be recognized as the only national language of the Jewish people. This debate—however tendentious between the advocates for Yiddish, for Hebrew, and those victorious ones who sought a middle path—reflected a new and profound sense of pride in both Yiddish and Jewish nationalism, a sentiment that was inconceivable just a decade prior when very few saw anything more than a utilitarian potential for Yiddish. Although not much was achieved in terms of tangible results, the conference's platform included planks that reflected the desire of the organizers to create lasting institutions for Yiddish culture.[67]

The conference was important less for its practical accomplishments than for how it proposed a new answer to a question that had confronted European Jewry since the beginning of the Enlightenment: what does it mean to be a Jew? If in the years prior to 1881–82, *maskilim* articulated a response that relegated Judaism strictly to the narrow confines of religious faith and to bring Russian Jewry more fully into the empire, the declaration at Czernowitz demonstrates well the national sentiment that had enraptured many during in these revolutionary times:

> If earlier, in the assimilationist period, it was a matter of respect for intellectuals to demonstrate their attachment to European civilization at every opportunity, then in our time a new moral imperative has evolved from that: to show with every breath and with the very pulse-beat of your heart your membership in the Jewish people and your solidarity with its historical destiny![68]

To proponents of Yiddishism, the Czernowitz conference represented a sea-change in the status of Yiddish. Yiddish scholarship itself is often said to have begun at the conference.[69] There, the amateur (albeit well-published) philologist Matisyohu Mieses (1885–unknown) delivered what is considered to be the first scholarly address in Yiddish. In a powerful speech defending the utility of Yiddish against its Hebraist and Germanist critics, Mieses drew from historical, philological, and sociological evidence to argue that Yiddish was equal to many languages and superior to the rest. The young (twenty-three years old) linguist lectured the assembled crowd of veteran political activists, writers, scholars, and reporters on the linguistic coherency of Yiddish and argued for its place within the family of languages. In an address that reportedly brought some of the Hebraists in attendance to anger and others to tears, Mieses methodically argued the case for Yiddish as the sole legitimate language for the modern Jewish nation. Mieses further set out to prove that the Hebrew language, which had long been abandoned as a spoken language, and was incomprehensible to most East European Jews, had little relevance in contemporary Jewish life, and was thus better restricted to synagogue and religious life. Only Yiddish could serve as a defense against the forces of assimilation and acculturation, and prevent the erosion of Jewish identity. Mieses even went so far as to link the very survival of the Jewish people to the survival of Yiddish, saying that the two were so intertwined, one could not endure without the other.

Despite the great amount of attention that has been paid to the conference by popular histories of Yiddish, the direct impact of Czernowitz on the subsequent development of Yiddish was quite limited. Like the case of

Di literarishe monatsshriftn, the gathering is best understood as auguring future changes in Yiddish in the period between the two world wars. On the one hand, several writers looked to the conference as a momentous occasion akin to the 1897 conferences that formed the Zionist and Bundist movements. On the other, while Mieses's arguments regarding the linguistic coherency of Yiddish would be echoed by later scholars, it is difficult to demonstrate any impact of his talk on most members of the first generation of Yiddish scholars. A number of factors may account for this lack of influence, among them the fact that the conference was generally panned in the press, Mieses's essay was never reprinted, the proceedings of the conference were never published, and they were only reconstructed more than twenty years later.

Although less strident in their ideological agenda than *Di literarishe monatsshriftn* and the Czernowitz conference, the post-1905 Revolution-era journals that combined Yiddish literature with articles covering a broad range of cultural and societal matters were where much of the expansion and modernization of Yiddish did occur. Modeled in large measure after Russian periodicals as well as a few highly successful Yiddish ones in the United States, literary/*gezelshaftlekh* journals such as *Lebn un visnshaft* (Life and Science, 1909–12) and *Di yidishe velt* (The Jewish World, 1912–16) not only featured some of the best new Yiddish fiction, plays, and poetry, but also contained articles on general and Jewish history, political essays on the state of Russian Jews, Jewish workers, and global politics.[70] Similar to the Hebrew periodicals of the early Haskalah, such as *Ha-Measef* (The Gatherer) and *Bikure Ha-Itim* (First Fruits), that Meyer Waxman argues served as "the seminary in which the early writers, poets, and scholars . . . of the second Haskalah period were nourished, trained, and prepared for their future activity," these journals served as a type of surrogate university for many early Yiddish intellectuals.[71] The folklorist, linguist, and newspaper editor Noyekh Prilutski credited the rapidly maturing Yiddish press as the most important factor in the transformation and maturation of the language:

> Thanks to the Yiddish press, our mame-loshen has quickly developed over the past few years. From the language of the marketplace, home,

folk creations, and belle lettres there has been created a language with which to speak of politics and diplomacy, the military and armored ships, social and communal questions, science and criticism, and sculpture and painting.[72]

Under the editorship of A. Litvin (pseud. of Shmuel Hurvits, 1862–1943), *Lebn un visnshaft* was founded with the expressed purpose of bringing popular works of science, culture, and politics to the broad masses of Russian-Jewish youth with limited access to formal university training. Like *Di literarishe monatsshriftn, Lebn un visnshaft* was unaligned politically and promoted culture as key to the Jewish national awakening: "cultural work in general and Jewish cultural work in particular must stand above all parties."[73] However, unlike the purely literary journal of Niger, Vayter, and Gorelik, Litvin's monthly was a forum for a wide variety of political views and sought a popular audience. The editor envisioned a journal that would serve as a bridge between the Jewish and the non-Jewish worlds: "we must have a Jewishly-educated and educated Jewish intelligentsia. And sadly, we barely even have this! Our educated intellectuals are almost entirely not Jewish and our Jewish intellectuals are too poorly educated."[74] *Lebn un visnshaft* was to remedy this unnatural condition.

Litvin's opening statement for the journal displays an almost *maskilic* conviction in the power of knowledge to emancipate the Jewish people. A full generation older than those who came of age in 1905, Litvin combined the Enlightenment embrace of science with the revolutionary geist of recent years:

> We proceed with this difficult work, because we know very well how our nation's youth—the young generation of the old "people of the book"— thirsts for a word of science, yearns for education, because we believe deeply in the strength of the science and education, because we are convinced that science—in the broadest sense of the term—is the unwavering fiery pillar that illuminates the dark path of life's desert and will one day bring general happiness to humanity.[75]

For several years, issues of *Lebn un visnshaft* contained writings from some of the best known novelists, poets, and scholars. Literary works by Dovid Einhorn and Avrom Reisen appeared alongside translations of Guy de Maupassant, Bialik, and Henry Wadsworth Longfellow. The journal included popular essays on nature, family dynamics and child rearing, and astronomy. Beyond popular contributions, however, *Lebn un visnshaft* was the forum for works by scholars such as "Dr. X" (pseud. for Ludovic L. Zamenhof, 1859–1917, the founder of Esperanto), Noyekh Prilutski, and the linguist Mordekhey Vayniger (1890–1929), who advanced proposals for Yiddish language reform (such as changing its alphabet from Hebrew to Latin, the use of proverbs, and the issue of *daytshmerizms*[76]). Others, such as Niger, Gorelik, and Prilutski contributed critical essays on Yiddish literature and theater.

Soon after the demise of *Lebn un visnshaft,* the literary/*gezelshaftlekh* journal, *Di yidishe velt* appeared on the Yiddish scene and quickly became the site of some of the finest and most influential pre–World War I Yiddish writing, expanding Yiddish even farther into the realms of *visnshaft*. The journal first appeared in St. Petersburg under the direction of the former *Fraynd* editor Shoyl Ginzburg (1866–1940). As Simon Rabinovitch has shown, in *Di yidishe velt's* first year of publication, it served as a "semi-official party organ" for Dubnow's Autonomist movement.[77] In addition, it published many mainstays of the established Yiddish literary scene, such as Abramovitsh, Dubnow, Horovits, An-sky, Spektor, and Peretz, as well as the best of the new generation of writers and intellectuals such as Asch, Einhorn, Niger, Prilutski, and Vayter. In its introduction, entitled "Our Path," the journal declared itself the organ for those Jewish intellectuals who desired to come into contact with the Jewish folk through culture and literature in a more thoughtful way than could be achieved in the daily press, by offering "a straightforward and honest literary journal, a forum for Jewish thought and creative-spirit, a meeting place for the folk and its intellectuals."[78] As Rabinovitch explains, *Di yidishe velt* was first launched in the wake of the collapse of the Russian-Jewish journal *Evreiskii mir* (Jewish World) by a group of young Yiddish activists who included Shtif, Niger, and Yisroel Tsinberg, among others, as well as An-sky and Horovits. "Abandoning the pretense of nonpartisanship, the new journal's editorial board reflected a particular folkist and Diaspora nationalist worldview. An-sky, Perel'man, Horovits, and Efroikin reconstituted the party in 1912, and thus *Di yidishe velt* was intended as a semiofficial party organ."[79]

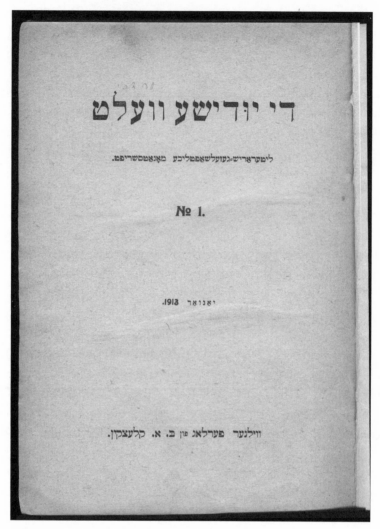

1. *Di yidishe velt,* no. 1 (Vilna, 1913)

Reminiscent of *Der fraynd*'s move to Warsaw, *Di yidishe velt*'s sudden transfer to Vilna in 1913 dramatically symbolizes the geographic and generational shift that was occurring as a younger generation of Yiddish intellectuals based in the Pale rose to the fore of the maturing Yiddish culture. In late 1912, the journal was taken over by the Boris Kletskin publishing house, its political partisanship was dropped, and Niger became editor. In its new, longer format, *Di yidishe velt* quickly was perceived as the premier Yiddish intellectual journal of its time. It included a broad range of literary criticism, lengthier discussions of political and social matters affecting Russian Jewry, scholarly works on Yiddish language development, the status of national minorities in the reshaping of Europe, and some of the finest works of Yiddish literature.[80] Throughout its five year lifespan (January 1912 to December 1916) and in its various incarnations, *Di yidishe velt* was unquestionably the finest Yiddish periodical produced in the years before World War I and is easily on par with any that succeeded it. With Niger as editor, *Di yidishe velt* offered a much fuller and more mature portrait of the Jewish intelligentsia than did its competition, and significantly raised the standard for future Yiddish journalistic and scholarly works. Like *Di literarishe monatsshriftn*, *Di yidishe velt* was not the instrument of any one political party, but served as a platform for the best Yiddish short fiction, poetry, literary criticism, and literary history, and included conversations from a broad range of Jewish national perspectives including Dubnow's liberalism, Zhitlowsky's socialism, and Borochov's Marxist-Zionism. It featured a steady stream of contributions by writers such as Peretz, Asch, Bergelson, Einhorn, and Yehoash (pseudonym of Solomon Bloomgarten, 1870–1927), economic and demographic essays by Jacob Lestschinsky and Moyshe Shalit, literary criticism and history by Borochov, Bal-Makhshoves, Nokhem Shtif, and Yisroel Tsinberg, and one of the first published works by the future head of the YIVO, Max Weinreich, who translated passages from Homer's *Iliad*. The journal also included writings by Niger, who spoke on a wide range of literary and cultural subjects, such as reflections on the contribution of Nathan Birnbaum to the Yiddishist movement, discussions on Romanticism and the Yiddish novel, and examinations of Yiddish writers such as Bergelson, Einhorn, and Morris Rosenfeld (1862–1923), and the Hebrew author Uri Nissan Gnessin.

Efforts to explore and chart the Yiddish language, its literature, culture, and history also found expression in the appearance of several new Yiddish language monographs and miscellanies. For example, in 1908 Zalmen Reisen published one of the first modern Yiddish grammars to prove to skeptics that such a task could be accomplished. As he wrote in *Yidishe gramatik* (Yiddish Grammar):

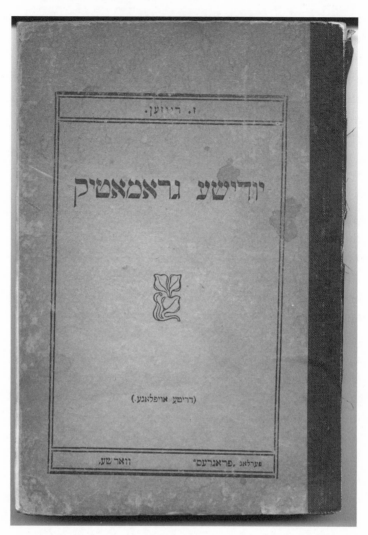

2. Zalmen Reisen, *Yidishe gramatik* (Warsaw, 1908)

Often discussed is whether it is possible [to create such a work]. I am inclined to think . . . that there has been imposed a veil of fear around that which is called "Yiddish grammar." . . . My grammar . . . which is, understand, only a first attempt, will demonstrate . . . that the fear is unnecessary—that a Yiddish grammar is *clearly* possible, and even relatively easy to write. . . . Mistakes, should they be found, will lead to the perfection of the Yiddish grammar. This is the path to the scientific basis of the Yiddish language.[81]

Along with the new emphases on Yiddish grammar, literature, and literary criticism came a renewed interest in folklore. Soon after the revolution, Noyekh Prilutski, for example, was motivated by a thirst for ethnography and published *Yidishe folkslider* (Jewish Folksongs) and Noyekh Prilutski's *Zamelbikher far yidishen folklor, filologye, un kulturgeshikhte* (Collections of Yiddish Folklore, Philology, and Cultural History).[82] His goal for the collections was to document and preserve the traditional Jewish world that was, by that time, clearly in its last days:

> I believe that the need for a special Yiddish organ for our folklore, philology, and cultural history has long been apparent. There already exist several such periodicals in German. The time has come, however, to produce a Yiddish ethnological periodical in the same language as the researched material.
>
> We request that you send to us 1) folksongs, folk stories, Purim plays, phrases, witticisms, colloquialisms, expressions, riddles, and the like; 2) folk stories about historical events and personalities; 3) odd documents, letters and family archives, pages from old store rooms [*genizes*], 4) descriptions and photos of old cemeteries, rituals baths, homes, house wares, kitchenware, and the like.[83]

The scholarly efforts that had been housed in the post-1905 Yiddish journals, miscellanies, and monographs attained their first independent forum with the 1913 publication of *Der pinkes: yorbukh far der geshikhte fun der yidisher literatur un shprakh, far folklore, kritik un bibliografye* (The Record: Yearbook for the History of Yiddish Literature and Language, for Folklore, Criticism and Bibliography). Under the editorial direction of Shmuel Niger, *Der pinkes* was such a tour de force of the new Yiddish scholarship that many scholars have credited it with launching the field of modern Yiddish scholarship.[84] Although its role in laying a foundation for subsequent scholarly investigations into Yiddish is undeniable, the volume must also be seen as the culmination of nearly a decade's worth of scholarly investigations into the Yiddish language, history, and culture of Russian Jewry. Published by the Kletskin press, this compendium is rich with the sort of linguistic, literary, folkloric, and bibliographic essays that were scattered throughout the Yiddish press since the 1905 Revolution. Not only was it the first volume to showcase the new Yiddish scholarship, but it also sought to establish the agenda for research by featuring a statement on the future of Yiddish language scholarship by Borochov. In his essay "Di oyfgabn fun der yidisher filologye" (The Tasks of Yiddish Philology), discussed at length in chapter 4, Borochov represented Yiddish language reform as a primary step toward national revitalization of the Russian Jewry.[85]

Der pinkes marked an important transition in Yiddish scholarship. The grandiose appearance of *Der pinkes,* fashioned with a handsome cover, ornamental typeface, and large pages, was an effort to take control of Yiddish language research and to tether it to the agenda of Jewish national liberation. Much like Borochov's treatise, the volume is itself a type of programmatic document that hoped to set the tenor and tone of future language research by infusing it with the pride developed during the 1905 Revolution. Indeed, the volume is largely a scholarly manifesto of the 1905 generation, despite the inclusion of older, more established Jewish scholars.[86] Beyond Borochov's "Oyfgabn," *Der pinkes* contained a broad range of articles on Yiddish literature and culture: essays on Yiddish phonetics and Hebrew sounds, memoirs and remembrances of literary figures, such as Mendele, Avrom Goldfaden, and Avrom Reisen, studies of the Yiddish theater, the early Yiddish press, Russian-Jewish folklore, and reviews of recent Yiddish scholarly work. The volume also closed with a bibliography of Yiddish philological works written by Borochov.

Although Niger's introduction to *Der pinkes* was brief, he articulated a bold agenda for the volume. He envisioned it as the first in an annual series that would serve as a permanent archive of the accomplishments of Yiddish publishing, and as an aid for comparative studies charting the growth and development of the language, literature, and literary studies. In effect, he was proposing that *Der pinkes* should be the first Yiddish scholarly institution, one that would not only preserve and store the wealth of Yiddish literary and scholarly activity, but would also preside over its development by setting standards for the budding discipline. Similar to the faith that

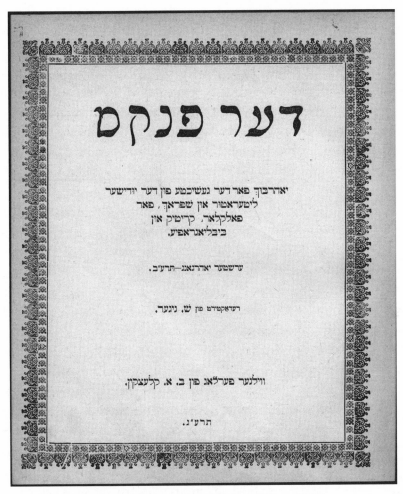

3. *Der pinkes*, ed. Shmuel Niger (Vilna, 1913)

he displayed in the Yiddish language five years earlier with *Di literarishe
monatsshriftn,* Niger intended that *Der pinkes* would further the legiti-
mization of Yiddish and its acceptance in the larger world. He saw it as a
vehicle that would set new standards for Yiddish orthography, establish
a regular grammar for the language, and lay the agenda for future scholarly endeavors. This agenda-setting impulse is most evident in the emphasis that Niger gave to the question of orthography. At the time, there was
no agreed-upon basis for spelling and each press tended to follow its own

standard, or in some cases, no identifiable standard at all. Niger named orthographic reform as among the first issues that needed to be addressed: "[*Der pinkes*] will be able to assist in answering the practical-scientific questions of Yiddish literary life. Among the most vital of these questions is without a doubt the question of its orthography."[87] Niger also hoped *Der pinkes* would serve Yiddish scholarship and the Jewish community in two additional ways: "by gathering and cultivating various material that has a relationship to scientific investigations of Yiddish literature and language in general," and "by collecting and systematizing the relevant materials of each year."[88]

Niger's vision for *Der pinkes* was partially successful. Although it could not be sustained beyond the 1913 volume, his goal for *Der pinkes* to begin a process of creating a broad variety of forums for scholarly research into the Yiddish language and Russian Jewry was achieved[89] and several of its contributions continue to inform Yiddish scholarship to this day.[90] More important, however, was the strident tone taken by the volume. *Der pinkes* confidently proclaimed that the Yiddish language and its culture was capable of the most sophisticated realms of intellectual expression, and its speakers were worthy of inclusion among the nations of Russia.

As much as it launched the field of *Yidishe visnshaft* as a serious field of modern Jewish scholarship, *Der pinkes* also represents the climax of a process of transformation of the Yiddish language that had been occurring over the previous half century, and which was accelerated and transformed by the 1905 Revolution. The language that once had to be abandoned by its native speakers for them to take up serious scholarly pursuits had become, by the eve of World War I, the language for some of the most critical, scientific studies into all aspects of Russian-Jewish life. Once marginalized as an immature jargon unfit for sophisticated works, it now stood at the very (indeed, crowded) center of a new national project.

Even with accomplishments such as *Di yidishe velt* and *Der pinkes,* there was little consensus on the scope, future, content, and ideological agenda of the new Yiddish science. The following chapters on Shmuel Niger, Ber Borochov, and Nokhem Shtif demonstrate that despite their shared commitment to Yiddish and belief in the authority of *visnshaft*, the ideological struggles that manifested themselves during the 1905 upheavals continued to exert their influence long after the revolution's demise.

3 Shmuel Niger and the Making of Yiddish High Culture

You are the *cultural critic* of our generation. . . .
—Ber Borochov to Shmuel Niger, 1912[1]

Shmuel Niger (1883–1955) was intimately involved with nearly every major Yiddish literary movement to appear during the first half of the twentieth century. More so than any other member in the cohort of Jewish cultural activists, scholars, and writers who came of age with the 1905 Revolution, Niger introduced generations of popular and educated audiences to the possibilities of an expansive Yiddish culture. He identified and fostered much of the Yiddish literature that appeared in the wake of the revolution, guided it to its heights of sophistication in the years after World War I, and chronicled its near total collapse in the decade following World War II.

In his youth, Niger was an activist and propagandist with the Vozrozhdenie group and the S.S. After the 1905 Revolution, he edited or contributed to almost every influential Yiddish literary journal that appeared from 1907 until his death in 1955. He was a contributor to major Yiddish dailies in Russia, Poland, and the United States, including *Der fraynd, Haynt, Moment, Der forverts,* and *Der tog.* He published significant studies on Abramovitsh, Sholem Aleichem, Peretz, the novelist and playwright Asch, and the renowned poet H. Leivik (1888–1962).[2] As an indication of his cultural range, Niger also promoted cutting-edge New York poetic circles like Di yunge (The Young Ones), and Di inzikhistn (The Introspectivists), and popularized Soviet Yiddish authors in spite of his opposition to the Soviet regime.[3]

Niger's contribution to the development of the new Yiddish culture extended well beyond his literary criticism. He was also among the first to identify the need for a scholarly approach toward the new Yiddish culture. In the years between the two Russian Revolutions, he not only edited several journals featuring the most significant works of early *Yidishe visnshaft*, but he also edited the 1913 volume *Der pinkes* and the first major lexicon of Yiddish writers. Upon moving to the United States after World War I, he became an active participant in the YIVO and an editor of its flagship journal, *YIVO bleter* (YIVO Journal). Niger's indefatigable activism for Yiddish influenced how other Yiddishists of his era understood their craft. As Max Weinreich, head of the YIVO for over forty years, credited him:

> Niger was a leader—a leader of a movement that he himself created. . . . Sh. Niger never once asked in his articles whether one could demand from a writer something other than writing, and yet from himself he demanded more than that. For his entire life he was more than a community thinker and a community worker, he was also a community leader.[4]

Niger's oeuvre includes fifty years' worth of articles in the Yiddish, Hebrew, Russian, and English presses and places him not just at the pinnacle of Yiddish literary criticism, but as a major figure within all of modern Jewish scholarship in spite of never holding an academic post. His influence was so vast and his rise to the top of the Yiddish intellectual world so swift that his writings were being gathered for republication while he was in his late twenties.[5] By the end of his career, a bibliography limited to his work on the topic of Jewish education contained over two hundred and fifty entries.[6] Upon his death in 1955, more than two hundred and fifty obituaries and tributes appeared in half a dozen languages.[7] As Leivik credited him: "Such a fifty year-long involvement and engagement with a national literature is rarely found among the greatest literatures in the world. Also rarely found is such an influence on a literature as was Sh. Niger's influence on Yiddish literature, even in those moments when one didn't agree with him, or even fought with him."[8]

In what is a profound indicator of the loss of the vibrant Yiddish intellectual culture that flourished in the first half of the twentieth century, no full-length study of Niger exists, and only a few essays examining his role

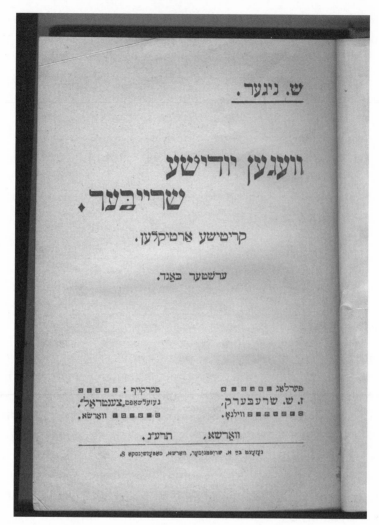

4. Shmuel Niger, *Vegn yidishe shrayber* (1912)

as a literary critic and cultural leader have been written.[9] After the brief outpouring of obituaries and memorials, scant attention has been paid to his contribution to modern Yiddish letters. Weinreich noted the need for a full study of Niger as indispensable to an understanding of all Yiddish culture:

There must be a book about Niger, not so much for the people of his generation as for those that come. It is difficult to explain him to a generation that is far from us, but it is not impossible, and it would be a service for those who are estranged. That generation will better understand its roots and its own self when they realize the greatness of Sh. Niger's mighty personality.[10]

Although this chapter is not the place for a comprehensive discussion of Niger's role in the creation of modern Yiddish culture, it does consider his early contribution to the formation of a *visnshaft* for Yiddish through his literary criticism, editorial stewardship, and support for institutions that would promote its maturation. After a brief biographical overview, this chapter explores the development of Niger's attitudes toward Yiddish literary culture and his turn to *visnshaft* in the period from the 1905 Revolution until his departure for the United States in 1919. In doing so, it investigates his efforts to shape a European Yiddish national culture that was a viable alternative to Jewish Orthodoxy, Russification, and even to the ideological constraints of the revolution itself.

Much of Niger's early activity was concerned with identifying a literary strategy that would elevate Yiddish letters to that of other European national cultures. An examination of his writings indicates that he spent these years struggling to find common ground between seemingly opposing ideological positions: between the competing loyalties of class and nation, between commitments to political and cultural activism, and most significantly, between the desires to create a Yiddish literary culture that would further the revolutionary cause and one that was strictly concerned with aesthetic values. In his quest for an approach to Yiddish literature, he identified the need for a new type of Jewish public intellectual—one who was committed to Yiddish culture, served the proletariat, stood opposed to the Haskalah, and held an artistic appreciation of Yiddish literature. A discussion of Niger further demonstrates that from its outset, *Yidishe visnshaft* was both a product of and a response to the changes brought about by the 1905 Revolution. If in the days of the revolution, the new radical Jewish politics provided much of the first organizational and ideological framework for the critical study of Yiddish, the revolution's collapse allowed for the new science to escape the confines of partisan politics and develop with greater ideological independence.

Shmuel Niger (pseudonym for Shmuel Tsharny) was born in 1883 in Dukor, a village located in the Minsk region of Russia (now Belarus). Niger's father, a fervent follower of Lubavitch Hasidim, died when Shmuel was six years old.[11] Among Niger's siblings were Baruch Charney Vladeck (1886–1935), a managing editor at the Yiddish daily *Forverts* and the founding president of the Jewish Labor Committee in New York, and Daniel Tsharny (1888–1958), the Yiddish poet, journalist, and memoirist. Like the other children in his household, Niger was provided with a traditional Hasidic education. He attended *kheyder* until age thirteen and was sent to Minsk to attend a Lubavitch yeshiva until he was seventeen years old. Considered an *ilui* (genius) by his teachers, Niger excelled in his studies and received *semikhah* (rabbinical ordination) in his late teens.

As a teenager, Niger began to take a strong interest in secular subjects. As in the case of Lestschinsky, his path away from orthodoxy was influenced by the writings of the Hebrew essayist and cultural Zionist Ahad Ha'am. While in yeshiva, he secretly learned Russian and studied texts of the Haskalah, Zionism, and Marxism. Soon, he abandoned the Hasidic world of his childhood and applied a comparable zealotry to the Jewish revolutionary movement. To Niger, the 1903 Kishinev pogroms were a sign of the persistent danger of Russian anti-Judaism and led to his full immersion in the revolution. He was a propagandist and a party activist in several early Labor Zionist groups in Dvinsk (now Daugavpils, Latvia), Warsaw, Kiev, and other cities in the Pale. Niger joined with the Vozrozhdenie group when it formed in 1903 and then with the S.S. in 1905. Niger's time in these short-lived groups provided him with his first opportunities to publish in Yiddish and to experiment with various approaches to Yiddish literary criticism.

Niger's initial contributions to S.S. publications focused on raising the awareness of Jewish workers to the revolutionary potential of a vibrant Jewish nation and were concerned with developing the party's synthesis of the ideologies of socialism and nationalism. Like Lestschinsky, Niger argued that as a consequence of its "unnatural" condition, the Jewish working class was stunted in its organic development, and that the newly politicized Jewish intellectual would be the agent to redeem it from its lowly status. However, as the 1905 Revolution began to falter, Niger's attention increasingly turned to questions of language and culture. By 1907, Niger was quickly moving away from advocating for any utilitarian functions for Yiddish, and instead advanced the possibility of a Yiddish literature that reflected the most current European modernist trends.

His first major essay for the S.S. was a widely distributed piece entitled "Vos iz der yidisher arbeter" (What Is the Jewish Worker) in which he hoped to awaken Jewish workers to class and national consciousness.[12] In it, he imparted to the Jewish proletariat a dual role as part of the international workers' movement that transcended individual national boundaries and simultaneously as part of the larger national "awakening" that embraced all Jews irrespective of class. He argued that only in recent days were Jewish workers becoming conscious of their status as a proletariat: "The Jewish worker is rousing himself from his nap. He is raising his head—and really not much more than his head—from his dark, drowsy cellar, from the desolate and dark ghetto air."[13] Although Jewish laborers shared many characteristics with workers throughout the Russian empire, Niger also insisted that they comprised a special case. Jewish proletarians were impeded by their lack of territorial concentration, which diluted their numbers, made them more vulnerable to the ravages of capitalism and political powerlessness, and prevented them from attaining full class consciousness. Several others factors contributed to their stunted growth: Jews were forced to live under unique legal constraints, were confined to the Pale, and were overly dependent upon the good will of their host communities. Finally, because most Jewish workers tended to work outside of Russia's large factories and instead languished in small isolated shops, "the Jews are not sufficiently developed to acquire the means for their own liberation. This leaves the Jews in an unnatural condition."[14]

In this widely distributed essay brimming with ideological bombast, Niger, like Lestschinsky, drew upon familiar Yiddish literary motifs to illustrate the evolving condition of workers in terms his audience might understand and thus inspire them to action. Speaking of the new national spirit developing among Jewish workers, he invoked the most famous of Peretz's characters, silent Bontshe, the symbol of Jewish passivity who was beaten down by a lifetime of hard labor, and who even in the afterlife was unable to speak on his own behalf. However, with the coming of the new age, even Bontshe is capable of being transformed into a man of action: "The old feelings and ideas, the old dark 'credos,' the old cold despairs, hide like shadows from the new warm and bright socialist light. Backs no longer bend under the pitiful heavy yoke as the [Jews'] meek subservience and muted patience disappears. As if in a dream, 'silent Bontshe' raises his voice, becomes a hero and a fighter. He dreams of a new life, he imagines a new world, and even a new heaven."[15]

Niger set out to achieve two goals with this essay. First, he had to convince Jewish workers of their responsibility to take part in the struggle of laborers everywhere to free themselves from the bondage of industrial capitalism. Despite that Jews were less proletarianized than workers of Russia's other national minorities, their degree of economic exploitation was nevertheless comparable. They had lost the means to support themselves economically and were forced to sell their own labor, an act that united them with all workers. Second, he cautioned them against separating themselves out of the larger Jewish fold. Rather, he argued, they stood at its vanguard:

> We must understand and treat the developmental path of the Jewish working class . . . , as an organic component, in truth as the most important and active component in the overall development of the Jewish national organism.[16]

and:

> If the history, if the awakening, if the origins of the Jewish proletariat is to be understood as bound up with the history of the entire Jewish nation, if the "today" of the Jewish proletariat has a close relationship to the present-day position of the entire Jewish nation, we must also, obviously, understand the problem of the Jewish proletariat's "tomorrow" no differently.[17]

Over the following year, in the midst of the revolution, Niger's contributions to the S.S. journal were concerned less with class struggle and more with questions of Jewish culture and language. Soon after writing "Vos iz der yidisher arbeter," Niger turned his attention directly to the issue of Yiddish culture in an essay entitled "Di yidishe shprakh un di yidishe inteligents" (The Yiddish Language and the Jewish Intelligentsia), in which he took the position that the greatest contribution Jewish radicals can make to their nation was in fact a cultural one.[18] Niger's goal was to convince the new generation of young Jewish intellectuals to champion the cause of Yiddish, both as a value unto itself and as a necessary component of the struggle of the Jewish working class. Yiddish, a language that was only then being thought of in some circles as a viable and legitimate medium for revolutionary propaganda, was for Niger a symbol of the downtrodden Jewish proletarian masses. The liberation of Yiddish was the key to the self-liberation of the whole Jewish nation, "Until now, Yiddish has not been freed," he writes, "It must become more meaningful, deeper, vital."[19]

Niger saw a parallel between the sorry state of Jewish workers and the Yiddish language. The "unending web" of capitalism not only stunted Jewish class consciousness, but also was responsible for the delayed development of their language and its culture. As he explained it, the capitalist system fostered the growth of a Jewish middle class that benefited from the new economic order. Among other nations, it was the bourgeoisie who took responsibility for developing and promoting their nation's culture. However, the Jewish bourgeoisie—whom he equated with the Haskalah—instead abandoned their national tongue and created Jewish cultures in the languages of their host societies. This led to the development of "unnatural" German-Jewish, Polish-Jewish, and Russian-Jewish cultures that severed bourgeois Jews from the organic Jewish nation. "Within our 'high society,' our jargon has become the symbol of exile, darkness and ignorance, the embodiment of material and spiritual poverty."[20] To Niger, even much of the Yiddish press (like *Der fraynd* of St. Petersburg), was created by those with assimilationist and *maskilic* intentions rather than out of a commitment to Yiddish, and therefore did not serve Jewish national interests.

Despite the apparent success of these hybrid cultures, Jewish laborers still universally employed Yiddish, leading to an ever greater "social differential" that prevented the unification of Jewish workers and the bourgeoisie into a nation. Workers, enslaved as they were by the capitalist system, did not have the resources to create a distinct national culture of their own and were left adrift. The remedy to this unnatural state was, of course, the growing Jewish labor movement that was building its own proletarian

Yiddish culture. At its forefront was a new type of Jewish intellectual who stood in opposition to the old bourgeois *maskil* and embraced both the revolution and the Yiddish language:

> For the folk, language is not some play-thing that it fabricates, but a tool, a weapon with which it forges its historical development. . . . The real proletarian socialist intellectuals who bind themselves to the folk-masses are with them as one body and one soul, flesh with their flesh, and blood with their blood. For the true proletarian intellectuals, the folk-language is not a means and is not an end, but is for them the very air that they breathe . . . which they neither idealize nor bemoan. [Yiddish is] an objective factor which they will and must make better, more beautiful, popular, and more productive.[21]

Once the political momentum began to fade in spring 1907, Niger distanced himself from attempts to forge a synthesis between the demands of Jewish nationalism and the working class. Although he continued to publish in the S.S. organ, his subsequent essays were less concerned with matters of party platform, the task of differentiating the S.S. stance from its Zionist, Bundist, and SERP competitors, or on crises in the government. Instead, as the tsar was dissolving the second Duma, Niger fully took up the cause for modern Yiddish literary culture. For the next several years, his writing was dominated by efforts to resolve the tension between a desire for a Yiddish literature that would serve the goals of the revolution and one that reflected the demands of European literary aesthetics. Niger's literary criticism in this period oscillated between promoting those writers whose work painted stark portraits depicting brutal working conditions under industrial capitalism and championing those who gave themselves over fully to the avant-garde. In these years, Niger began to fall under the sway of nineteenth-century Russian literary theorists of Realism such as Vissarion Belinsky, Nikolay Dobrolyubov, and Nikolay Mikhaylovsky who struggled to balance social goals and artistic considerations. Later, as a university student in Bern, through exposure to the writings of French literary critics Charles Augustin Sainte-Beuve and Hippolyte Taine, Niger attempted to divorce Yiddish artistic forms from all utilitarian functions, and judge them only by their artistry.[22] Increasingly, he came to insist that artistic expression must exist outside of any practical political and economic realms—"no timely, national or social ends,"—and answer only to its own internal demands.[23]

Niger's first attempt at Yiddish literary criticism was a review of Sholem Asch's drama, *Meshiekh's tsaytn* (Times of the Messiah).[24] The essay, "Vegn der tragedye fun goles" (On the Tragedy of Exile), was Niger's initial attempt to place himself at the forefront of the new Yiddish literary culture as well as to introduce the still largely unknown Asch to a much broader audience.[25] The fact that Niger was so young at the time of this publication (just twenty-four years old), with little secular training, and no higher education, this work was a remarkable accomplishment. The overly didactic and ideologically driven prose that defined his political essays just a year before is greatly diminished, but not entirely absent from this essay. The result is a review that is alternatively sophisticated and naïve, insightful and doctrinaire.

Niger saw Asch's play as a meditation on the need to reconfigure Jewish messianic hopes in an increasingly secular and uncertain time. As he saw it, the play's greatest contribution was its depiction of the multifaceted exilic status of Jews, "just as each age has its own Messiah—so too must each generation carry the yoke of its own particular exile."[26] Each of Asch's characters has his or her own understanding of the Messiah, and each represents a particular manifestation of the Jews' exilic condition. To Niger, the characters in Asch's play were symbols of the tragic and fractured lives led by the Jews of his day because they were stuck in circumstances and ideologies that left them no opportunity to remedy their condition. The exception to this is the character Rabbi Kakhan—the patriarch of the drama who is its most complete figure. A throwback to traditional Orthodoxy, Kakhan believes deeply in the coming of the Messiah and therefore, does not suffer from his own exilic circumstance. He is the embodiment of the eternal pain of Jewish exile, but is so deeply convinced of its joyous end that he is the only character to possess inner harmony. Trapped as he is in the past, however, he provides no model for the legions of post-traditional Jews of the twentieth century.

Kakhan's descendants, Niger explained, are less fortunate. No longer able to maintain their ancestral faith, Kakhan's children and grandchildren look for ways to remedy their condition and find a home in their world. "Each symbolic-type that Asch created in *Meshiekh's tsaytn* embodies a more or less *artistic* answer to that eternal Jewish question: *Where is our home?*"[27] Rabbi Kakhan's son, Moyshe, is forever stuck in the present. Like Peretz's silent Bontshe, Moyshe is incapable of improving his situation and simply moves with the times. He has no usable past and no hope for the future. Another son, Ben-Zion, is an old style *maskilic* Zionist with a belief so thin that he cannot even imagine the possibility of Zion. The young Justine spends her time wandering the Polish woods, making her home among the poplars, and is barely human herself.

Niger's critique of the character Khaym, a young socialist revolutionary who "destroys old worlds and builds new ones," demonstrates that in spite of his attempts, Niger's literary approach was not entirely disassociated from the influence of revolutionary politics. Although he praised Asch's ability to convey the Jewish condition in purely artistic terms and for distancing his literary efforts from immediate utilitarian considerations, Niger expressed betrayal at Asch's portrayal of Khaym as a lost, hapless soul with an inclination for naïve, flowery speeches. He scolded Asch for depicting Khaym as an internationalist far removed from the Jewish nation rather than as a complicated figure who could point the way to a heroic postexilic future for the Jews.

Niger's subsequent essays for the S.S. organ continued this vacillation between what were for him the increasingly exclusive demands of politics and aesthetics. His continued loyalty to the Jewish proletarian revolution is evident in his portrait of the poet Hershele (pseudonym for D. Danilevitsh, 1882–1941).[28] Although Niger had focused his attention largely upon aesthetic questions in his review of Asch's drama, he characterized Hershele's strident revolutionary poetry as representing the true spirit of the new Yiddish proletarian poets. In his review of *Hershele's lider* (Hershele's Poems), Niger returned to the political bombast of his earlier essays and declared that the best of the new generation of Yiddish poets were those who dedicated their work to the cause of the Jewish worker: "[t]he young Yiddish-'jargonistic'-poetry is a people's poetry not because it serves the folk, but because it belongs to them, because it is blood with its blood and marrow with its marrow. The Jewish poets who speak with the national voice are truly folk-poets . . . because they *go* to the people; they *come* from the people."[29]

However, just three weeks after this review, he changed course once again and distanced himself from any utilitarian function of literature in a feuilleton that marked his first programmatic statement for Yiddish literature, "Shmuesen vegn der yidisher literatur" (Talks on Yiddish Literature):

> The most noble and most intimate creations of humankind's personality must develop freely and broadly only as an end unto themselves, not as a means for something else. This is an old, a very old rule. And Yiddish literature is naturally no exception. Yiddish literature, the oldest and youngest of all literatures, must become an end for itself and its self-worth; it must stand on its own feet, with broad, unfolded wings.[30]

In this essay, Niger attacked much of the pre–1905 Revolution Yiddish literature and set out a clear agenda for its future. He took the generation of *maskilic* Yiddish writers before him to task for not employing Jewish languages for their own sake, but rather to encourage assimilation. He recounted that, in the past, Hebrew had been employed to demonstrate the ease with which one could learn Russian and that Yiddish had been used to persuade its speakers to abandon it. He charged those authors with writing in Yiddish strictly for practical purposes and without any concern for aesthetics, and for diminishing the language as a result. It was the task of his generation, therefore, to bring an end to such assaults on the Jewish national language. His hope—and increasingly, his life's mission—was that by elevating Yiddish literature to the standard of major European literatures, Jews would simultaneously be cohering into a nation. To Niger, the best of this new writing was produced by those who published their works in innovative Yiddish journals and miscellanies such as *Di naye tsayt, Di velt,* and *Goldene funken.* Along with a tribute to Abramovitsh, Peretz, and Spektor—who paved the way to creating the language's modern forms—Niger heralded the work of figures such as Asch, Avrom Reisen, Hirshbeyn, and Weissenberg as embodying the very best of the new Yiddish writing. The new national literature served the folk masses best, and resisted cultural assimilation most, he argued, when it lost its ideological thrust and focused on artistic forms. Paradoxically then, the effort required to normalize and liberate the Jews required adopting a literary strategy that was at odds with the very overt political campaigns in which he was active during the 1905 Revolution.

In this respect then, the failure of the revolution can be said to have freed Niger intellectually, by providing him an opportunity to divorce himself from the ideological constraints of Jewish partisan politics and to explore a broader range of literary strategies. The appearance in 1908 of *Di literarishe monatsshriftn*, rather than being a sharp break away from revolutionary politics, was (at least in Niger's case), a consequence of his struggle to distance himself from a utilitarian conception of Yiddish literature. This disengagement had a clear impact on his writing style as well. Niger not only abandoned the formulaic prose that characterized much of his early essays, but he increasingly matured as a writer as he came to believe that with his criticism, he was fostering new artistic forms.[31]

As discussed in chapter 2, *Di literarishe monatsshriftn* was a joint project of three former political activists, Niger (S.S.), A. Vayter (Bund) and Shmarya Gorelik (Zionist). Widely recognized as having begun the Yiddish literary "renaissance," this short-lived but highly influential journal was the first attempt to create a Yiddish literary forum devoted purely to the cultivation of aesthetic values, absent any party ideology. Central to *Di literarishe monatsshriftn* was a series of four essays by Niger on the Yiddish authors Peretz, Nomberg, Avrom Reisen, and Asch. Like the journal in which they appeared, Niger's essays introduced a new critical tone into modern Yiddish culture. For perhaps the first time in its modern history, Yiddish is treated as a language on par with all others, without apologetics. There are neither defenses of Yiddish, discussions of "the language question," nor instrumental motives imparted to it. Quite simply, Yiddish is taken seriously as a medium of intellectual discourse. The essays themselves are remarkable on several additional fronts: they outline a bold new vision for Yiddish literature and championed a new generation of Yiddish writers, rail against ideologically driven literature, and advance aesthetic ends as the sole legitimate source of artistic motivation.

The best models for the new Yiddish literature were, according to Niger, those offered by the examples of Peretz and Asch. As he saw it, Peretz was the leader of a new generation of Yiddish writers. His Romantic vision of Yiddish was a much needed effort at national mythmaking and provided a basis for a healthy, vibrant, post-traditional Jewish life. Although Niger dutifully credited Abramovitsh as the founder of the Yiddish literary renaissance, he argued that Peretz was the first to divorce himself fully from the didactic Haskalah ideals that characterized nineteenth-century Yiddish writing. To the young Niger, Abramovitsh did not offer his readers a usable future, only a clear portrait of the world they had left behind. By contrast, having broken free of such *maskilic* constraints, Peretz was free to express his artistry fully and, in doing so, provide the literary foundation for a modern, secular Jewish nation. Peretz's neoromantic interpretations of Jewish mysticism paved the way for a new generation of Yiddish writers to take on more experimental forms: "As the father of the Yiddish short story, Peretz is the most Jewish of all Yiddish writers."[32] Peretz's greatest disciple was Asch, "the prophet of the earth."[33] More so than Nomberg, whose work Niger admired but believed would not endure, Asch wrote directly from his soul, as if bound to the earth itself. "Asch is the poet of the simple people, the sign of his God is the ordinary."[34] A writer of stillness and quietude, Asch embodied the very best of the new Yiddish writing: "Asch teaches us belief, Asch teaches us love."[35]

In a reversal of his characterization of the revolutionary Hershele a year earlier, Niger now cited Peretz as the true people's-poet who "carries inside of him the day-to-day experiences of the people, their everyday pathos."[36] At the same time, Niger bristled against poetry that was composed with the goal of advocating on behalf of downtrodden Jews, and that sacrificed artistic authenticity in favor of immediate and pragmatic ends. This was the basis of much of the criticism he leveled at Avrom Reisen's poetry, which he deemed simple and sentimental, and he chided Reisen for employing trite themes in order to tug at his reader's heart strings. Women and children might weep at his poems, Niger wrote, "but Reisen is not my poet. . . . Not for me, for us, for many of us intellectuals."[37]

As Niger noted several decades later, the failure of *Di literarishe monatsshriftn* after only four issues came as a rude awakening to him and his coeditors. The editors were so deeply committed to its agenda that they could not see its limitations.[38] In the violent and uncertain period following the failed revolution, there was little patience among many Jewish readers for retreats into the realm of "pure" culture. No longer able to rely upon the financial support of the defunct S.S., Niger found himself moving from city to city to assume short-lived editorial and journalistic positions. After a very brief stay in Berlin in 1910, Niger joined the growing community of Russian-Jewish émigrés who took up residence in Bern, Switzerland and enrolled in the university. Since the 1890s, Bern had been a regular gathering place for young Russian-Jewish intellectuals in search of university training. The entrance examinations were widely known to be easier at Bern than at other European universities, and there was no *numerus clausus* like that prohibiting most aspiring Jewish students from studying in the Russian empire.[39] Bern also had a reputation as a meeting ground for some of the best and brightest of the new generation of Jewish cultural activists who had fallen under the influence of Chaim Zhitlowsky, (who had lived there in the late 1890s). As Niger's brother Daniel Tsharny recounted in his memoirs, figures such as Asch, Nomberg, and Einhorn were regulars in Niger's apartment.[40]

Niger remained in Bern through the end of 1912. His literary criticism during this time was largely an extension and expansion of the agenda he outlined in the final days of his affiliation with the S.S. and in his essays in *Di literarishe monatsshriftn*. The records of Niger's coursework also provide some indication of his training. Along with seminars on the history of philosophy, including materialism and pragmatism, he enrolled in a variety of courses on French and German theories of literature and art. He continued to publish much in Yiddish, but seems to have made no substantial progress on his planned work on Schopenhauer.[41] The bulk of his activity remained directed toward advancing Yiddish culture on several fronts: building a canon of modern Yiddish literature, promoting the new Jewish intellectual class, and fostering a high-literary style of Yiddish-speaking writers. In his role as literary editor for Litvin's *Lebn un visnshaft,* Niger was in a position to publish, promote, and review works by some of the greatest names in Yiddish letters, including Sholem Aleichem, Der Nister, Weissenberg, Bal-Makhshoves, Bialik, and Pinski. During this time he also published substantial essays on Isaac Meir Dik's (1814–1893) Hebrew writings and on Hebrew poetry.[42] Consequently, because of his prodigious output, close relationships with modern Yiddish authors, and seemingly boundless energy, during this period he began to be heralded as the most renown and influential Yiddish literary critic, topping his one major rival, Bal-Makhshoves.

Niger's greatest ire in this period was directed not at the growing Hebrew literary cultural scene (to which he was an occasional contributor), nor even at the Jewish intellectuals who tried to continue the political revolution (with whom he at times collaborated). Rather, the danger he saw to the development of a Yiddish high culture was the persistent legacy of the Haskalah. Niger believed the Haskalah remained a barrier to Jewish nationalism and represented all that he fought against: assimilation, Russification, and bourgeois democracy. His fear was that Jews would destroy themselves from within by denying their national spirit, a far more insidious threat than anti-Jewish hatred.

Niger's 1911 essay "Kultur un bildung: vegn der yidisher inteligents" (Culture and *Bildung:* On Jewish Intellectuals) exemplifies well his continuing struggle against the assimilatory legacy of the Haskalah.[43] In it, he made a sharp contrast between the demands of culture and those of *bildung*, and insisted that Jewish intellectuals dedicate themselves to enriching the former while combating the latter. In both its German and Yiddish connotations, the Haskalah conception of *bildung* signified both education and moral edification, and reflected not only the abstract aspiration of Jews who wanted to modernize themselves according to Enlightenment values, but also by adopting the host society's cultural practices and national identities as their own. Many Jews, however, took the step of leaving the Jewish fold altogether through conversion. From the point of view of Jewish nationalists like Niger, *bildung* was a betrayal of Jewish national aspirations. By contrast, culture was seen as possessing the necessary force to maintain and strengthen Jewish national identity through the development of Jewish languages, institutions, and artistic forms. To Niger, the task of creating a viable national culture fell to the new class of young intellectuals:

> I speak of the intelligentsia because, to me, the question of Jewish culture is a question for the Jewish intelligentsia. If we don't have a Jewish intelligentsia . . . we will not have any Jewish culture. If we don't have Jewish intelligentsia, we will [continue] to have only Jewish benefactors and advocates of the Haskalah. Our position is that these proponents of

the Haskalah, who have no other goal besides philanthropy and democracy, will not create Enlightenment among us, but will only create heresy, careerism, and de-nationalization. Real enlightenment will come to us when these "cultural carriers" will stop existing for their own sake and will instead become a step in the path toward Jewish culture, when those who want to help the masses will do so by helping our culture, [which is] the future of the nation; . . . when those who are concerned with charity or with abstract democratization . . . will assume the natural functions of an intelligentsia, . . . and will be flesh with the flesh of the folk and spirit with its spirit, and their life will be its life and their future, its future.[44]

Niger likewise saw the continued presence of Haskalah attitudes as a threat to contemporary Yiddish writing. As he explained in a 1912 essay, in spite of recent accomplishments in Yiddish literature, Yiddish was being plagued by the "affliction" of *daytshmerish*.[45] *Daytshmerish* is the term commonly given to a style of Yiddish that employs words from contemporary German (Yiddish: *daytsh*) in the hopes of assuming a "higher" or more cultivated literary tone. Although to some degree understandable in the time before the development of a modern literary Yiddish idiom, the fact that Yiddish writers still turned to Germanisms in the second decade of the twentieth century was abhorrent to Niger. He considered it yet another holdover from the age of the Haskalah, when the adoption of German was seen as among the highest values of "civilized" Jews and was employed by early nineteenth-century Yiddish writers like I. M. Dik. In Dik's time, "one could not speak in simple Yiddish about '*erhabene*' [German: 'elevated, exalted'] matters. . . . Until the recent period . . . Yiddish was a language without a 'literary' style, and one needed a surrogate, and employed daytshmerish. Daytshmerish was a sign of 'courtesy' of 'worldliness' and daytshmerish carried a sense of romance."[46] However, by the end of the nineteenth century, when figures such as Zhitlowsky and Bal-Makhshoves, (who had lived much of their adult lives in German-speaking lands), managed to write in straightforward, unadulterated Yiddish—the practice of using Germanisms was viewed in some circles as a threat to the development of Yiddish literature, "Mendele, Sholem Aleichem, Peretz—the entire literature of the past 50 years shows that one can also create a literature that is worthy of the name beautiful without daytshmerish."[47] The problem, however, was that too many writers still assumed that Yiddish was a language that one did not need to cultivate, "it is clear that daytshmerish is an affliction from which we must be freed."[48]

With his growing reputation as the leading critic of Yiddish literature, and on the heels of the publication of a two volume collection of his articles, Niger returned to Vilna in 1912 at the request of the publisher Boris A. Kletskin, who hired him to edit *Di yidishe velt*. In taking this post, Niger now stood at the center of Yiddish letters, and from 1913 to 1916, he achieved perhaps his greatest impact on its development. Niger also seemed to have settled his debates on how best to advocate on behalf of Yiddish by adopting a strategy that placed him for a time above many of the partisan debates on its future direction. Most important to the history of *Yidishe visnshaft*, during these years, Niger edited three landmark publications that established the first framework for Yiddish: the literary/*gezelshaftlekh* monthly *Di yidishe velt*, the scholarly volume *Der pinkes*, and the first edition of Zalmen Reisen's *Leksikon fun der yidisher literatur un prese* (1914).[49] Looked upon as a whole, these works represent an important milestone in the development of Yiddish scholarship in that they were the forums for its most sophisticated discussions, created a repository for the best of its scholarly productions, and set a new canon of its writers and intellectuals.

In part, what marked Niger's *Di yidishe velt* as being so distinctive was its dedication to Yiddish language planning and development. Niger envisioned *Di yidishe velt* would serve functions akin to a language academy in the absence of any recognized institutional authority over Yiddish. From the beginning of his editorship, the journal advanced a potent vision that included language reform, the preservation of the Jewish communal record, and a commitment to Jewish folklore studies. For example, at the end of the first number that appeared under his direction, Niger made three requests of his readers: to report details of Jewish life in isolated provinces; to help expand the vocabulary by sending in little-known Yiddish words (mostly technical terms from various occupations) for use in a planned Yiddish dictionary; and to donate Jewish cultural artifacts for a planned Jewish cultural museum.[50]

As editor of the most influential journal of Yiddish letters, Niger also tried to influence debates on a wide range of cultural issues. A case in point is his essay on the proposal for a Jewish university in Palestine, made at the eleventh Zionist Congress in Vienna (1913) by Menahem Ussishkin (1863–1941) and Chaim Weizmann (1874–1952). In light of Niger's strong enthusiasm for *visnshaft* and the cultivation of a Jewish intelligentsia, it is surprising to read an essay in which he comes out in strong opposition to suggestions that Jews needed to establish their own national university. In "Tsu dem rayen tsu shafn a yidisher universitet" (On the Notion of a Jewish University), he argued that although the idea may seem like a simple and logical response to the lack of options for Russian Jews seeking higher education, it was in fact, a wrong headed reaction to anti-Jewish discrimination.[51] Niger, no enemy of university training, was not proposing to deny Jews access to centers where they could obtain the best education. However, he was more concerned with the motivation of its proponents and saw it as a threat to Jewish cultural life in the Diaspora.

First, Niger suggested that such an institution would only serve wealthy Jewish families who wanted a university education for their children, but who had found that they were barred from attending the great Russian academies. Such an institution would simply reinforce the ghetto experience—it would amount to a university for Jews and not a Jewish university. Because the proposed university was not an outgrowth of a natural desire among Jews to create secular centers of learning, but was instead a reaction to Jewish hatred, Niger feared that it would do nothing to serve Jewish national interests and only be, "a factory for diplomas."[52] Second, Niger saw the new "Yavne" (as the Zionists called it) as a direct attack on Jewish Diasporic interests, because such an institution threatened to delegitimize Russian Jewry and deny them much needed resources.[53] He was angered that Zionists would seek to dedicate scarce resources to such a lofty project when the support was much more needed in Jewish communities throughout Russia. The Jewish renaissance could not be served from such a distant outpost, Niger argued, and a university in Palestine would only interfere with the project of Jewish nation-building: "A national university is not a factory for diplomas. A national university must, first of all, create and cultivate certain objective cultural values. The 'doctors' must help to develop and disseminate these cultural values." In a university in Palestine—which would likely be conducted in Hebrew and therefore would be inaccessible to most Jews—the values would not be those of the Jewish nation, but rather "Palestinian values" that reflected only the needs of Zionists who sought to uproot Diaspora Jewry. In what might be an appropriate truism for the whole of *Di yidishe velt* under his direction, Niger declared without equivocation: *"The Jews are a Diaspora people."*[54]

Niger's second and most significant contribution to the development of *Yidishe visnshaft* was his involvement in *Der pinkes,* the first forum dedicated to Yiddish scholarship. While officially *Der pinkes*'s sole editor, Niger was greatly assisted by Ber Borochov, who had a hand in shaping the volume by helping with everything from editing contributions, advertising its release, and solving questions of the new orthography.[55] In addition to his introduction (discussed in chapter 2), Niger's contribution to *Der pinkes* was a lengthy piece entitled, "Shtudyes tsu der geshikhte fun der yidisher literatur" (Studies of the History of the Yiddish Language).[56] He had intended that this would be a multipart essay, with further installments presumably appearing in subsequent volumes of *Der pinkes*.[57] The first (and as it turned out, the only) chapter was entitled "Di yidishe literatur—un di lezerin" (Yiddish Literature—and the Female Reader), a dense essay with rich documentation that was the first comprehensive examination of Yiddish literature to concern itself with questions of gender.[58]

In the essay's introduction, Niger called for inquiries into the social context of Yiddish literary culture, and repeated the by-then familiar refrain that Yiddish literature has unique needs because of its special character. Although each literature could benefit from a critical study of its chronology and bibliography, Yiddish, he asserted, requires a higher level of attention:

> So that the facts of Yiddish literature should not be hollow and arid, but be like rings in the chain of our spiritual development, or like limbs of an entire organism, so that its chronological and bibliographical data should become data for its literary history, it is necessary to know and research the time and condition of its particular facts and data. This is necessary in all literatures, in Yiddish literature it is more necessary than anything else.[59]

Niger pointed to the need for investigations into the context within which Old Yiddish—which he referred to as "Ivri-taytsh" (Hebreo-German)—developed in order to examine its relationship to German and Hebrew literature of the same period. He saw that for much of its existence, literature in Yiddish was composed not for its own sake, but rather as a means of introducing material from other literary traditions to uneducated Yiddish-reading audiences, "This is why the matter of context is nowhere as important as it is in the scientific investigation of the literature of Ivri-taytsh."[60] In particular, he hoped to understand the audience for these works, "above all one must know who were the people in various times and places who had an effect upon the development of Yiddish literature, who they were economically, socially, religiously, morally, etc."[61]

As a way to access the readership of Old Yiddish literature, Niger focused his attention on its main audience—Jewish women. He began his essay by declaring that the common perception that Yiddish literature only existed for the sake of women and *amoratsim* (simple ones, ignoramuses) was an exaggeration. Pointing to the scholarship of the folklorist Noyekh Prilutski, whose collections provided ample evidence of Hasidic leaders' use of Yiddish in prayers, Talmudic lessons, and stories, Niger argued for the presence of a long tradition of learned, erudite Jewish men who employed Yiddish in many realms of life.[62] Niger likewise referred to the famous Yiddish legends of Rabbi Nachman of Bratslav (1772–1810) and the common use of Yiddish as the instructional language in all-male religious schools. With this evidence he concluded, "Therefore, both in its creation and in its prolific uses, teachers, rabbis, and pious Jews had a share in Yiddish folklore, not only women and simple Jews."[63]

However, after acknowledging that Yiddish was a language that had been employed by Ashkenazic Jews of all sorts, regardless of sex or education, he stated unequivocally that the perception of Yiddish as feminized is wholly accurate: "The opinion that the only readers of Old Yiddish literature were women and simple men is a bit of an exaggeration. *The opinion is however, a correct one.*"[64] The rest of his essay investigated the influence of women readers on the development of Old Yiddish until the early nineteenth century, when it was increasingly used by *maskilim* to promote the Haskalah among male readers, "Women were not the only readers of Old Yiddish literature.

They were, however, the most important, the most secure, the most characteristic readers of it, and they left their stamp upon its content."[65]

In particular, he showed that premodern Yiddish literature developed less in response to women's religious needs than it did as a means to restrict their social and economic standing. In an echo of his essay from 1906, in which he drew attention to the "social differential" that existed between classes of Jews, he identified a language differential that contributed to the religious segregation of women. He addressed the ways that by restricting Jewish women's access to literature in Hebrew, (in particular, to discussions on Jewish law) women were disenfranchised within the community. Because in premodern Jewish society, social status was awarded in large part on the basis of one's scholarly erudition, denying women the ability to learn Hebrew effectively shunted them to its margins. Women were relegated to serving as the economic foundation of their families and not gaining any concomitant status or power:

> Not withstanding the great role that the Jewish woman played in economic life, . . . in the spiritual realm where the Jewish man lived, she had no free access. This did not amount to the economic emancipation of the woman, such as in the present day where it would lead to a sort of spiritual emancipation: this amounted to the economic *exploitation* of the woman."[66]

Because women were restricted to the Yiddish language and literature, Yiddish itself became identified with them. A consequence of this was the "feminization" of Yiddish, as it became the means through which sacred Jewish literature was translated and amended for women.[67] As Niger described, Old Yiddish literature was analogous to the *zogerke* ("speaker" or "caller"). In the past, *zogerke* was the title given to those women who would lead other women in Hebrew prayers in the synagogue. In doing so, they would render what would otherwise be inaccessible texts into comprehensible prayers that spoke to their concerns.[68] Because it was the linguistic medium through which Jewish women gained access to sacred texts, Yiddish itself served a comparable function:

> women most of all required a literature that was written in the language that they were able to read, in a literature that would mediate between them: the sinful women and the holy texts, in a literature—a zogerke.[69]

The bulk of Old Yiddish literature was, Niger argued, composed of religious texts published by men for women's consumption, and reflects the attempt to isolate women from religious discussions.[70] Old Yiddish literature was largely confined to loose translations of the Old Testament, prayers, homiletic works, and Aggadah (ethical literature, parables, bible stories, etc.), leaving discussions of Jewish law untranslated and inaccessible. Because mastery of Halakhah was a strong determiner of one's status in Jewish communities, its absence from women's literature contributed to their second-class status. Whereas men's literature (in Hebrew) was largely occupied with "straightforward-Halakhah," the strategies designed to curb women's access to it made a "deep impression in the entire appearance and character of the literature."[71]

In recent years, Niger's essay has made an impact on Yiddish studies, as scholars such as Chava Weissler, Naomi Seidman, and Sheva Zucker have cited it as laying a foundation for a critical understanding of Yiddish through the lens of gender.[72] In more general terms, Niger's essay was also groundbreaking in that it was one of the first studies of Yiddish that took the issue of its readership seriously, examining the interplay between the text and the audience. In doing so, Niger's contribution charted a new course for Yiddish literary history away from its prior role as a resource for the study into other Germanic languages and toward the study of Ashkenazic Jewry as a subject of its own worth.

Soon after the publication of *Der pinkes* came Niger's third major prewar contribution to the development of *Yidishe visnshaft,* the editing of Zalmen Reisen's *Leksikon fun der yidisher literatur un prese* (Lexicon of Yiddish Literature and the Press).[73] Although Reisen's 1914 one-volume *Leksikon* would be overshadowed by his 1926 four-volume edition, the initial text stands as a compelling record of the attempt to craft a history of Yiddish cultural development. The *Leksikon* consists of 657 entries of key Yiddish writers, scholars, and cultural activists. In addition, it includes the first complete compilation of Yiddish periodicals (dating back to the late seventeenth century), as well as a list of anonymous Yiddish texts. As Reisen described it, the task of the *Leksikon* was to provide, "a more or less complete and precise report of Yiddish literature and the press."[74]

Similar to Ber Borochov's 1913 "Bibliotek" (which appeared in *Der pinkes* and is discussed in the following chapter) the *Leksikon* includes entries from a broad range of Yiddish writers (as well as scholars who wrote on Yiddish in other languages), dating back more than four hundred years from the time of its publication. Unlike Borochov's ideologically charged "Bibliotek"—which was limited to works of Yiddish scholarship—Reisen's *Leksikon* is broadly conceived, and includes entries on a wide range of authors, regardless of their standing within the literary ranks. Biographical descriptions of major figures active in the Yiddish literary scene appear alongside the up and coming (such as the novelist Weissenberg and the historian Y. Y. Trunk, 1887–1961), the much maligned (like the romance novelist Shomer, pseudonym of Nokhem-Meyer Shaykevitsh, 1846–1905, and the literary historian M. Pines, 1882–1942), and the long forgotten. Most of the entries are of figures from the distant Yiddish past, such as premodern Yiddish writers dating from the sixteenth century, early scholars of Yiddish, translators of Hebrew texts, poets, Hasidic storytellers, publishers, and writers from the Haskalah.

In adopting a broadly inclusive stance toward Yiddish culture, the *Leksikon* was not only creating a new Yiddish literary canon and providing a tool for Yiddish researchers, but was also establishing a new Yiddish historical tradition by charting its past, present, and future. By placing all of these figures into a single volume and declaring them united to one another by a common literary tradition, they were in effect setting the boundaries of a newly identified culture. Although such a historiographical impulse toward Yiddish culture would become one of the hallmarks of *Yidishe visnshaft* in the two decades after World War I, the *Leksikon*, along with Pines' widely read (and disparaged) *Di geshikhte fun der yidisher literatur* (The History of Yiddish Literature) and Borochov's soon-to-be published multipart essay in *Di yidishe velt* by the same name, were among the first attempts to convey a history of Yiddish to an audience of Yiddish-speaking Jews.[75]

In editing *Di yidishe velt*, *Der pinkes*, and *Der leksikon*, Niger made his most significant contributions to the formation of *Yidishe visnshaft*:

identifying Yiddish as a legitimate realm of study, raising the standards of Yiddish scholarship and literary culture, and laying the groundwork for the establishment of cultural institutions that appeared in the decades after World War I. Soon after the appearance of these three works, Jewish life in Eastern Europe once again began to unravel. Despite the tumult and uncertainty, the years of war and revolution continued to be productive for Niger. While continuing to edit *Di yidishe velt,* he also assumed the position of editor at a new journal, *Di vokh* (The Week).[76] At the beginning of 1916, with mounting instability in Vilna (it had been recently captured by the German Army and the Russians were preparing an assault), Niger began to edit *Di yidishe velt* from Petrograd (renamed from St. Petersburg) until the journal was finally forced to fold at the end of that year. Niger also published a memorial volume to the recently deceased Sholem Aleichem (in 1916), contributed to the Russian-Jewish journal *Voskhod* (Dawn), and wrote for many other publications. Having abandoned the life of the pure aesthete that he idealized nearly a decade earlier when editing *Di literarishe monatsshriftn,* during the war Niger threw himself into work on behalf of the increasingly threatened Jewish community. He worked with refugee organizations, self-help groups, and participated in a Yiddish language people's university. In 1918, after the successful 1917 Revolution, Niger briefly edited the weekly *Kultur un bildung,* which was released by the Jewish Commissariat, and a year later, he was an editor at *Di naye velt* (The New World).

Despite this long commitment to Russian Jewry, the volatile situation at the end of World War I and the Bolshevik rise to power made the situation in Russia untenable for him. An incident in April 1919 in which his houseguest and one-time collaborator of *Di literarishe monatsshriftn,* A. Vayter, was murdered by Polish soldiers, compelled Niger to leave Europe permanently. For three days Vayter's corpse lay in the street outside of Niger's apartment, because pogroms raging through the city made it impossible to remove. Niger was also arrested and briefly imprisoned. Soon after his release, he left with his family and resettled in New York City.

The years that Niger spent editing *Der pinkes, Di yidishe velt,* the *Leksikon,* and other journals during World War I and the 1917 Revolution represented in many ways the logical outcome of his earlier concerns to elevate the Jewish people to the global community of nations and to identify a middle position between the poles of politics and pure aesthetics. "The Yiddish World" that Niger imagined was scattered across the continents, and yet was linked by the common language of workers and their cultural artifacts, narratives, and folk tales. Having helped to transform Yiddish from a jargon of the home, marketplace, and sweatshop into a language in which Jewish artists and intellectuals could undertake literary projects that incorporated the highest European standards, Niger left for the growing community of Russian-Jewish émigré intellectuals in the United States. Far from the political upheavals and social tumult that would soon threaten Eastern European Jewry's very existence, Niger continued his project of Jewish cultural renewal from the relative safety of the United States. This move allowed him to be one of the few members of the 1905 generation of Yiddish literary activists to survive the twin assaults on European Jewry by the Nazi Holocaust and Stalinism.

4 Ber Borochov

Science in Service of the Revolution

He was representative of an entire generation of Jewish intellectuals
who did not adhere to the "Torah," who did not follow the "command-
ments." This was a devoted generation, a generation that when its
detailed history will be written, one will see how rich it was in its
creative strength, in intellectual initiative, in spiritual ventures.
—Shmuel Niger, 1938[1]

Shmuel Niger's characterization notwithstanding, Ber Borochov's path
to Yiddish activism was remarkably unrepresentative of that followed by
most of his contemporaries in the 1905 generation. He did not champion
the possibilities of Yiddish during the first Russian Revolution and in fact,
only came to learn the language well in the years following the revolution's
collapse. He was not a participant in many of the seminal moments in the
development of the Yiddishist movement, including the 1908 Czernowitz
conference or the publication of *Di literarishe monatsshriftn*. He did not
join the circles of Russian-Jewish émigrés in Bern or Berlin, was not a follower of Zhitlowsky, Peretz, or Ahad Ha'am, and he battled rather than
supported the Vozrozhdenie. Nevertheless, the events of 1903–7 not only
led Borochov to promote a *visnshaft* for Yiddish, but also drove him to
become its most passionate and authoritative spokesperson in the years
between the two Russian revolutions, and to play a decisive role in setting
the stage for its politicization ever since.

Borochov (1881–1917) is the only founding figure of Yiddish scholarship who consistently remains a subject of interest by scholars, although
generally not for his efforts on behalf of the language. Instead, it is his

role as the chief theoretician of Marxist-Zionism and as the charismatic leader of the Poalei Zion that has attracted the attention of historians and political theorists. By contrast, Borochov's contribution to the field of Yiddish studies—a task that occupied him for the last half decade of his brief life—has been largely overshadowed by his political activity. Furthermore, in those comparatively rare instances when his work on behalf of Yiddish is examined, studies tend to venerate and extol his memory rather than critically assess his role in crafting a scholarly agenda for Yiddish.

Throughout his lifetime Borochov advocated a variety of ideological stances concerning the future of Russian Jewry. Consequently, after his death in 1917, his legacy was available to be claimed by a wide spectrum of Jewish nationalists, including general Zionists, the left and right wings of Labor Zionism, Marxists, and Yiddishists. Because his accomplishments were so influential, his treatises so compelling, and the fact that he seemed to arrive at ideological positions at the very moment when they were most in need of passionate articulation, Borochov is regularly viewed as an icon whose authority and stature are evoked even in the present day.

Despite his multifarious political allegiances, for many decades he was widely memorialized within Zionist circles as a somewhat intellectually static figure. This is because Borochov died young, after a decade of exile from Russia, and on the cusp of what many followers anticipated would be his reappearance to the center of the Jewish revolutionary stage. Yet, as more contemporary scholarship has shown, he was also a dynamic thinker who had by no means settled upon a single solution to the question of Russian Jewry. In recent decades, scholars have moved beyond monolithic representations of Borochov's thinking and have offered nuanced understandings of his political course.[2] However, similar work remains concerning Borochov's activity on behalf of Yiddish language development. A goal of this chapter, then, is to engage his efforts to create a *visnshaft* for Yiddish and in doing so, to demonstrate that, in contrast to the commonplace representation of Borochov as its "pioneering" founder, he was fully a part of the linguistic national currents that were transforming Russian Jewry in the early twentieth century.

Like many of his contemporaries, Borochov's hope for a Jewish national renaissance rested with the Jewish masses, who, along with their language, were underdeveloped and under assault by the twin forces of assimilation and industrial capitalism. As he understood it, in preindustrial times, the Jewish folk were those who created and maintained the Yiddish language, who stood opposed to and alienated from an elite rabbinic leadership, and who were the most authentic representatives of the Jewish people. In modern times, the folk consisted of the Jewish proletariat who labored under the pains of industrialization and were the raw material of the emerging nation. What united them was Yiddish, and their language held for Borochov the key to their national character. He believed in the potential of Yiddish to define, unite, and ultimately bring about their emancipation. In his conception, the function and task of *Yidishe visnshaft* was to elevate, commemorate, and legitimate the Jewish masses through the standardization and enrichment of their native language. The study of Yiddish, therefore, became another weapon in the struggle for the liberation of the Jewish nation, making the philologist and poet as indispensable as the revolutionary. Unlike his German-Jewish predecessors who—in his conception—had founded *Wissenschaft des Judentums* to promote the Haskalah goals of individual Jewish emancipation and assimilation, Borochov's ultimate goal for *Yidishe visnshaft* was the liberation of the Russian-Jewish masses.

Born June 21, 1881 in the small community of Zolotonosha in Ukraine's Cherkasy region, Ber Borochov's family soon moved to nearby Poltava.[3] This sedate town without an industrial base lacked a working class, and partially for that reason, the Russian government would periodically exile political radicals there. Additionally, Poltava was home to a strong Zionist Jewish community. Borochov's father, a Hebrew teacher and *maskil* who was a member of the Hibbat Zion, made a conscious decision along with his mother *not* to speak their native Yiddish in front of the children, and so from the age of two or three, Russian was spoken in Borochov's home. However, it is reasonable to assume that Borochov continued to be exposed to Yiddish by his extended family and community.

Befitting a Zionist *maskilic* upbringing, Borochov received an education that was a mixture of private tutors, the state school system, and secular Jewish learning that provided him with regular access to banned Zionist materials. As he described it, "a Hoveve-Zionist education at home and an assimilatory one in gymnasium."[4] From an early age, he was proficient in learning ancient languages, including Sanskrit. Heavily influenced by the Zionist milieu of Poltava, Borochov twice attempted (at the ages of ten and sixteen) unsuccessfully to leave for Palestine. Likewise, he fell under the sway of the region's radical figures and immersed himself in philosophy (in particular Karl Marx and Richard Avenarius). He graduated from gymnasium in 1900 but reportedly was refused academic honors because he was Jewish, which resulted in him being prevented from pursuing a university education in the empire.[5]

Rather than go abroad to continue with his studies, Borochov moved to the city of Ekaterinoslav, a strong center of both Social Democrat and Zionist activity, where he quickly gained a reputation as a powerful lecturer on both subjects. Initially, he aligned himself with the Social Democrats but was soon expelled from the party (in May 1901) because of his persistent engagement with questions of Jewish nationalism. Instead, he found a home on the opposite end of the ideological spectrum and joined with the Zionists. In Ekaterinoslav, the Zionist movement was under the leadership of Menachem Ussishkin, a "practical" Zionist of the Hibbat Zion tradition who favored agricultural settlement as a necessary step for the colonization of Palestine. Soon, Borochov was working on behalf of the general Zionists in Russia, speaking widely across the Pale of Settlement, publishing in the Zionist press, and distancing himself from the various socialist-Zionist groups in Russia that had been gathering under the name Poalei Zion.

Borochov returned to Poltava in 1902. Soon after the 1903 Kishinev and Gomel pogroms, his family joined his sister in the United States, but he stayed behind and quickly involved himself in Zionist and Jewish self-defense activity. In particular, the support that railroad workers gave to the 1903 pogroms shocked him. He saw their participation as marking the failure of the RSDWP program, because despite the workers' exposure to it, they nevertheless participated in the anti-Jewish violence.[6] In July 1904, he was arrested for the first time (a result of his earlier association with the Social Democrats), but was soon released because of a lack of evidence. Still a strict Palestine-centered Zionist who shunned revolutionary politics, Borochov maintained his association with Ussishkin while in

Poltava, and much of his activity was focused on persuading other Jewish youth not to get caught up in diasporist or revolutionary politics. As late as the Seventh Zionist Congress in Basle in summer 1905 (on the cusp of the October Manifesto and subsequent pogroms), Borochov took part in harsh exchanges with delegates from the various Territorialist camps (including the Vozrozhdenie), that were gaining ground among young Zionists because of their attention to the immediate crises facing Russian Jewry rather than the Palestine-centered programs that he was advocating.

Just as the 1903 violence revealed to Borochov the failure of the RSD-WP's program to curb Jewish hatred, the violence of October 1905 demonstrated to him the weakness of the general Zionists' program to provide for the immediate needs of Russian Jewry, thus prompting another shift in his ideological position. Abroad in Switzerland and Germany, powerless to assist his fellow Jews, in despair over the assaults, and realizing that the political tide was getting far ahead of him, Borochov began raising money for arms for self-defense groups and composing increasingly radical essays. The most renown and influential of these was his landmark Russian language treatise "The National Question and the Class Struggle," an attempt to synthesize the seemingly irreconcilable ideologies of Marxism and Zionism.[7] This text, which solidified his position as the chief theoretician of the new Jewish revolutionary generation, offered a materialist conception of the relationship between nation and class and concluded by asserting that Jewish hatred was a permanent fixture of diasporic Jewish life. He argued that all efforts should henceforth be directed toward fostering Jewish emigration to Palestine for the sake of creating a national homeland where the Jewish working class would eventually rule the means of production.

Returning to Russia at the end of 1905, Borochov quickly asserted his place among the Jewish revolutionaries. After further disputes with the Territorialists and witnessing the destruction of Jewish communities first-hand, he began to concede that work on behalf of Jewish life in the Diaspora was as necessary as building a future state in Palestine. Frankel describes this time as a traumatic one for Borochov, when he underwent a "philosophical and psychological break" with the general Zionists.[8] Unable, however, to come to full agreement with the Vozrozhdenie and the recently formed S.S.

over their visions of Jewish autonomy, Borochov founded the Poalei Zion—
the founding text of which was his second momentous Russian language
essay, entitled simply, "Our Platform."[9]

Although he remained a Palestine-centered Zionist revolutionary,
Borochov's increasing commitment to Jewish life in the Diaspora (and
his later turn to Yiddish) can be seen in his changing stance on the question of whether to cultivate Jewish emigration to Palestine.[10] In his 1905
essay, "Class Struggle," Borochov asserted the need for immediate efforts
to encourage emigration from the empire and to dissuade Jews from par-
ticipating in revolutionary activity in the name of overthrowing the aristocracy. By contrast, his 1906 essay—which adheres to a stricter Marxist
analysis and was deliberately antiromantic in its stance toward Palestine—
concludes that emigration would only occur spontaneously after economically determined processes had manifested themselves and the rest of the
world closed its doors to the Jews. In the meantime, energy needed to be
directed toward stabilizing Jewish life in the Diaspora, overthrowing the
tsar, and furthering the overall revolutionary cause. The situation had
shifted so much in the previous year that he no longer considered Jewish
hatred as inevitable, but understood it as a consequence of Jewish political
powerlessness. Instead, he argued that the Jewish minority was similar to
other national minorities and (until the time when Jews actually do emi-
grate to their own territory), they too deserved the right of self-determination and to organize themselves along national lines in the lands in which
they were located.[11] The violence of the revolution, the failure of the Social
Democrats to curtail it, and the arguments of the Territorialists in favor of
Jewish national autonomy in Russia helped turn Borochov into a committed Labor Zionist who saw the fate of the Jews as intertwined with Russia's
other national minorities:

> colonizing a territory is a prolonged process, during which we must also
> defend our needs in the galut [Diaspora]. We must assume that a large
> part of the Jewish people, including a part of the proletariat, will always
> remain in the galut as an ordinary national minority. For that reason we
> include in our program, along with territorial demands, the demand for
> the maximum protection of our national needs in the galut. Explicitly,
> this means national political autonomy for the Jews in all galut lands.[12]

In June 1906, just a few months after founding the Poalei Zion (and on the same evening the tsar dissolved the first Duma), Borochov was again arrested for revolutionary activity. He sat several months in prison and was then expelled from Russia for the next decade, settling first in Vienna and later New York. Far removed from the revolutionary center in Russia and from the growing community in Palestine, Borochov struggled to maintain his influence over the Zionist movement and to chart a different course than many of his followers and comrades. While others in the party were making their way to Palestine to create a Hebrew-speaking Jewish society, Borochov began to investigate the Yiddish language and to commit himself to building up Yiddish-speaking diasporic life. During this time, the Yiddish language became central to his vision for the Jewish future. He likewise struggled with other factions of the Poalei Zion over the course of development of Jewish life in Palestine, whether to join the Socialist International and whether to remain part of the World Zionist Organization.

In Vienna, Borochov turned his attention to the possibilities of Yiddish. He arrived in the city just as its short-lived encounter with modern Yiddish culture was beginning to flower and his presence there played a central role in that brief moment. As Gabriele Kohlbauer-Fritz relates, in the aftermath of the 1905 Revolution, many émigrés, refugees, and political exiles helped to bolster the Yiddish language press in Galicia, which had been developing at a comparatively much slower rate than in Russia. Yiddish in Galicia was benefiting from the aftermath of the Czernowitz conference and all Jewish parties encouraged their supporters to declare Yiddish as their native language in the 1910 Austrian census. When Borochov moved the Poalei Zion's center to Vienna, its organs, *Di yidishe arbeter* (The Jewish Worker) and *Dos fraye vort* (The Free Word), quickly came to dominate the Yiddish scene.[13]

Like so many Russian *maskilim* and Jewish revolutionaries before him, Borochov began to take Yiddish seriously only after realizing amidst his political activism that he would have to convey his message in the language of his intended audience. The literary historian Sh. L. Tsitron (1860–1930) once asked Borochov how he came to Yiddish. Borochov recounted that when graduating from gymnasium, he knew nothing of Yiddish and only came to realize its importance through his political work. "I became interested in Yiddish because of the Poalei-Zion and *through* it."[14] Reflecting on his Yiddish activism, Borochov's colleague in the Poalei Zion, Ya'akov Zerubavel (1886–1967), offered the explanation that for Borochov, the turn to Yiddish was more than just a strategy for connecting with his followers. Rather, it was an attempt to access the very center of the Jewish people.[15] In 1907, at the age of twenty-six and far from the Russian-Jewish masses, he took on the task of learning the very language that his Zionist *maskilic* parents had hoped to dissuade him from speaking. Very soon, Yiddish for Borochov became more than a way of occupying his time while in exile or as a means of communicating with Jewish workers, but as a scholarly pre-occupation that was increasingly central to his vision of Jewish autonomy. Given his proclivity for languages and what was most likely his prior exposure to it, he quickly began writing Yiddish essays and conducting research into its historical development. His first work in Yiddish, an examination of the national question in Belgium, appeared in 1908.[16]

Borochov's greatest contributions to Yiddish studies occurred in these years of exile from Russia. While traveling on behalf of the Poalei Zion, he spent much of his time in European libraries, looking for sources of premodern Yiddish literature. The results of his investigations were published in a groundbreaking bibliography of Old Yiddish literature and literary studies entitled "Di bibliotek funem yidishn filolog: 400 yor yidishe shprakh-forshung" (The Library of the Yiddish Philologist: 400 Years of Yiddish Language Research). This contribution, as well as a treatise, "Di oyfgabn fun der yidisher filologye" (The Tasks of Yiddish Philology), appeared in 1913 in *Der pinkes* and were ultimately as consequential to the burgeoning field of Yiddish studies as his 1905 and 1906 essays were to Jewish revolutionary politics. Although his association with Yiddish scholarship was relatively brief—approximately half a dozen years—he covered a wide range of philological, bibliographical, and literary topics. Along with his investigations into premodern Yiddish sources and his agenda-setting essays, he also tried to impose a new orthographic system onto Yiddish spelling and to standardize its corpus of words. He closely assisted Shmuel Niger with editing *Der pinkes,* wrote criticisms of contemporary writers including Asch, Opatoshu, and the literary group Di yunge, and began a comprehensive history of the language and its literature.[17]

After being expelled from the Austro-Hungarian empire with the onset of World War I, Borochov traveled to New York and was based there from 1915 to 1917. His time in New York marked the period of his greatest isolation. Far from the Poalei Zion movement in Eastern Europe, he spent his time clashing with political opponents, writing for the Yiddish newspapers *Di varhayt* (The Truth) and *Di yidisher kemfer* (The Jewish Fighter), and working on his history of the Yiddish language. It was with great joy that he returned to Russia with the overthrow of the tsar in 1917. His excitement was short-lived, however. He quickly clashed with his fellow Poalei Zion members at the third Conference in Kiev in September 1917 when he adopted positions that seemed to hark back to his by-then antiquated pre-1906 stances in favor of active settlement and socialist experimentation in Palestine. Within a few months of the conference, he became ill with pneumonia (it is suspected) and died in Kiev on December 17.

One characteristic that distinguishes Borochov more than any other figure who was central to the creation of *Yidishe visnshaft* is a long legacy of relatively uncritical acclaim of his accomplishments on behalf of Yiddish. Since the early 1920s, scholars and commentators have praised him nearly universally for his "pioneering" efforts on behalf of Yiddish. Several factors have contributed to this depiction of Borochov. Coming so relatively late to Yiddish and Yiddish advocacy, he managed quickly to take control over the agenda of the burgeoning scholarly discipline by linking it to Jewish mass culture and politics. In doing so, Borochov conceived of *Yidishe visnshaft* as a tool to build the Jewish nation, and he insisted that Yiddish scholars concern themselves with the immediate needs of the Jewish people and not disconnect the study of the language from those who spoke it, thus giving them a way to carry on the ideals of the revolution through their Yiddish research. His insistence on recognizing the Jewish folk masses as a legitimate field of research helped to counter what he perceived to be the increasingly wide gulf between Jewish intellectuals and the Jewish people. The former, he felt, were either too wrapped up either in dispassionate, apolitical research, or too enchanted with fashionable literary trends. The latter were in need of an intelligentsia who would chart a path to a new national identity. However contentious a figure he was during his lifetime, his work challenged his fellow intellectuals to focus their attention back on the continuing crises facing Russian Jews after the disappointments of the failed 1905 Revolution.

In addition to the urgency of his program, by the time Borochov took up the cause of Yiddish, his stature among present and former Jewish revolutionaries was so great that his efforts were taken with great seriousness. His involvement with Yiddish scholarship gave the field prestige at a critical juncture in its development. When his death coincided with the moment of the long-awaited emancipation of Russian Jewry and the opportunity to craft a culture based on the Yiddish language, his memory was as ripe for veneration in Yiddish scholarly circles as it was in Zionist ones.

The near-universal posthumous reverence of Borochov as a Yiddish theoretician stands in contrast to the reception of his work during his lifetime. Although he was praised for his efforts on behalf of the language while alive, few of his fellow Yiddishists would have considered themselves "Borochovists."[18] Some welcomed his initial forays into Yiddish language research, but others were also put off by key elements of his work, and chastised him for the absolutist tone with which he issued his decrees for Yiddish. He was criticized on several fronts: for the overbearing nationalism of his program by those who were concerned with how it would interfere with the "pure" science of linguistics, by those who rejected his insistence on a standardized orthography for Yiddish and the consequential disregard for regional dialects, by Hebraists who thought his advocacy for Yiddish was a betrayal of Zionist values, and by fellow researchers who deemed his work sloppy and prone to error.

As in Zionist circles, among Yiddishists, Borochov is also known and remembered largely through the programmatic, foundational treatises that marked his entrance into the field. Similar to how his 1905 and 1906 essays "Class Struggle and the National Question" and "Our Platform" secured his status as leader of Marxist Zionism, his landmark essays on Yiddish, "Di oyfgabn" and "Di bibliotek," established him as the first theoretician of *Yidishe visnshaft.* Both works appeared in *Der pinkes,* the volume that culminated nearly a decade's worth of intellectual activity on behalf of Yiddish, and announced the arrival of Yiddish studies as a scholarly discipline.

Unquestionably, much of the enduring significance of *Der pinkes* is a consequence of Borochov's contributions. "Di oyfgabn" outlined an agenda for future Yiddish scholarship and "Di bibliotek" was presented as the ideologically correct model for the new scholarship.[19]

Borochov's manifesto was a call for philological examinations into Yiddish on behalf of Jewish national renewal. In it, Borochov sketched out a broad agenda for Yiddish research. His tasks ranged from the practical: creating a standardized Yiddish dictionary and grammar, researching the origins and development of the language, and establishing a language institute; to the lofty and abstract—the "nationalizing and humanizing" of the Yiddish language and its speakers. The manifesto begins by echoing the oft-heard demand that Yiddish be elevated to the level of a language equal to all others. Just as the editors of the 1908 *Di literarishe monatsshriftn* had written of the need for the Jewish nation "to bind its own unique page into the great book of the world" through the creation of a refined Yiddish literary aesthetics, Borochov argued for the need to apply scientific methods to ensure that the Jews had a mature language like the "Finns, Latvians, Estonians, . . . Croats, Slovenes, Czechs, and Slovaks."[20]

What set the "Di oyfgabn" apart from earlier efforts to modernize Yiddish was Borochov's coupling of the specific case of the Jewish national revolution to the scientific discipline of philology. Like his programmatic works of 1905 and 1906 in which he forged the antinationalistic theory of Marxism together with Zionism into a coherent ideology of Jewish liberation, in the 1913 essays he paired yet another set of seemingly incongruous ideas in service of Jewish national interests. Borochov argued that the "objective" discipline of philology—with its authority to establish a uniform orthographic standard, word corpus, and grammar—would be among the most powerful, necessary, and essential tools for realizing the national aspirations of the Jewish people, "As long as a people remain 'illiterate' in their own language," he wrote, "one cannot yet speak of a national culture."[21]

As novel as his argument was to the cause of Jewish liberation, Borochov drew deeply from ideological currents that had long been in vogue among nationalists. By the early twentieth century, philological examinations into language were widely viewed as essential to the national "revivals" taking place across the Russian empire.[22] Rather than creating a program out of whole cloth as he has so often been credited, Borochov's contribution to *Yidishe visnshaft* is more correctly understood as the creative application of established models of philological research to the specific case of the Yiddish language. Although he was hardly the first to bring philology to the cause of national liberation, he was among the first to render them serviceable to Russian Jews. Borochov himself acknowledged this point several times in "Di oyfgabn" as he discussed the ways philology had been employed among other national groups in Europe, and noted that Jewish national development was stunted in comparison to those nations that took pride in their philological institutions.[23]

In fact, by the early twentieth century, philology's utility in shaping in shaping European nationalisms was reaching its end. In his study of race and language, the historian Maurice Olender reminds us that already by the first decades of the eighteenth century, "it became impossible to speak of nations or national histories without discussing the instrument with which they maintained their identity over time and conveyed ancestral values from generation to generation: namely, language."[24] By the time Borochov came to champion philology, however, its definition had grown so vast that it had begun to fragment and its practitioners to specialize. Philological investigations increasingly gave way to the growing field of linguistics. As the scholar Karl D. Uitti notes:

> By the end of the nineteenth century the very term "philology" had come to mean ... all university-standard activity related specifically to the study of language; the term covered textual criticism, general linguistics, historical reconstruction of texts and languages ... lexicography, sociolinguistics, and language geography."[25]

Nevertheless, Borochov insisted upon making distinctions between philology and linguistics. Despite linguistics' increased dominance over philology by the turn of the twentieth century, Borochov attacked it as a narrow-minded apolitical general science concerned solely with the form of the language. Philology, he asserted, was part of a national project that had the ability to reveal the "cultural-historical worth" of a language and to determine its future national potential.[26]

Not only was Borochov adopting philology as a tool of Jewish liberation at a time when it was becoming increasingly unstable, he also employed the racialist approach that was by then intrinsic to it. For much of the seventeenth, eighteenth, and nineteenth centuries, philology had been employed in the search for the roots of European civilization, locating them first in Hebrew and then in Sanskrit.[27] Long before it was appropriated as a tool for national liberation movements, philological methods were used as a way of working through theological debates on the origins of Christianity, Europe, and the various "races" of the world. Philologists divided languages into the broad categories of Semitic and Aryan/Indo-European. In time, philology provided much of the vocabulary for the racial categories that reinforced a vast divide between West and East. One consequence was that Semitic languages—and by extension the Jews (for bequeathing Hebrew)—came to be represented either as static or in a state of deterioration, and Indo-European languages—and by extension, "native" Europeans—as dynamic, healthy, and progressing. Although Jews were credited as the creators of the *ur* language, the future of civilization was squarely in the hands of the Europeans. By the 1870s, comparative philology was providing the language, terminology, and part of the scientific justification for the racialization of European society.

Philology was widely used in what was often the brutal process of unifying disparate peoples under a single linguistic rubric. In his study of the modern roots of European nationalism, the historian Patrick Geary argues that philology led to the "virtual invention" of languages, resulting in the elimination of countless oral traditions and the hegemony of one central (often state) authority over language standards:

> Thus, everywhere, individuals, families, and communities found themselves isolated from the "national language" and under pressure to give up their traditions of speech. This could mean anything from simply adopting vocabulary, standard pronunciation, and modified systems of inflections, as in the case of the inhabitants of Holland, to abandoning dialects or ancient linguistic traditions such as Provençal in the south of France.
>
> Language became the vehicle for teaching the national history of the "people" whose language this was and whose political aspirations the

language expressed. However, the new philology allowed nationalist educators and ideologues to go even further: It made possible the creation of a national, "scientific" history that projected both national language and national ideology into a distant past.[28]

By aligning himself to a discipline steeped in such practices, the consequences of what Borochov was proposing—"the Yiddish language must become purified, become enriched, become reformed"—were profound and had the potential to challenge several fundamental assumptions of both philology and nationalism.[29] First, given that Yiddish contains both "Semitic" and "Aryan" elements (Hebraic and Germanic), it was unclassifiable according to extant philological categories. A Yiddish philology, therefore, would potentially force the creation of a third category that bridged the two by representing the Yiddish language, and by extension its speakers, as a hybrid Oriental/Occidental people. If at the heart of Borochov's project was the unification of the Jewish people by crafting them into a nation through their mother tongue, engaging philology in service of this goal was certainly a bold choice. Resisting the tendency of philologists to restrict languages to discrete linguistic designations, Borochov asserted that the admixture that was Yiddish was in fact its strength and should force a reconsideration of how languages were conceived. He went on to argue that Yiddish was not alone in being a "mishmash" of a language, and cited other languages that were made up of various linguistic components (like English and Japanese).[30] However, none of the examples that he pointed to bridged the seemingly vast divide between Semitic and Aryan.

Despite the frequency and availability of successful models, Borochov's attempt to apply philological methodologies to Yiddish would be no easy task. Compounding his difficulties was that Yiddish would have to serve double duty. Because Eastern European nationalist movements in the late nineteenth and early twentieth centuries still tended to rest upon the twin pillars of native language and territorial sovereignty, Borochov's plan for the landless Jewish nation would ultimately require rendering Yiddish substantial enough to satisfy both of these demands. In effect, what he was hoping to do was to turn Yiddish into a state language in the absence of a state. It would therefore, be the task of the Yiddish philologist to forge a collective national identity not only by giving Jews a standardized means through which to communicate with one another, but by instilling in them a shared historical narrative, demarcating the nation's borders, and determining—by virtue of fluency—one's status as a "citizen." In order to achieve this expansive role for Yiddish, Borochov cast his net as wide as possible and made the case that not only the Yiddish language, but all aspects of Jewish life and culture that were expressed in Yiddish must be the philologist's focus of study. As he wrote to Niger in 1912 during the editing of *Der pinkes,* "My goal is not language, nor literature, and not social development—but *culture,* which includes everything. And we see that all of our goals lie within culture."[31]

In addition to the theoretical implications of his "Tasks," Borochov himself pointed to a series of practical challenges facing the Yiddish philologist. He maintained that as a consequence of their statelessness, the language of the Jews lacked political and scientific terminologies. Therefore, when Jewish intellectuals tried to employ Yiddish, they often turned, he argued, to *daytshmerish* rather than terms drawn from the Yiddish language corpus. Such a tendency of Jewish intellectuals to model their Yiddish upon contemporary German was antithetical to the national project because it brought them increasingly further away from the Jewish folk, whom he saw (however ungrammatical and unstandardized their Yiddish) as the true source of the organic development of the language. He accused his contemporaries of mimicking German orthography and of incorporating German syntax into their sentence structure. Borochov concluded that far from being corrupted German, it was Yiddish that was being corrupted *by* German.[32] Furthermore, he challenged the long standing conception of Yiddish as a substandard language by dismissing common-place characterizations of Yiddish as a "jargon," and as lacking a grammar or orthography—but he also acknowledged that it would be for the philologist to disprove these conceptions scientifically.[33]

To bring Yiddish to the point where it could fulfill these unifying functions, Borochov outlined three levels of tasks for future Yiddish philologists. The most basic of these was eradicating regional Yiddish variants and replacing them with a universal orthographic, lexical, and grammatical standard. He maintained that by determining the appropriate spelling, pronunciation, and meaning of Yiddish words, philologists could bring an end to the mishmash as the language emerged from chaos and came into its authentic national identity. Borochov proposed an orthography based upon the Lithuanian variant of Yiddish because, as he conceived it, *Litvish* allowed for the closest match between written and spoken word. He also called for philologists to ascertain the place of each linguistic group within Yiddish to understand what role the Germanic, Hebraic, and Slavic components play in the language and to overturn long-standing misconceptions about their functions.

Its composite structure notwithstanding, his second level of tasks was the "purification" and "enrichment" of Yiddish.[34] Adopting the racialist language common to late nineteenth and early twentieth-century philology, Borochov argued that Yiddish needed to be purged of its foreign elements and supplemented with words drawn from its native stock. Philology would thus discern the origins of these disparate elements, trace their introduction into the language, and determine whether to include them in or to expel them from the corpus of acceptable words. In effect, the philologist would determine which words could and could not be uttered in the Jewish national language.

Some of this work to standardize, enrich, and purify Yiddish was already being done before Borochov's call to action, albeit without the overt ideological thrust. One brief example is Zalmen Reisen's 1908 *Yidishe gramatik* (mentioned in chapter 2), which was an effort to demonstrate that Yiddish *had* an identifiable grammar.[35] Written four years before Borochov's call to arms, Reisen's text discusses the relationship between letters and sounds, the construction of tenses, nouns, phrases, plurals, passive and active forms, etc. In his introduction, Reisen, like Borochov, declared that the time had come for such an effort, and located the authority and need for his grammar in the increasingly strong Yiddish literary tradition that began with Abramovitsh and ran through the literary and journalistic efforts of the subsequent decades. His work was an attempt to bring "scientific proof" of the veracity of Yiddish to those skeptics who insisted that it was not a full language like others.[36]

Borochov's third and most "supreme" level of tasks for the Yiddish philologist was the "nationalization and humanization" of Yiddish:

> Nationalizing Yiddish, turning it into a true national language, means
> purifying the language thoroughly and enriching it extensively, so it can
> express all aspects of Jewish creativity. Humanizing the language in a
> broad sense means turning it into a tool for incorporating the cultural
> values of the modern development of mankind into the Jewish people.[37]

Humanizing Yiddish, he insisted, would transform it into an instrument that
could express the full range of Jewish national creativity: "Yiddish philology must assist in making the Yiddish language become *a national cultural-
medium and an educational-medium for the people and for intellectuals.*"[38]
The best examples of this process, he offered, were those set by Abramovitsh
and Peretz, even though they did not adopt a "scientific" outlook to the
prose language. To Borochov, Abramovitsh was the "Columbus" of Yiddish
who discovered the rich possibilities of cultural creativity in the language
and Peretz was its "Napoleon" who brought to it the best European forms.[39]
Their work paved the way for Yiddish to become the means through which
the Jewish people could reach the heights of their innate creativity. The philologist's task then, was to cultivate works of national genius and bring order
to the chaotic creative process of nationalizing the language. By working
scientifically, philologists could complete the task begun by these authors,
first by identifying an authentic Yiddish literary tradition from its scattered
remains, and then by mining it for use by future generations:

> Philology must excavate the hidden layers of the people's creativity, it
> must unearth the treasures of our national creativeness that lie scattered
> in western-European libraries. Old Yiddish literature has its classical
> works like the *Shmuel bukh* [Book of Samuel], the *Mayse bukh* [Book of
> Stories], and the *Sefer hamides* [Book of Attributes], that have served as a
> paradigm for many generations and even used to be translated into foreign
> languages. The people possess a mass of words in their aphorisms, jokes,
> songs, stories, and riddles, and generally in their folklore, which philology
> should investigate and cultivate. These philological methods will enrich
> the language, and the people will become acquainted with their literary
> past and will learn to profit from its concealed wealth.[40]

Borochov's program for Yiddish left as many questions unanswered
as it tried to solve, such as how to reconcile the fact that increasingly large

realms of the Jewish world were not made up of Yiddish speakers and would therefore be excluded from the Jewish nation that he hoped to forge. As well, he left undiscussed the mechanisms through which the new Yiddish standards would be enforced, or how to respond to the challenge of other Zionists who insisted on the centrality of the Hebrew language and the land of Israel as the unifying factor of Jewish nationalism. Despite these limitations, "Di oyfgabn" remains a significant text, less in that it set forth an agenda that was subsequently followed by subsequent scholars, but in that Borochov foresaw so many of the challenges necessary to transform Yiddish into the basis of a Jewish national culture.

Borochov's second major contribution to *Der pinkes* was "Di bibliotek funem yidishn filolog," a catalog of the then extant studies on Yiddish—totaling 501 entries and spanning several centuries and languages. If "Di oyfgabn" was concerned with the future agenda of Yiddish studies, "Di bibliotek" was an exploration of its past. Like "Di oyfgabn," "Di bibliotek" was not a straightforward scholarly contribution to *Der pinkes*. At its most elemental, "Di bibliotek" was a reference guide intended to introduce future Yiddish philologists to prior scholarly research in the field. Representing several years of Borochov's investigations in libraries across Europe, his bibliography was by far the most comprehensive survey of Yiddish scholarship to date. It contained a broad range of items, including manuscripts and printed materials, monographs, dictionaries, journal articles, and encyclopedia entries from the sixteenth to the twentieth century in many languages, including Latin, Hebrew, German, Russian, Polish, English, and Yiddish. Entries include the sixteenth-century Jewish convert to Christianity Paulus Fagius, the seventeenth-century Christian linguist Johann Christof Wagenseil, the nineteenth-century Germanist Friedrich Christian Benedict Avé-Lallemant, practitioners of *Wissenschaft des Judentums* such as Leopold Zunz (1794–1886) and Moritz Steinschneider (1816–1907), as well as members of the 1905 generation including Shmuel Niger, Zalmen Reisen, and Noyekh Prilutski.

As much as it was meant to be a reference tool, "Di bibliotek" was also a continuation of Borochov's argument in "Di oyfgabn": for too long, Yiddish language research had been held captive by its enemies. The time had arrived for Yiddish philologists to wrest control over Yiddish language studies and liberate the language. In the process, Yiddish scholarship would at last be acknowledged as a serious academic discipline. His contempt toward most prior Yiddish research is evident by his categorization of scholars in the pre-Borochovian era, whom he placed into six realms: (1) Christian scholars in the sixteenth to eighteenth centuries who were motivated to explore Yiddish either out of Humanist or missionary impulses; (2) "Jewish scholars of the same period who had no interest in Yiddish itself, but wanted to enlighten the simple rabble"; (3) "Shund" (Rubbish) linguists who consisted of apostates and Judeophobes; (4) Liberal Christian researchers of the nineteenth century who wanted to understand Yiddish as a dialect of German; (5) assimilated Jews who treated Yiddish as a corrupt German dialect; and (6) "Writers of the new Jewish generation who understand the cultural or at least the educational value of the Yiddish language and strive to develop its culture."[41]

Because Borochov assessed the merit of prior Yiddish research almost exclusively in terms of its value to Jewish national development, "Di bibliotek" was also a concrete articulation of the principles that he outlined in 'Di oyfgabn." He divided the entries into two general chronological categories: "Primitive Philological Writings" and "Philological Literature from the XIX and XX Centuries." Within each, he then created various subcategories such as "Christian scholars," "Sensational writings on Yidish-taytsh," "Writings by Jewish authors," "Articles in Encyclopedic Dictionaries," "Bibliographic Newspapers," and "Yidish-Taytsh Linguistics." Very few works of research met with Borochov's full approval. He even dismissed several of his contemporaries from the 1905 generation. For example, Zalmen Reisen's 1908 *Yidishe gramatik* was chastised for not possessing enough of a philological imperative, and Noyekh Prilutski's *Materialn far yidisher gramatik un ortografye* (Material for Yiddish Grammar and Orthography), although "interesting," was relegated to the category of "Linguistics," as were contributions by leading Yiddish advocates such as Shmuel Niger, Chaim Zhitlowsky, and Judah A. Joffe.

Not all pre-Borochovian works were met with scorn, however. Most notably, he praised the work of Philipp Mansch (1838–1890)—to whom he also dedicated "Di oyfgabn"—as the sole legitimate precursor to authentic

Yiddish philology. Mansch, an obscure attorney from Lvov, who, in his capacity as editor of the German language newspaper, *Der Israelit*, published a history of Yiddish that for Borochov symbolized the first attempt to take Yiddish seriously as an independent language.[42] Borochov depicted Mansch as "the most noble community-leader in Galicia, a devoted friend of the Yiddish language, literature and theater . . . ," who wrote with "great love, with a deep philosophical and philological perspective."[43]

Borochov's apparent disdain for earlier investigations into Yiddish raises the question of why bother to publish such a complete catalog? In an echo of Moritz Steinschneider, the nineteenth-century Jewish bibliographer of the *Wissenschaft des Judentums* school, one senses that Borochov's primary agenda was to give prior studies on Yiddish a decent burial. In effect, he was declaring them artifacts of outmoded attitudes toward Yiddish. Worthwhile to consult for clues to the development of Yiddish, these works would be maintained as relics whose primary value was to demonstrate the legacy that future Yiddish studies will have overcome. In effect, Borochov's catalog was an attempt to do to previous examinations of Yiddish what he felt they had done to Yiddish. Just as prior studies were an account of the efforts to demonstrate the illegitimacy of Yiddish as a language, "Di bibliotek" was an attack on their authenticity as scholarship.

Reviewing *Der pinkes* in *Di tsukunft,* the linguist Judah Joffe hailed the compendium as the fulfillment of his long held desire for a home for Yiddish philological studies. Not only was this an achievement for Yiddish scholarship, it was an achievement for the Jewish people. At the same time however, he recoiled from Borochov's overtly nationalistic agenda for Yiddish, viewing it as a betrayal of scholarly objectivity and as a delegitimization of the field of Yiddish philology, "one must abandon the romanticism of passionate love for Yiddish—which remains a relic from the ancient past, and one must look upon one's task with the sober eyes of a strict scientific undertaking."[44] Reflecting on Borochov's plan to reform the language and its vocabulary into a small, accessible set of grammatical rules, Joffe criticized his lack of awareness of the complexities of such a task and the lack of any scholarly consensus on basic issues concerning the language:

[Borochov] speaks at length about the *purity* and enrichment of the language. But it is superfluous to speak about such a thing because what looks pure to one looks overly polished in another's eyes, and to a third looks messy. And I don't mean in the eyes of simple Jews, but indeed in those who write about Yiddish. One person might think that all Slavic words in Yiddish are a type of abscess that has to be excised or cut out—they would rather import words from German. A second person screams that this is daytshmerish and not Yiddish, better instead to bring in words from Hebrew. And who is right? Who can determine the right rule as long as it depends upon one's taste, and "how one feels?" Above all, philological grammars rest upon the rule of rules: "if it sounds good."[45]

Joffe was not uniformly critical of Borochov, however. In his review of Borochov's bibliography of Yiddish scholarly research, he hailed it as the single most important piece of work in *Der pinkes*. Despite its occasional errors, he deemed it "a treasure of information on the entire field of Yiddish."[46] Borochov's inventory, reflecting years of archival research, better represented for Joffe the type of somber approach that scholars should adopt.

Joffe was by no means Borochov's only critic. In a long review of *Der pinkes* (discussed in chapter 5), Nokhem Shtif challenged Borochov on several fronts, most notably his coupling of political ends with scholarly ones in "Di oyfgabn," as well as for an abundance of bibliographic errors in "Di bibliotek."[47] Borochov's insistence on the need to impose a single orthographic standard also earned him the ire of journalists. According to Tsitron, at the Eleventh Zionist Congress (Vienna, 1913), Borochov was working as a correspondent and other journalists would tease him by regularly asking how correctly to spell various words in "a quiet protest against Borochov as an innovator in the field of Yiddish orthography."[48] A debate between Borochov and journalists was joined by Nathan Birnbaum and other delegates over the matter of Borochov's proposed orthography. Nearly all were opposed to it but, according to Tsitron, only Borochov had mastery over the material. "Like a ga'on [genius], who throws successive Gemoras and commentaries and responsa . . . ," Tsitron recounted, Borochov "drew from Yiddish and non-Yiddish incunabula that almost none of us had ever even heard of."[49] Borochov was also criticized at the Congress by Klausner at a meeting of Jewish journalists. According to Tsitron, the question arose as to whether the union should include Hebrew and Yiddish journalists, or be limited solely to the Hebrew ones. Despite Borochov's impassioned plea that "Hebrew and Yiddish are like a body and a soul" he was attacked for his defenses of Yiddish.[50]

In spring 1913, Borochov began a project that was never completed: a comprehensive history of the Yiddish language that would reflect the values he articulated in his contributions to *Der pinkes*. Borochov believed the true history of the Jewish people remained unknown, despite more than a century of efforts by modern Jewish historians to write it. The vast Yiddish-speaking Jewish masses were left unrecognized, unacknowledged, and confined to the margins of the Jewish past. The way to access their story was through their national language and, therefore, the task of writing it fell less to the historian than it did to the philologist. Borochov's solution was to write the first "scientific book concerning Yiddish" that would be both "truly scientific" and "truly Yiddish."[51] Central to his endeavor was overcoming the many deficiencies in prior attempts to write the history of Yiddish, especially those composed by linguists and bibliographers. As he told Niger, he planned to surmount their legacy by writing a broad history that would be "not only scientific, but as far as possible be literary and popular" to encompass the full range of the language, its speakers, and their customs.[52] Although he would continue to write shorter pieces on Yiddish literature and culture, including a lengthy entry for a Russian encyclopedia, bibliographies of Peretz and Sholem Aleichem, and examinations of early modern Yiddish texts and literary criticism, "Di geshikhte fun der yidisher literatur" (The History of Yiddish Literature) was his greatest effort to reimagine the Jewish people as a nation with the Yiddish-speaking folk at the center.

Although he never completed his goal of writing a full history of the Yiddish language before his death in 1917, Borochov published a blueprint for it in a five-part essay that appeared in 1915.[53] In proceeding with this task, Borochov envisioned himself a pioneer by accessing this untold history of the Jewish people. Although he acknowledged Moritz Steinschneider as the "*ga'on* of Jewish bibliography," Borochov accused him of not recognizing the literary value of the works that he cataloged. He likewise dismissed the philologist Leo Weiner's 1899 *The History of Yiddish Literature in the Nineteenth Century* as having "no great scientific worth" because Weiner "sinned against the chief-demand of historical scholarship" by not researching libraries for source material.[54] Others, such as the historian Gustav Karpeles (1848–1909), the Romanian philologist Lazar Saineanu (1859–1934), and the author of a recent survey of Yiddish literature, Meyer Pines (1881[?]–1942), were discounted as "'self-crowned' historians" who did nothing more than copy the title pages of Yiddish works into their studies. Instead, by bringing together the treasure-trove of Old Yiddish materials from the great libraries of the world, Borochov hoped to effect "an ingathering of the exiles of Yiddish literature," into a unified history of the language.[55]

Crafting even this abridged study—the first attempt at a comprehensive history of Yiddish composed in the Yiddish language—presented Borochov with a series of hurdles. Putting aside the question of whether or not there existed an identifiable Jewish folk, writing a unified history of Yiddish in order to tell their story was hampered by the fact that unlike most national groups, Jews had spoken many languages throughout their long history. In this regard, he compared Jews negatively to Germans, for whom "German literature is German not only in its content, in its purpose, but also in its form. It was created *from German, for German, in the German language*," but Jewish literature—containing everything written both by and for Jews—was too vast and imprecise a concept to provide the basis of a national culture.[56] Prior attempts to solve this dilemma typically resulted in broad surveys of Jewish literature through its many languages. Although they might have been far more comprehensive than what he was proposing, he argued that Yiddish literature was most often unfairly subsumed within larger narratives that did not reflect its central role in Jewish folk life. The emerging Jewish national consciousness, he asserted, demanded a new conception of Jewish literature: one that was written not only by Jews, for Jews, but also written in their national language.[57]

Despite his identification with Yiddish, Borochov acknowledged that there were in fact two genuine Jewish *national* languages—Yiddish and

Hebrew—and unlike many of his linguistically partisan contemporaries, he did not seek to deny one for the other. Whereas Matisyohu Mieses had dismissed the centrality of Hebrew to Jewish national life at the Czernowitz conference in 1908, Borochov argued in his "History" that *both* Yiddish and Hebrew were essential to Jewish cultural development. In an echo of his earlier assertion that the diversity of linguistic components within Yiddish was the language's strength rather than its deficiency, he likewise saw the duality of Jewish languages as a sign of his nation's strength. Hebrew was a means for Jews to connect back thousands of years to their ancestral past, whereas Yiddish was a way of Jews connecting to one another during their time in the Diaspora. "Therefore," he wrote, "everything belongs to our *national literature* that is created *both in oral and written form, by Jews for Jews in the Hebrew and in the Yiddish language.*"[58] Despite this gesture toward inclusiveness, he adopted a stance that put him at odds with his comrades in the Poalei Zion by insisting that the language that would forge them into a unified nation would be Yiddish and not Hebrew.

A second obstacle facing his project was the dearth of Yiddish sources from the premodern era. Because Yiddish was not considered a proper language by its speakers for most of its history, it was not the medium for most legal, commercial, scientific, or religious texts. In spite of the centrality of religious texts to Jews, to Borochov, they were marginal to the topic of his study. Because he identified the nation with the masses, and the masses with their language, it was not these elite materials he was concerned with when trying to tell his nation's history. Instead, by charting the development of Yiddish, he hoped to examine "the living, popular, and artistic products" of the folk culture in all of its "provinces," his term for the many realms of literature that were comprised in Yiddish, including folklore, drama, scientific literature, the press, and rhetoric.[59]

Borochov's "History" provided him with a way to demonstrate that there existed a Jewish past as yet undiscovered by scholars who were willing to take the Jewish masses seriously. By keeping his sights set squarely on those sources that were written in Yiddish, his work at its best reveals the possibilities of a rich, unexplored Jewish past that is evidenced not by the responsa, *halakhot,* and philosophical writings of great Jewish rabbis and thinkers, but by the spells, legends, folk remedies, exorcisms, and superstitions that had informed the lives of most Jews.[60] He hoped to show that by inverting this relationship between elite and popular materials, one could reconceptualize Jewish history in a way that placed the great masses of Jewish people at its foundation.

To make this case, Borochov pointed to the premodern Yiddish texts that he had researched in libraries while making his way across Europe. For example, he cited an early sixteenth century love poem written in Old Italian (in Latin letters) in the Ambrosia Library in Milan that had a bill of sale written in Yiddish (in Hebrew letters) on the reverse side. The poem was composed by the late fifteenth-/early sixteenth-century Italian scholar (and later cardinal) Pietro Bembo and the Italian handwriting was thought to be that of his mistress, the daughter of Pope Alexander VI, Lucretia Borgia. This text, when viewed in light of a similar undated love poem in Old Yiddish elsewhere in the collection, demonstrated the high level of engagement of Jews with Renaissance culture.[61] In another instance, he called attention to what he believed to be a twelfth or thirteenth century text handwritten in "Yidish-taytsh" that contained medicinal incantations that were still in use among the "bubbies" of his time as recorded in 1909 by Sh. An-sky in the Russian-Jewish journal, *Evreiskaia Starina* (Jewish Past).[62]

Elsewhere in his "History," Borochov traced dialectical shifts within the language and charted the development of its sounds, orthography, pronunciation, and word usage in an effort to establish that Yiddish developed along a path that was distinct from—yet related to—other Germanic languages.[63] More than this however, Borochov demonstrated how searching along the lines of Yiddish allowed for a new periodization of the past. In what he referred to as a "philological-archeological introduction," he divided Yiddish history into five epochs to demonstrate the degree to which the histories of the Yiddish language and the Jewish nation were intertwined: (a) the Classical period of Old Yiddish Literature; (b) its decline; (c) Hasidic Yiddish; (d) *maskilic* literature for the Yiddish-speaking folk of Russia; and (e) the new Yiddish literature that began with Abramovitsh. Adhering closely to the ideals of late nineteenth-century national Romanticism, Borochov's narrative posits a Golden Age of Yiddish during the sixteenth and seventeenth centuries, its decline at the hands of Enlightenment-inspired assimilationists during the eighteenth, and its subsequent renaissance in the modern period as the Jewish people reclaimed their national form in the late nineteenth.

As he represented it, the history of Yiddish followed a familiar pattern of rise, fall, and rebirth. For a full two hundred years during the sixteenth and seventeenth centuries, Yiddish literature contained the "greatest, most beautiful, and most widespread works" of Jewish folk literature."[64] Its hegemonic centers were in German and Bohemian lands where the great masses of Yiddish-speaking Jews were located. Following a principle that he referred to as the "emigration-factor" in Yiddish literature, the greatest works of its first Golden Age—such as the *Shmuel bukh, Sefer hamides, Sefer yosifon* [Book of Josephus]—emanated from Jews in Italy and others were composed in Polish lands.[65]

Beginning in the eighteenth century with the rise of the Haskalah and the subsequent linguistic "assimilation of the German Jewish intelligentsia and barbarization of the Jewish masses," Yiddish cultural productivity entered into a period of severe decline.[66] To Borochov, like Niger, the Jewish enlightenment represented little more than an attack on the Jewish folk masses and their culture and brought their vernacular to its lowest point.

Just as Eastern European Jews, who had always looked westward for guidance, were left "spiritually orphaned," when their brethren became sickened with "assimilation-gangrene," Yiddish was saved by the rise of the Hasidic movement in Polish and Russian lands in the eighteenth century and its emphasis on popular (if religious) literature.[67] Hasidic Jewry filled the gap left by assimilated German Jews and they nurtured Yiddish in Slavic lands. Under Hasidic influence, the language that had taken root and subsequently withered in German lands began to flower in the East. With the rise of the Haskalah in the early nineteenth century and its subsequent reluctant turn to Yiddish, the language was increasingly purified. By the 1880s Yiddish once again assumed its rightful status as the Jewish national language.

Although he was hampered by a lack of access in Vienna to important Yiddish sources, Borochov's blueprint for a history of Yiddish literature was his greatest effort to challenge conventional—and competing—renderings of Jewish history. Absent from his version are the familiar concepts of chosenness, the Jewish spirit, or the idea of an exiled Jewish nation striving to reach its homeland. Missing from his cast of characters are the great rabbis, sages, and mystics (except when they wrote in Yiddish). Instead, Borochov's history was one in which the masses of Jewish people stood at center stage as their folk legends, incantations, spells, poems, and songs replaced Halakhic rulings, philosophical tracts, and Talmudic discourses as the key products of Jewish culture.

Borochov never lived to see the fulfillment of his efforts to forge a scholarly discipline for Yiddish. It would be nearly a decade before Yiddish scholars were able to create an institutional structure influential enough to effect the broad changes in the language that he envisioned. Additionally, the geopolitical reshuffling in the aftermath of World War I meant that Russian Jewry was now divided among many states, and each of them brought new opportunities and limitations to expand Yiddish scholarly work. Although Borochov's thinking on how best to achieve Jewish emigration to Palestine was still in flux at the end of his life, one conclusion he had reached was the centrality of the Yiddish language in the forging of Jewish nationalism. Unlike many of his fellow members of the Poalei Zion, Borochov did not turn his attention to the development of Hebrew culture, nor to the complex realities of establishing a socialist Jewish state. Unlike his fellow Yiddishists, he remained insistent that Yiddish scholarship exist not for its own sake nor as a means to elevate Yiddish literary aesthetics, but rather as a central component of the revolutionary agenda he came to promote on account of his experience in the 1905 upheavals.

5 Nokhem Shtif

A Contrarian's Yiddishism

He either wandered as if in a world of chaos, or else was imprisoned as
if in a cage.
—Shmuel Niger[1]

Nokhem Shtif (1879–1933), the Yiddish linguist, philologist, and literary
historian, was one of the most influential and provocative figures involved
in the project to transform Yiddish into a modern language capable of
sophisticated scholarly activity. Like Niger, Borochov, and many others
of his generation, Shtif championed a variety of ideological solutions to
the question of the status of Russian Jewry over his lifetime. Unlike most
of his peers, however, Shtif never settled into an ideological or geographical home from which he could, even for a short time, comfortably pursue
his intellectual and political agendas. In spite of his intimate involvement
with radical Jewish politics and Yiddish cultural projects, his combative
personality and rigid insistence on objective scholarship put him regularly
at odds with his fellow activists during the politically charged formative
period of the Yiddishist movement. Although he would reconsider his
opposition to ideologically motivated scholarship in his later years and
become an active participant in the Sovietization of Yiddish, in the years
before the 1917 Revolution, Shtif's commitment to an authentic approach
to *visnshaft* led him to demand that its practitioners submit themselves to
the standards set by the disciplines of history, linguistics, and philology,
and prohibited them from conducting their work on behalf of temporal or
elite causes. To that end, he quickly earned a reputation as a severe and

135

uncooperative critic of the efforts to bring about new and mature forms of the language.

Similar to Niger and Borochov (with whom he alternatively collaborated and clashed), Shtif's relationship to the Yiddish language was in flux throughout most of his youth. Although he wrote his first propagandist works in Russian and held very little faith in the ability of Yiddish to express sophisticated thoughts and ideas, he began to consider its value as a means to agitate for change in the Russian empire in the years immediately prior to the 1905 Revolution. By the time of his association with the Vozrozhdenie, he had come to view Yiddish as central to his vision of a liberated Russian Jewry, and by the end of the revolution, he had become an impassioned Yiddishist. Shtif abandoned partisan politics in the decade between 1907 and 1917 and poured his creative energies into the development of Yiddish. In the years between the two Russian Revolutions, he attempted a variety of occupations (including working as a journalist and in a bank), yet most of his efforts were dedicated to exploring how Yiddish literary criticism and scholarly research could bring about the revitalization of Jewish national life. A tendentious and often confrontational intellectual, he engaged in polemics with Shoyl Ginzburg, Ber Borochov, and Chaim Nachman Bialik over the course and direction of Yiddish. With the onset of the 1917 Revolution, Shtif became politically active in Dubnow's reconstituted Folkspartey, and he once again joined the struggle for the advancement of Jewish minority rights. With the subsequent consolidation and eradication of Jewish political parties under Bolshevik rule, he joined the growing community of Russian-Jewish émigré intellectuals in Berlin and took up Yiddish scholarship and translation as his primary vocation. After writing the essay that led to the creation of the YIVO in 1925, he accepted an academic post in the Soviet Union's Academy of Science in Kiev, quickly distanced himself from the YIVO circle, and joined the Soviet effort to reform the Yiddish language.

Despite their not infrequent wrangling, Max Weinreich spoke of Shtif's deep commitment to build a Jewish world based upon Yiddish: "His path was Yiddish. His goal was a humanistic Jewish life. His path and his goal were intertwined and not disconnected."[2] Shtif tried to "create a new tradition. [He believed that one] must give faith back to the people and create an aristocracy that is neither wealthy nor bookish, but of the people."[3] Niger recounted Shtif's tortured efforts to find a base from which he could continue his work, and described him as a tragic figure, a "restless man" who was unable to identify a place for himself in the complex and uncertain world of modern Jewish culture. Nonetheless, he credited Shtif as the most energetic figure in Yiddish language and literary scholarship, but noted that his life was often defined by intellectual rootlessness.[4]

Shtif's vast oeuvre encompasses several hundred works on a wide range of political, communal, literary, and scholarly topics. As an impassioned Yiddishist, Shtif was active in nearly all realms of Eastern European–Jewish intellectual life: he conducted early investigations into Old Yiddish literature, wrote innovative works in Yiddish linguistics, philology, and literary criticism, published a study of the 1919 pogroms in the Ukraine, translated literary and historical works from Russian into Yiddish, and was a central figure in Soviet Yiddish circles.[5] He is best remembered for his 1925 essay, "Vegn a yidishn akademishn institut" (On a Yiddish Academic Institute), a text that successfully argued for the formation of the YIVO in Berlin later that same year. Despite his prodigious scholarly output, Shtif has only received scant attention since his death in April 1933, and rarely has he been the focus of sustained study. The discussions of his work that do exist are chiefly concerned with the final decade and a half of his life, when he took up scholarship as his primary vocation.[6] Because he was one of the most embattled of all Yiddishists in the 1905 generation, an examination of his peripatetic career illustrates the possibilities and hazards faced by those who tried to carve out a home for themselves within the world of secular Yiddish culture.

This chapter will consider Shtif's intellectual development in the early years of the efforts on behalf of the rejuvenation of Yiddish. After a brief sketch of his prerevolutionary activity, it traces his Yiddish writings from his time as a propagandist for the SERP, through his period as a Yiddish literary critic, as a increasingly passionate advocate for Yiddishism, and culminates with his initial efforts to define himself as a practitioner of *Yidishe visnshaft*. An investigation of the formative period of Shtif's life demonstrates that although scholars have often depicted the inter-revolutionary years as being marked in particular by battles between Hebraists, Yiddishists, and

Russianists to determine which language would best define Russian Jewry, the battles within the Yiddishist camp were often equally divisive. In the case of Shtif, his contrarian and defiant stance toward many of the early major venues of Yiddish literature and scholarship was not an attack on Yiddish from without, but by one of its most passionate and articulate champions. His often relentless criticism of Peretz's Warsaw circle of writers, the newspaper *Der fraynd, Di literarishe monatsshriftn* and even *Der pinkes* provides an alternative way to regard the formative period of modern Yiddish culture. Looking at these cultural productions not from the perspective of their accomplishments, but from the point of view of one of their most consistently severe critics, illuminates many of the tensions that were present at the outset of the Yiddishist movement, such as whether to continue with the revolution or make a break with it, to forge a high Yiddish culture or a popular one, and by which measure the new scholarship should be assessed.

Shtif was born in 1879 in the city of Rovno, Volhynia province (now in Ukraine), to parents who had been strongly influenced by the Haskalah.[7] His maternal grandfather had been an early teacher in the official Russian government schools for Jewish students and he gave a modern education to his sons. Although Nokhem studied religious texts (albeit with secular tutors) until the age of thirteen, and spoke Yiddish at home, most of his secondary education was in the Russian school system. In spite of his father's efforts to make a Russified Jew of his son, Nokhem was increasingly attracted to questions of Jewish nationalism, and he became an ardent Zionist in the wake of the First Zionist Congress in 1897. Upon enrolling at the Kiev Polytechnikum to study engineering and chemistry, he spent his time agitating on behalf of radical Zionist organizations.

Shtif began writing propaganda from his earliest encounter with Zionism in 1897. According to his memoirs, he wrote primarily in Russian in the pre-1905 revolutionary days for a variety of radical groups such as Yung Yisroel (Young Israel) and the Vozrozhdenie. In particular, his 1903 brochures (published in Yiddish and Russian) on the failed Jewish assassin Pinchas Dashevsky gained him a measure of notoriety for their boldness and support of violence as a weapon in the struggle for Jewish emancipation.[8] They also earned him six weeks in a Minsk prison. With his training in Russian schools and the near-total absence of Yiddish political and scholarly materials available to Russian-Jewish students in the late nineteenth century, Shtif at first found it nearly impossible to imagine a future for himself as a Yiddish-speaking intellectual. As he later recalled, he once believed, "as did all of my friends, that I did not know Yiddish."[9] He began to reassess his stance toward Yiddish in his early twenties after hearing Sholem Aleichem read at Zionist gatherings in Kiev.

Like many young Jewish activists, the Easter 1903 Kishinev pogroms prompted Shtif to move his politics away from a Palestine-centered Zionism and toward a Diaspora-based Territorialism, and he joined in with those forming the Vozrozhdenie group. After his second arrest and imprisonment (for possessing banned materials), he fled Russia in fall 1904 and lived in Bern and Geneva for a year. It was during his time among the Russian-Jewish émigré community in Switzerland that Shtif joined followers of Sh. An-sky and Chaim Zhitlowsky. He turned to Yiddish both as a practical means of spreading revolutionary propaganda and as an ideology upon which to form his politics. In what he describes as a "vision" around the time of the 1905 Revolution, he became a fervent believer in the potential of Yiddish.[10] In 1906, he returned to Kiev on a false passport and worked as a party activist for the SERP.

Shtif's dreams for Yiddish were influenced in large measure by his hero and mentor, Zhitlowsky. As he recounted, Zhitlowsky's essays, such as "A yid tsu yidn" (A Jew to Jews) and "Tsienizm oder sotsializm" (Zionism or Socialism) that made the case for a vibrant Diasporic Jewish life, became foundational texts for the movements of Diaspora Nationalism and Yiddishism. Shtif credited Zhitlowsky with imparting to him the conviction that the success of Diaspora Jewry depended upon the unification of then-divided Jewish national and labor movements and that Jewish intellectuals would be the link to join them. At a time when many young, radicalized Jews like Shtif saw no real possibility for themselves within the established Jewish community and often gravitated toward Russian revolutionary groups, Zhitlowsky showed them a way to combine Jewish nationalism and radical politics. As Shtif related:

Dr. Zhitlowsky was the first to attack the criminally assimilationist attitude toward the Jewish people and he called upon the Jewish intelligentsia to return to the people . . . and to join with Jewish workers in a uniquely Jewish social-political program on the basis of the Yiddish language and Jewish culture and to join in the historical fate of the entire people. If one comes to accept this stance toward the Jewish worker and his language, and if one begins to consider the Jewish worker as an end unto himself and his language as equal with all others, (at least in a practical sense) one must acknowledge the courageous and consistent theoretical and practical literary efforts of Dr. Zhitlowsky.[11]

With his Yiddish propaganda on behalf of the SERP, Shtif spent much the 1905 Revolution seeking to realize Zhitlowsky's vision of a socialist diasporic Jewish national existence.

As a member of the SERP, Shtif began writing essays that considered the possibilities of Yiddish as a medium for political thought. In spite of his earlier concern that he could not compose works in Yiddish, he consciously struggled to cultivate a popular style, hoping to make his politics accessible to Jewish workers. He remarked that from his earliest Yiddish essays, he began to earn a reputation as a stylist, and his articles were praised in many circles. He later pointed to this period as the time when his commitment to Yiddish crystallized—"[in] that revitalized Jewish environment, in particular in the naturally Jewish atmosphere of the workers' party and with my literary work, Yiddish became a culture for me."[12]

Under Zhitlowsky's influence, the SERP differentiated itself from other Jewish revolutionary organizations, most notably the Bund and the S.S., with its commitment to the idea of Territorialism. Territorialists argued that not only should Jews seek the cultural autonomy demanded by the Bund, the S.S., and some liberal Jewish parties, but they should expand their agenda to call for political independence for Russia's minority groups through the establishment of various national parliaments. Although the SERP recognized that the Jews were too dispersed throughout the Pale to demand their own sovereign state, its members argued that they would comprise a large enough amount of the population in the regions they resided in to gain a significant measure of political power. Because Jews amounted to only a tiny minority within the whole of the Russian empire, the chances of them ever gaining political rights were minuscule, they argued, as evidenced by the poor showing of Jewish representatives to the Duma elections. Within, however, a future Ukrainian or Polish state, where Jews would comprise a much more significant percent of the population, the SERP contended that Jews would be much better able to gain substantial political rights.[13]

It was in the pages of the SERP's biweekly journal, *Di folksshtime* that Shtif first articulated many of the ideological convictions that were to govern his politics. As a regular contributor to the *Di folksshtime,* Shtif often defended his party's stance against its main rivals. He frequently criticized the Bund and the S.S., charging them with lacking a commitment to democratic politics, refusing to demand political sovereignty for the Jews, and (in the case of the Bund) subordinating themselves to the RSDWP. He criticized the mainstream Zionists for their unwillingness to focus on the immediate problems facing Russian Jewry in favor of political negotiations aimed at securing land abroad. Finally, like other radicals of his generation, Shtif charged the liberal parties with being vestiges of an outmoded, *maskilic* system that denied the integrity of the Jewish nation in favor of bourgeois attempts at assimilation into Russian society.

In an article he wrote in late 1906, Shtif urged his fellow Jews to follow the SERP position and to take an active role in the 1907 elections to the second Duma.[14] As mentioned in chapter 1, Jewish radical groups boycotted the elections to the first Duma (which convened in May 1906 and was dissolved by the tsar just ten weeks later).[15] Despite the fact that Jewish participation remained restricted in the elections to the second Duma, many radical organizations shifted course and joined with other Russian revolutionary parties to support the efforts to elect a legislative body in the hope of continuing the revolution from this front.[16] Shtif hoped to convince his fellow Jews to take part in voting for the second Duma, and to use the election as another tool in the war against the tsarist regime, and as a tactical move to build coalitions with other parties that were increasingly alienated by the government. Although "the pulse of the Jewish street beats weakly," Shtif noted in this essay, the Jews could not afford to ignore the electoral campaign this time.[17] He decried the government's tactics of dividing the workers, separating peasants from factory workers, and seeking to turn the Duma into a base for the forces of reaction. He advanced a strategy of uniting Jewish and non-Jewish parties as well as radicals and liberals against the growing strength of the government and called upon the Jewish Voting Committee to develop a clear program to unify Jewish voters and agitate on behalf of community interests.

In 1907, just before the revolutionary moment began to fade, Shtif meditated on the growing strength of Diasporism within the Jewish national movement. In a feuilleton entitled "Fun minsk biz helzingford," (From Minsk to Helsingfors), Shtif considered the monumental ideological shift that had taken place within the Zionist movement in the time between the second conference of Russian Zionists, held in Minsk in September 1902, and its third conference, which took place in Helsinki in December 1906.[18] The outcome of the third conference confirmed for him both his generation's mission to chart a new direction for Russian Jewry and the supremacy of the Diaspora Nationalist stance.

The 1902 conference had been dominated by a dispute between two factions over how best to direct Zionist energies in Palestine. The competing sides eventually reached a compromise and thwarted the possibility of a split in the Russian Zionist movement. To Shtif, however, the Minsk conference represented not a triumph for Zionism, but rather the final attempt of an older generation of *maskilic* Zionists to maintain their control over the Jewish national movement. From his point of view, both sides were at fault for ignoring the immediate, physical needs of Russian Jewry and for getting caught up in debates over an unattainable utopian Jewish life in Palestine. Although the first years of the Zionist movement had been filled with wild hopes and unrealistic expectations of an imminent Jewish state, ("All believed that the end of the exile was near and the Messiah was at the door"), the violence that raged since 1903 showed that Zionist energies of the movement were misdirected and needed to be reoriented toward the immediate needs of Jews in the empire.[19]

The years immediately following the Minsk conference saw the landscape of Russian Jewry dramatically altered. The Zionist leader Herzl, unexpectedly died soon after proposing the highly divisive Uganda plan and the 1903 Kishinev pogrom and the October 1905 violence highlighted the increasingly vulnerable situation of Russian Jewry.[20] By 1906, a new generation of leaders, infused with radical visions of socialist revolution, now dominated Jewish politics and put the case for Jewish national rights within the Russian empire at the forefront of the Zionist agenda, "the Russian Revolution opened broad new ideas, new hopes were born and were aloft like butterflies in the Jewish street."[21]

To Shtif, the 1906 Helsinki meeting was a clear affirmation of the Diasporist position and a triumph for revolutionary nationalism. In contrast to the 1902 conference, the 1906 gathering saw its participants largely unconcerned with the world diplomacy of Herzlian Zionism but were focused instead on debating how best to respond to the immediate threats facing Russian Jewry, agreeing to shift their efforts toward *Gegenwartsarbeit* (present-day work) in order to ease the suffering of Diaspora Jewry. Building up a strong Jewish community in the Diaspora was accepted by the delegates as a necessary precondition to the future resettlement of Jews in Palestine. For Shtif, the Helsinki conference was a validation of his party's commitment to Diaspora Jewry:

> Minsk and Helsingfors! They traverse a small distance—only 4 years—and yet a great transformation, nearly a revolution in the Zionist world. Minsk and Helsingfors—they are two symbols of contradictory ages in the Zionist system. The first ended the age of "untainted Zionism" that existed without a trace of shatnets [impurity], and held the greatest scorn for the Diaspora. The second began . . . the Zionism of despair and forced a reconciliation with the Diaspora. . . . Between these two points lay a long road.[22]

To Shtif, the terrible events that had occurred between the Minsk and Helsinki gatherings forced the Zionist movement to reconsider its stance on two competing demands—the land or the people. Until 1906, the movement had always favored the acquisition of land, but it had at last chosen the people. In addition, Zionists had begun to recognize the role of the Jewish working class in leading the movement of Jewish liberation. Once at the forefront of the Jewish national movement, the Zionists were now forced to catch up to the position of those revolutionary groups that wanted to rebuild Jewish life in the Diaspora, "and thus Territorialism is growing and ascending, it has grasped the hearts and minds of the workers and the intelligentsia, and joined together the social ideals of the working masses with its national aspirations for freedom and independence."[23]

Despite the outcome of the Helsinki conference, Shtif's triumphalism was short-lived. The Territorialist movement that he and his comrades had begun could not sustain the onslaught that came in spring 1907 when the tsar began to reassert his authority and crack down on revolutionary activity. Shtif continued his agitation on behalf of the SERP throughout the first half of 1907, writing on the elections to the third Duma and the international Socialist Congress held in Stuttgart.[24] His brief but powerful affiliation with the SERP lasted until the summer, when the tsarist crackdown on radical groups made further revolutionary work all but impossible. By 1908, the SERP had all but ceased to exist. As Shtif related in his memoirs, "the reaction began, [and] party life was snuffed out."[25] With the waning of the revolution in spring 1907, Shtif began turning his attention away from political activity.

He did not, however, repudiate his commitment to diasporic Jewish life. Like Shmuel Niger and many other members of the 1905 generation, Shtif continued to focus his attention on Yiddish cultural work during the decade of reaction. However, unlike Niger and those around him who spent much of these years creating new literary forums to advance Yiddish aesthetics, Shtif positioned himself as one of their severest critics. Although he frequented the same cultural circles and published in the same journals and newspapers as did other Yiddishists, with his combative personality and unrelenting insistence that modern Yiddish culture not be divorced from the masses of speakers (in favor of what he called an "uncontrived, free folk-language"), Shtif repeatedly found himself at odds with his peers.[26] From this point on, more so than Zionism or Territorialism, Yiddishism became the cornerstone of his Jewish identity. As the historian Lucy Dawidowicz noted, "in the study of Yiddish and in advocating for it a central place in Jewish life and thought, Shtif found his identity as a Jew."[27]

In fall 1907, Shtif and his new wife moved to St. Petersburg, and he quickly became engrossed in the small but active Yiddish literary scene that was located in the capital. In the years just following the 1905 Revolution, St. Petersburg experienced a brief resurgence as an important center of Russian-Jewish intellectual life. Although Shtif did not remain there for long, (he left in 1909) he took part in the intense cultural debates that raged within the Jewish community. The contentious divisions between the liberal and radical Jewish camps that had been so potent during the 1905 Revolution found a new focus during the years of political repression. The clashes between Russia's liberal and radical Jews that had occurred over issues of political strategy were replaced with debates over questions of culture and language. Such struggles often took place within Jewish institutions such as the Society for the Spread of Enlightenment among the Jews in Russia, the Jewish Historiographical Society, the Jewish Literary Society, and the Society for Yiddish, as well as in the Russian and Yiddish press.[28]

Shtif positioned himself in these disputes as a guardian of a popular Yiddish culture that responded to the political and spiritual needs of the Jewish masses, and that kept the forces of elitism at bay. He saw attacks on Yiddish as emanating from many quarters: from Hebraists who championed a return to a modernized ancestral language, from advocates of an increasingly archaic Haskalah who saw Yiddish as a barrier to the agenda of liberalism, and from those who hoped to incorporate European modernist styles to Yiddish literature. He defended Yiddish against each with a great passion and as a consequence, found himself increasingly isolated and with few allies in his efforts to advocate a populist, unadorned path for Yiddish.

Against those who insisted that a modern Jewish revival would best occur in Hebrew—Shtif replied that the truest, most sincere expressions of the Jewish people could only be in their mother-tongue:

> If we want to speak about the living folk-culture that is created by the people, from its deep internal treasury, that contains the deepest impressions of its life, thoughts, feelings, hopes, and fantasies, and that which develops organically—such a culture is possible in Yiddish and only in Yiddish.[29]

To those who argued that Yiddish suffered from a deficient vocabulary and a sparse literary tradition and was therefore incapable of expressing the sophisticated thought necessary of true intellectuals, Shtif remained undeterred. He made a comparison to Russian, which, despite its rich vocabulary and history as a language of scholarship, still borrowed from other languages:

> Even until today, the Russian language possesses little original political and scientific creations. . . . In particular it nourishes itself with translated literature. This hardly injures the national self-conception of the Russian intelligentsia.[30]

One of Shtif's first actions that earned him a measure of notoriety as a contrarian on behalf of Yiddish was an attack on *Der fraynd* for its insufficient support of Yiddish, which stemmed, he argued, from its decision to abandon its experiment with radical politics (that it had taken up during the revolution) and to return to its more moderate ideological stance in the name of reaching a mass audience in an increasingly crowded marketplace. Since arriving in St. Petersburg, he had been writing for the city's only Yiddish daily newspaper. In October 1908, when *Der fraynd* was on hiatus while it relocated to Warsaw, he published an article in the Russian-Jewish journal, *Razsvet* (Dawn) that was sharply critical of the newspaper.[31] He chastised it for its wavering editorial positions and refusal to take up seriously the cause for a Yiddish renaissance. In particular, he argued that it was stuck in its antiquated, prerevolutionary stance: "I showed that it was dying from excessive respectability: idealistic without an ideal, radical without a clear political face, literary without literary content (in recent years), Yiddish without any feeling for Yiddish, etc. . . . everything respectable." It was a paper only for intellectuals, "without an understanding of and without any interest in the great reading masses" and thus did not serve the interests of the Jewish street.[32] Later, he described this essay as "untactful" and reflected on how his brashness cost him the support of its editor Shoyl Ginzburg, who refused to publish any more of his submissions or to speak with him for many years afterwards.

The main target of his attacks during these years, however, was not the prior generation of *maskilim* (for whom he would later express much sympathy), but rather his own peers who were promoting the modernist styles favored by the writers of Peretz's Warsaw circle and hailed by Niger, Gorelik, and Vayter. He chastised them for mimicking cosmopolitan forms and he exhorted his fellow Jews to look instead to their own traditions for sources of creativity. His opposition manifested itself in many ways: through attacks on projects like *Di literarishe monatsshriftn,* in his own literary criticism, and through his promotion of the few authentic Yiddish writers whom he could identify.[33] In his autobiography, Shtif defended his fulminations against critics who tried to raise the prestige of those he considered to be inferior Yiddish writers:

> In particular, among the literary critics, I attempted to release myself from the communal perspective that dictated that our critics offer compassion and treat each mediocrity with velvet gloves, simply because it was "ours"; gazing with wide eyes at each trifling. I stood on behalf of the artistic-aesthetic point of view: the standards of world literature: ideas, emotions, literary techniques, style, that pertained to us as much as it did all others. I was certain that I truly served the literature. . . . For my entire time in the literary cliques I was a sort of outsider, like a visitor, in part because of my estrangement from the Warsaw crowd and their ways.[34]

His resistance to European modernist literary forms left him with few authors to champion as a critic. Rather than promote the writers around Peretz, he instead turned to Sholem Aleichem as a more appropriate model for aspiring Yiddish authors. One of his earliest attempts at literary criticism was a celebration of the author, whose folksy style, according to Shtif, spoke from within the Jewish tradition yet was contemporary enough to connect with broad masses of Jewish readers. Unlike more esoteric writers, he argued, Sholem Aleichem typified the very best "democratic" writing, whose works improved the entire lot of the Jews:

> His goal is not the higher fashions, the more-developed tastes, like Peretz, for example. He is the *democrat,* he knows well that he writes for all the people.
>
> Sholem Aleichem's language conforms to his manner. It is a rich, simple folk-language that doesn't use contrived words or expressions that grate on the eyes [like those found] in Peretz and even more so among our "young ones." His language is easy, gentle, and calm.[35]

Favoring a realist approach that accurately reflected the lives of Russian Jews, Shtif continued with this theme as he launched forceful attacks on the Yiddish literature being produced by members of his own generation.

In an essay entitled "Vegn unzere 'yunge'" (On our Young Ones), Shtif derided the modernist fashions that were being advanced by figures such as Asch, Hirshbeyn, Nomberg, and Weissenberg.[36] Although he saw them as competent writers, he also felt they were naïve, uneducated in their craft, and produced bad imitations of European forms. They were trying to create literature using techniques with which they had no skill, and produced second-rate material that, in Shtif's mind, was consistently dreadful in its pretentiousness, "thus is created a brainy literature by tiny minds."[37] He saw the efforts to employ decadent imagery as "painful" and "annoying" and a provocation that wasted the time and attention of its readers.[38] He railed against the use of mystical, dark images that viewed the world only in blacks and grays, and did not portray the colors that illuminated the world. He chastised them for retreating into psychological excursions at the expense of the material world around them, and for not obtaining the training needed of first-rate authors:

> Where are the eyes of our "young ones?" They are not only distant from the human world, they have shut their eyes to the material world too. . . . The young painter undergoes a particular training. One places before him a model: a foot, a head, an ornament, limbs, muscles, etc. . . . and has him look, in order to notice each point in great detail. One teaches him perspective. In a word, one disciplines his eye and then develops his style. Guy de Maupassant underwent a similar type of writing school with Flaubert. Where can our "young ones" benefit from such a writing school?[39]

To Shtif, at stake in the battle for Yiddish was nothing less than the future of Russian Jewry. His concern was that by divorcing its literature from the richness of Jewish history and by subjecting it instead to the ephemeral standards of European literary trends, it would not become sufficiently substantial to serve as the basis of a renewed Jewish existence. In an inspirational essay entitled "Betokhn" (Faith), he lamented the absence of the once proud faith that had existed among the Jews.[40] He could not locate it among religious leaders, political figures, or most sadly for him, within the new Yiddish literature beginning to take form. Instead, contemporary Yiddish writers primarily offered their readers uninspiring works of gloominess, grayness, and misery in a cheap mimicry of European trends.

He called upon them to return to the well of Jewish faith during dark times and again pointed to the model offered by Sholem Aleichem, whose character Tevye the Milkman was to him the epitome of Jewish conviction, who demonstrated that faith—"a beautiful Jewish virtue"—was the essential tool for Jewish survival.[41]

Shtif's advocacy of Diaspora Nationalism and Yiddish ultimately brought him to the nascent Yiddish scholarly movement. Although he would not fully engage Yiddish linguistics and literary history until after World War I, Shtif began his research into Yiddish with his move to St. Petersburg in 1907, with regular visits to the collections of Hebrew and Yiddish manuscripts at the city's Asiatic Museum. He wrote of the "tremendous impact" made upon him after first encountering a copy of the *Shmuel bukh*, a fifteenth-century Yiddish epic tale.[42] At the time, he attempted to write a scholarly work on the history of Old Yiddish literature, but without proper training in philology, he found it nearly impossible and abandoned the project. In what would be a criticism that he would often levy against other scholars throughout his career, he concluded that his project would have had "more propagandistic than scientific ends," and decided not to continue with it.[43]

In 1909, while studying law, Shtif began to gather Old Yiddish materials, including rare manuscripts and collections of responsa with Yiddish glosses, as well as a library of Yiddish philological and bibliographical texts, mostly composed in German.[44] These texts informed the basis of much of his early knowledge of Yiddish literary history and was the beginning of his lifelong engagement with the historical development of the language. In what was the first of several tragedies in his career, he lost the entire collection at the end of World War I when a friend who was entrusted to guard it was forced to sell the materials in order to fend off starvation.[45]

Just prior to World War I, Shtif attempted to take up Yiddish scholarship as his primary intellectual pursuit. He was only able to publish two scholarly articles before the outbreak of World War I and the 1917 Revolution put a temporary halt to his work. The first was a lengthy book critique published in the 1913 compendium, *Der pinkes,* and the second was a critical review of *Der pinkes* itself. Both submissions were provocative, antagonistic efforts to defend the standards of Yiddish studies against what he saw as tendencies toward sloppy, ideologically driven research. Likewise, both pieces were a continuation of the contrarian stance that he had adopted as a literary critic.

Shtif's contribution to *Der pinkes* was an examination of Meyer Pines' two volume survey, *Di geshikhte fun der yidisher literatur (The History of Yiddish Literature)*, a Yiddish translation of Pines' doctoral dissertation completed at the Sorbonne.[46] Edited with an introduction by the literary critic Bal-Makhshoves, *Di geshikhte fun der yidisher literatur* was a comprehensive study of the development of Yiddish literature from its (then) earliest known sources in the first decade of the sixteenth century until the first decade of the twentieth. Pines, a former S.S. candidate to the second Duma and a leader in the Jewish Territorialist Organization of Israel Zangwill (1864–1926), was a Yiddish writer and journalist who helped publish (with Bal-Makhshoves) the Yiddish newspaper *Di yidishe shtime*. Despite that *Di geshikhte* was a translation of a work written in French, the fact that its author was an active Yiddish journalist from the 1905 generation meant that his book was widely viewed as the first historical study of Yiddish to be written from within the Yiddishist camp.

It was also wholly scorned by its Yiddish language reviewers, including Niger and Borochov, who, like Shtif, found the work to be amateurish, naïve, and derivative of more important studies done in the field.[47] Even the editor Bal-Makhshoves sensed that the work would not be received well by its Yiddish language readers. In his introduction, Bal-Makhshoves remarked that although the "attentive reader [may] find some faults in it," they should not diminish the reader's love for the Yiddish language.[48] Bal-Makhshoves then listed many of the text's weaknesses and deficiencies. Overall, however, he claimed that the work provided a much-needed examination of the historical foundations on which modern Yiddish literature was built. He likewise remarked that such an accomplishment as Pines' was only possible given the new appreciation for Yiddish literature that had occurred over the previous decade.

Shtif summed up his review by concluding that Pines' survey held, "little familiarity with the historical material, lengthy discussions on trivial matters, [and] half-words about important phenomenon."[49] Rather than dismiss it off-hand, however, Shtif used his contribution to *Der pinkes* to set forth high standards for Yiddish scholarship. Like Borochov's "*Di oyfgabn*" that appeared in the same volume, Shtif's essay was highly programmatic and advanced a very particular vision of the growing discipline. Unlike Borochov's essay, however, Shtif's review strenuously argued against tethering Yiddish scholarship to overt ideological goals and instead, tried to hold it to the standards of objective research.

Given his substantial library of Old Yiddish texts and time spent in the Asiatic Museum, Shtif was in a unique position to review Pines' work. Having abandoned a similar effort at Yiddish literary history himself because he felt that he lacked the proper skills, it is clear that Shtif wished Pines had made a similar choice. Although he agreed with Bal-Makhshoves that Yiddish was at last mature enough to have its own history in its own language (even if in a translation), Shtif thought the volume a poor example of the scholarly potential of Yiddish. He saw the book as evidence that, despite its growth and transformation over the previous decade, the language was not being treated seriously as a subject for scholarship.

Shtif accused Pines of a host of missteps: giving short shrift to the formative period of the Yiddish language and its literature while devoting an entire volume to six contemporary writers (of mixed influence), having inconsistent orthographic standards, and confusing literary criticism with literary history. He went on to charge him with offering sloppy evidence (with countless errors of dates, places, and attribution), misreading his sources (claiming the opposite of what other scholars have concluded), relying too heavily on secondary sources, advancing fantastic, unsubstantiated theories of the origins of Yiddish, ignoring the category of folklore entirely, and accepting the conclusion that Yiddish was a form of corrupted German: "What they called corrupted, we call developed, in a particularly Jewish way!"[50] He also chastised Pines for his use of dogmatic Marxist logic, and for passing off social history as the literary history he purported to present.

Even worse was Pines' lack of historiographical literacy, a trait he felt Pines shared with too many Yiddish intellectuals: "The majority know nothing of what has already been done, that learned Christians and Jews, philologists, historians have studied and researched our Yiddish."[51] Whereas

Pines was ignorant of much of the historical, philological, and linguistic research that went on before him, and Borochov scorned most of it as relics of a defeatist anti-Yiddish posture, Shtif insisted on its usefulness to literary historians. Rather than disdain studies by early modern and modern scholars of Yiddish such as Wagenseil, Avé-Lallemant, Steinschneider, and Güdemann, he saw great value in their work, even if he disagreed with their scholarly orientation. Like Borochov, Shtif insisted that scholars of Yiddish take the language seriously as an entity unto itself and not as a corrupt form of German. Nevertheless, he saw merit in the scholarship conducted by Germanists. He remarked that it was absurd to discount the findings of pre-Yiddishist scholars who conducted research into Yiddish when they were engaged in the study of the development of German.

At the root of Shtif's critique of Pines was a strong resistance to scholarship that was governed by ideological demands, even ones with which he shared an affinity. Given Shtif's subsequent involvement with the highly ideological language reform projects of the Soviet Union in the late 1920s and early 1930s, it is remarkable that at the outset of his scholarly career, he tried to forestall the co-optation of *Yidishe visnshaft* for partisan causes. In this review, he positioned himself squarely against those who engaged Yiddish research as an instrument to further causes other than itself. He argued for the necessity of scholarly dispassion: for researchers to consider the full range of available materials, to examine each piece of literature anew, and to provide proper attribution of sources.

One of the most surprising outcomes of Shtif's insistence that scholars rid their work of ideological didacticism was his volte-face concerning the legacy of the Haskalah. Pines, with his unflinching Marxist/nationalist perspective, had joined with those who condemned *maskilim* as enemies of Jewish national aspirations and as proponents of assimilation and embourgeoisement. By contrast, Shtif adopted a much more conciliatory stance and sought to rehabilitate their legacy. To the postrevolutionary Shtif, who had himself criticized Jewish liberal parties during the 1905 upheaval as outmoded remnants of the Haskalah, the *maskilim* were in fact the forefathers of the new nationalistic ethos. He recast the Jewish Enlightenment as the initial attempt to liberate the Jews and as "the first stirrings of a sleeping, frightful, backwards people to a better life, to a modern world-view, to a struggle for its human rights."[52] He dismissed Pines' blanket denunciation of the Haskalah as not the opinion of a serious "historian" but as one who "treats it like a political adversary, as a Marxist and 'Yiddishist'" who is bound to a particular jargon.[53] "He has here the whole arsenal of trite brochure-like phrases about the *maskilic* assimilation, about their 'patriotism', about their flowery-language, etc."[54]

Instead of joining the chorus of denunciation of the *maskilim* that was nearly obligatory among his generation, Shtif adopted a more forgiving stance and strove to understand them in their historical context. Even if they were not motivated by national sentiments and followed a "false path," they added a "positive value" to Jewish lives because they began the process of liberation that was now culminating in Jewish national movements. Because it was only the 1880s when Jews began seriously to consider their own national movement, chastising *maskilim* for their attempt to secure a better future for the Jews was anachronistic as well as "childish and naïve":

> The time is long since past for national, polemical and not in the least unhistorical positions vis-à-vis the maskilim. It must be acknowledged that they were the first to point out a new broad path in the large world, and we have to thank them greatly for the political and cultural rebirth of our people. If they erred, it was out of historical necessity, they were in their own time the best of our people and worked for their ideal with devotion. And if we today have for ourselves a phenomenon such as *A History of Yiddish Literature* that attacks the *maskilim* boldly and without compassion, it is in no small part because of such "jargon-users" as [the founder of the Russian Jewish Enlightenment] Isaac Ber Levinsohn.[55]

Shtif continued with this approach to the new Yiddish scholarship in 1914, in a lengthy review of *Der pinkes* published in *Di yidishe velt,* the journal edited by Niger. By this time, Shtif had moved to Vilna to work for the Boris Kletskin publishing house, which issued both *Der pinkes* and *Di yidishe velt*. Despite any fealty he may have had toward his new employer, Shtif had many harsh words for the volume.[56] Although he praised it as marking a new era in Yiddish scholarship and as a vital step in the development of the young discipline, he concluded that it, like Pines' *Geshikhte,* fell far short of the rigorous standards demanded of serious scholarship. As he did with Pines' study, Shtif used his review of *Der pinkes* to advocate for a more intellectually rigorous approach to *Yidishe visnshaft* and to attack what he saw as spurious, unscientific approaches that posed a threat to its success.

Shtif related that up until the appearance of *Der pinkes,* scholarship on Yiddish suffered from the triple faults of (a) being written in a foreign language, (b) being scattered throughout hundreds of newspapers and journals and thus inaccessible to most scholars, and (c) not being composed for the sake of the language, but as a by-product of other linguistic studies. Unlike Borochov, however, Shtif did not dismiss prior Yiddish scholarship as without value to future Yiddish researchers, but saw it as a base upon which to build a new science dedicated to the study and development of the language. Although *Der pinkes* strove to provide a solution to these problems, Shtif pointed to the many flaws he found in the text. His first criticism was that despite its pretense of being a forum for serious scholarly studies, the volume was marred by the presence of "reading material" better suited for popular literary journals. He argued, for example, that although works like M. Tshemerinski's essay on Yiddish phonetics were perfectly suited to *Der pinkes,* the poet Sarah Reisen's reflections on her brother Avrom had no place in a collection of such monumental importance.[57] Instead, Shtif believed that only memoirs with a clear historical or philological significance were appropriate, like those of the Jewish businesswoman Glikl of Hameln (1646 or 1647–1724). He recognized that although restricting the annual in this way would limit its potential audience, there was no other way to maintain a consistently high standard of serious scholarship, "It is true that a 'scientific library' would have a small circle of readers, but it must be so."[58] He likewise was wary of Niger's contribution on the role of women in Yiddish literature, seeing it less as a historical study than as a "literary-psychological" one.[59]

In a brief rebuttal, Niger defended his choice to include literary memoirs in *Der pinkes.* He noted that because so little was known about the lives of Yiddish literary figures, it was an appropriate and accepted practice to include them. He pointed out, for example, that despite his importance to Yiddish literature and his vast oeuvre, no useful biography of Mendele

Moykher Sforim (Abramovitsh) existed, as well as other key figures of the new literature. Further, he argued that the mixture of popular and scientific material in a single volume was a necessary choice given the paltry state of Yiddish letters.[60]

Shtif took his severest aim at Borochov, and devoted the bulk of his thirty-page critique to Borochov's programmatic statement, "Di oyfgabn" as well as to his catalog, "Di bibliotek."[61] He criticized Borochov on nearly every account: for his use of an "experimental" orthographic system that differed from that used in the rest of the volume; for his dismissal of extant Yiddish scholarship; for his lack of a systematic program for the "defense" of Yiddish from its Russianist and Hebraist foes; and finally, for his poorly collected "Bibliotek," which Shtif found full of errors, omissions, and inappropriate entries.

His primary concern with Borochov's insistence on his own orthography was that a scholarly journal was the wrong forum for experimentation. He noted that in the introduction to *Der pinkes,* Niger had explicitly remarked that it was not going to be the place to test out new spelling systems, and yet Borochov was given leeway to do just that. "One thing is clear to me," he wrote, "that such a system in which each stands apart cannot lead to the improvement and refinement of our spelling, but only to greater and more dangerous barbarization. If Borochov is permitted, why not Prilutski, the brothers Gordin, and why not a 'Yiddishist' from Yehupetz and Terebendiev?"[62] For Shtif, the entire question of orthography was something to be deferred until the time when a Yiddish language academy could be formed to decide matters of such monumental importance.

Shtif also contested Borochov's agenda for Yiddish research. As Shtif saw it, the first activities of Yiddish scholars had to be strictly practical. Although he concurred that creating an authoritative institution for Yiddish was necessary in order to expand the language, he feared that without methodical, deliberate action, the new science was at risk of failing in its infancy. In contrast to Borochov's overly ideological agenda, he argued that the first step was to gather and make available all the previous work on Yiddish that had been conducted, "One must create the possibility for our young researchers who do not have an academy nor an academic mission in the great European libraries to have the entire material in their hands."[63]

He advocated collecting the relevant articles, monographs, bibliographies, manuscripts that were scattered across Europe in many languages, and translating them into Yiddish, "Who among even our scientific scholars, for example, has read the *Shmuel bukh,* around which there already exists an entire literature?"[64]

He also attacked Borochov's "Bibliotek" as being but a poor rehash of more comprehensive bibliographies composed in previous years by figures such as Moritz Steinschneider, or the well-known linguist Alfred Landau (1850–1935).[65] He saw it less a catalog of philological articles than a series of entries on the "Yiddish Question." He chastised Borochov for not discerning between those articles that had a scholarly merit, those that were brochures for general audiences, and those that were notoriously full of errors and therefore valueless.[66]

Shtif's Yiddish scholarship was halted with the onset of World War I and he did not have another opportunity to continue until the early 1920s. As he described it, the period from 1915 to 1921 was "unlucky" because his efforts to pursue his scholarly ambitions were continually thwarted on account of war.[67] Although he was unable to produce a substantial body of work in the years preceding World War I (in great contrast to his prodigious output in the decade and a half after the war), his early criticisms of the burgeoning Yiddish literary and scholarly culture provide a useful counterbalance to the ideologically infused productions that often characterized the first efforts of the Yiddishist movement. Although he was as much a product of the 1905 Revolutionary generation as was Niger and Borochov, and was as deeply committed to the flowering of modern Yiddish culture, his critique of the projects to which they were so wedded and his resistance to experimentalism and innovation placed him as an outsider among the new Yiddish intelligentsia. Rather than champion such initiatives as *Di literarishe monatsshriftn, Der fraynd,* and *Der pinkes,* he insisted on holding them to rigid and uncompromising standards. As an impassioned ideologue committed to diasporic Jewish life, he waged a regular battle for the enrichment and viability of the Yiddish language, but did so through the language of caution and restraint. As a result, he frequently found himself on the margins of scholarly circles, and never found a home where he could pursue his work unencumbered by material concerns. Despite his setbacks and false starts, his insistence that Yiddish must serve the needs of the Jewish masses often served as a useful corrective to those who wished to make the language more exclusive, esoteric, and out of reach to most readers.

Conclusion

Once Jews became citizens in the Soviet Union and the newly independent Poland in the aftermath of World War I, the Yiddish language and culture stood at the center of Eastern European–Jewish popular and intellectual life. Over the next two decades, Yiddish reached its greatest heights of scholarly, cultural, and political expression and dominance. This was the moment when Yiddish fully came into its own as a cultural idiom and became the foundation of a secular Jewish renaissance, replete with vibrant Yiddish school systems, presses, and theaters. This was the age of important Yiddish literary circles like Di khalyastre (The Gang) and Yunge vilne (Young Vilna) and renowned writers such as Kadya Molodovsky (1894–1975), Peretz Markish (1895–1952), Uri Tsvi Greenberg (1896–1981), Itsik Fefer (1900–1952), Itsik Manger (1901–1969), Bashevis Singer (1904–1991), and Avrom Sutzkever (1913–).[1]

The signing of the Treaty of Versailles and the Minorities Treaty in 1919 led many Eastern European Jews to believe they might finally realize their decades-old aspirations for cultural and political autonomy within a modern state. With legal barriers to political and communal activism in Poland now removed, political parties such as the Poalei Zion, the Bund, and the Folkspartey embraced what was termed by one scholar as the "new Jewish politics" as they sought to make a definitive break with traditional Jewish political strategies that seemed to them too accomodationist.[2] In the process, they came to be among the most active promoters of secular Yiddish culture. In the Soviet Union, Yiddishist visions of state-supported cultural and educational activities seemed to be realized, prompting scores of Yiddish-speaking scholars and authors living abroad to return in the 1920s.[3]

Despite the far-reaching influence of Yiddish culture, resources for its scholarship were often quite scarce and were dependent upon either the marketplace (in Poland) or the state (in the Soviet Union). Building upon the work first begun during the 1905 Revolution, three major institutes devoted to *Yidishe visnshaft* were founded with the task of sponsoring scholarship, training students, reforming the language, creating archives, hosting conferences, and writing pedagogic materials: the YIVO in Vilna, the Institute for Jewish Proletarian Culture of the Ukrainian Academy of Sciences in Kiev, and the Jewish Department of the Belorussian Academy of Sciences.[4] Their journals, such as *Yivo bleter, Di yidishe shprakh/Afn shprakhfront* (The Yiddish Language/On the Battle Lines of Language), and *Tsaytshrift* (Periodical), covered the fields of history, demography, economics, linguistics, and folklore, and showcased the work of scholars of the 1905 generation such as Lestschinsky, Prilutski, Shtif, Niger, Kalmanovitsh, and Tcherikower, as well as a younger generation who came to prominence after the war such as Jacob Shatsky (1893–1956), Max Weinreich, Max Erik (1898–1937), Raphael Mahler (1899–1977), and Emanuel Ringelblum (1900–1941).[5]

The post–World War I careers of the 1905 generation (and in the case of Borochov, his legacy), were often as complicated and discordant as the lives they led before the war. In the case of Niger, however, he continued his Yiddish cultural activity unabated soon after arriving in the United States. He became a member of the staff of the Yiddish daily *Der tog* (The Day), writing weekly columns until his death in 1955 and maintaining his status as the doyen of Yiddish literary criticism, as Marcus Moseley has called him.[6] He was an active member of nearly all major Yiddish cultural projects to take place in New York, including serving as a contributor to the journal *Di tsukunft* (The Future), as a lecturer in Yiddish pedagogic seminars, as president of the Sholem Aleichem Folk Institute, as editor with Zhitlowsky of *Dos naye lebn* (The New Life), and as a member of the Central Yiddish Culture Organization. During this time, he also published many of his most significant critical studies, including works on Abramovitsh, Sholem Aleichem, and Peretz. Although he was based in New

York, Niger also played a strong role in the development of the YIVO, and contributed to many of its publications. In 1948, Niger helped to found the Congress for Jewish Culture. He also contributed to the first major Yiddish encyclopedia project, *Di algemeyne entsiklopedye* (The General Encyclopedia) and was an editor of its English-language variant, *Jewish People: Past and Present*. In 1954, he began to edit *Leksikon fun der nayer yidisher literatur*. He died on Christmas eve, 1955, leaving a legacy unmatched in all of Yiddish letters.

Following his death in 1917, Borochov quickly became the subject of much lionizing, in particular after World War I when the Poalei Zion split into Left and Right factions, and both sides sought to base their authority on his stature.[7] Having died young, with several foundational texts to his name and a mass of inspired followers eager to draw from his legacy, he was a figure ripe for memorialization and idolization at a time when hopes for Jewish freedom and national liberation seemed to be on the horizon.[8] Even in more recent times, Borochov's memory often remains shrouded in myths that are much greater than the man.[9] These attitudes dominated the historical literature to such a degree that it was nearly six decades before scholars began reflecting critically on his political activity. In 1976, Matityahu Mintz's biographical studies of Borochov were soon followed by Jonathan Frankel's lengthy chapter on Borochov in his 1981 *Prophecy and Politics* and Mitchell Cohen's 1984 introduction to an English translation of Borochov's political writings.[10] These insightful works provided a much-needed contextualization of Borochov's political thought and have convincingly made the case of Borochov as being a highly complicated political theoretician whose thought, far from static and unwavering, was as dynamic and varied as the times in which he lived.

Yiddishists likewise elevated Borochov to that of a prophet soon after his death. With their discipline on more solid footing by the mid-1920s, Yiddish researchers began reflecting on the history of their discipline and often spoke of Borochov as the "pioneer" and "father" of modern Yiddish studies. For example, the linguist Zalmen Reisen hailed him as the "groundwork layer" of Yiddish studies, as the figure who liberated Yiddish studies from the hands of the Germanists and the Hebraists, and as the one who set the research agenda that led directly to the YIVO. At the same time, the historian Tcherikower referred to him as "the fighter for Yiddish, the first-born child of our language-science." Shmuel Niger hailed Borochov for paving the way for all future research into Yiddish: "Chiefly, he is a pioneer and the foundation-layer of our young scientific culture." Max Weinreich referred to him as a "pioneer" with "visionary gaze." Even many of those who earlier had criticized him, and who likewise played instrumental roles in creating the field, later crowned Borochov as the originator of their movement.[11]

Of all Borochov's contemporaries, the literary historian Nachman Meisel (1886–1966) did the most to promote him as the founder of Yiddish studies by publishing the collected works of Borochov's writings on Yiddish.[12] In this volume are reprinted the full range of Borochov's writings on the future of *Yidishe visnshaft*, his philological explorations, literary histories, tributes to the Abramovitsh, Sholem Aleichem, and Peretz, critical reviews, and letters to colleagues. In the introductory essay, Meisel elaborated upon this characterization of Borochov as the founder of Yiddish scholarship and offered an insightful chronology of Borochov's Yiddish activism, concluding that he was "the genius, the wonderful thinker, researcher, the discoverer of new worlds, of new ideas, 'the Columbus of Yiddish scholarship,' as Zalmen Reisen called him."[13] In more recent years, this representation of Borochov continues to be echoed. Only recently have critical examinations of Borochov's Yiddish activism begun to appear.[14]

With the onset of the 1917 Revolution, Shtif moved to Petrograd and joined the growing circle of Yiddish activists who had gathered there, which included Niger, Kalmanovitsh, Weinreich, and Yudel Mark (1897–1975). It was at this time he first began to articulate the idea of creating a Yiddish scholarly institute.[15] In order to support himself and his family, Shtif returned to journalism and took up a variety of editorial positions with journals such as the St. Petersburg journal *Folksblat* (People's Paper), for which he again wrote literary criticism, and *Fun tsayt tsu tsayt* (From Time to Time), where he pressed the case for Jewish national autonomy within the new postrevolutionary state.[16] Additionally, like many of his colleagues who had turned away from political activity with the end of the 1905 Revolution, Shtif returned to politics at the onset of the 1917 Revolution and was active in several pro-Diaspora groups, including the Folkspartey.

With the end of the war, Shtif resumed his scholarly work and moved with many of his fellow activists to Kiev, a city that was, for a brief period, a major center of Yiddish cultural activity, not in the least because of the work of the Kultur-lige, an organization established to support a variety of Jewish cultural projects.[17] During his time there, Shtif, like several others who formed the first cohort of YIVO scholars, wrote a study of the pogroms that devastated Jewish communities throughout the Ukraine after the end of the war.[18] By 1922, he moved to Berlin. In 1925 he wrote his most influential essay, "Vegn a yidishen akademishn institut," which made the case for the founding of the YIVO. In 1926, impoverished and desperate for employment, Shtif returned to Kiev, where he assumed the Chair in Yiddish Studies at the Academy of Sciences.[19] There, he took up Yiddish linguistics as his primary focus of study and he engaged in fierce ideological polemics with the YIVO circle over issues of language reform, to the point where he declared a *shprakhfront* in the campaign against his former colleagues, and recanted many of his earlier "errors" regarding the language.[20] In particular, he was deeply involved in efforts to reduce the Hebraic component in Yiddish because it was characterized by the Soviets as representative of a lingering bourgeois element of the language. As Rakhmiel Peltz has shown, the last years of his life were "very trying" for Shtif and he unsuccessfully sought to step down from his post and faced a barrage of criticism from abroad. Shtif died at his desk in April 1933.

The efforts of the generation that included Niger, Borochov, and Shtif to create a *visnshaft* for Yiddish and to locate the language at the center of Jewish national consciousness never had a chance to face the test of time. Whereas the violence and destruction of 1881–82, 1903–5, and World War I helped to accelerate the expansion and modernization of Yiddish, the Holocaust brought these processes to a near complete halt. In the post–World War II hegemonic centers of Jewish life—the United States and Israel—the Yiddish language and its science were no longer appropriate to the tasks of nation building, revolution, or enlightenment. Instead, Yiddish scholarship has become an academic discipline that is distant from most native speakers of the language (the majority of whom are ultra-Orthodox), is expressed mainly in languages other than Yiddish, and is concerned nearly exclusively with the examination of its historical development.[21]

NOTES

BIBLIOGRAPHY

INDEX

Notes

Introduction: Yiddish as Instrument and Ideology

1. Simon Dubnow, *Fun "zhargon" tsu yidish un andere artiklen: literarishe zikhroynes* (Vilna: B. Kletskin, 1929), 9.

2. Simon Dubnow, *Weltgeschichte des jüdischen Volkes: von seinen Uranfängen bis zur Gegenwart* (Berlin: Jüdischer Verlag, 1925–30). On Dubnow's political program for Russian Jewry at the time of the 1905 Revolution, see David E. Fishman, *The Rise of Modern Yiddish Culture* (Pittsburgh: Univ. of Pittsburgh Press, 2005), 62–79; and Simon Rabinovitch, "Alternative to Zion: The Jewish Autonomist Movement in Late Imperial and Revolutionary Russia" (PhD diss., Brandeis Univ., 2007).

3. Dan Miron, *A Traveler Disguised: The Rise of Modern Yiddish Fiction in the Nineteenth Century* (New York: Schocken, 1972), 27–28. Dubnow was at one time highly skeptical of the literary possibilities of Yiddish. See Emanuel S. Goldsmith, *Architects of Yiddishism at the Beginning of the Twentieth Century: A Study in Jewish Cultural History* (Rutherford, N.J.: Fairleigh Dickinson Univ. Press, 1976), 57.

4. For a discussion of Dubnow's generation, see David H. Weinberg, *Between Tradition and Modernity: Haim Zhitlowsky, Simon Dubnow, Ahad Ha'am, and the Shaping of Modern Jewish Identity* (New York: Holmes & Meier, 1996).

5. See Jonathan Frankel, *Prophecy and Politics: Socialism, Nationalism, and the Russian Jews, 1862–1917* (Cambridge: Cambridge Univ. Press, 1981).

6. Weinberg, 3.

7. The Yiddish term *"visnshaft,"* like its German cognate, *"Wissenschaft,"* does not have an easy equivalent in English. Just as *"Wissenschaft des Judentums"* has been translated to mean "the science of Judaism" or "Jewish scholarship" or "Jewish studies," *"Yidishe visnshaft"* can mean "Yiddish science," "Yiddish scholarship," or "Yiddish studies," and I use them interchangeably in this work. Complicating matters further is that in Yiddish the word *"Yidish"* can mean either "Yiddish" or "Jewish." See the discussion of the term *"Yidishe visnshaft,"* below.

8. Michael A. Meyer, "Two Persistent Tensions Within *Wissenschaft des Judentums,*" *Modern Judaism* 24, no. 2 (May 2004): 105–19.

9. Abraham Ascher, *The Revolution of 1905: A Short History* (Stanford: Stanford Univ. Press, 2004), 82. Abraham Ascher states that "All in all, according to the most reliable estimates, 690 anti-Jewish pogroms occurred, primarily in the southwestern provinces; 876 people were killed and between 7,000 and 8,000 injured."

10. Frankel, *Prophecy and Politics*, 329.

11. Mikhail Krutikov, "Reading Yiddish in a Post-Modern Age: Some Trends in Literary Scholarship of the 1990s," *Shofar: An Interdisciplinary Journal of Jewish Studies* 20, no. 3 (2002): 4.

12. Krutikov, 8. Krutikov is quoting from the Preface to the reprint edition of Dan Miron, *A Traveler Disguised* (Syracuse: Syracuse Univ. Press, 1996), xviii–xix.

13. See, for example, David Shneer, *Yiddish and the Creation of Soviet Jewish Culture: 1918-1930* (Cambridge: Cambridge Univ. Press, 2004); Gennady Estraikh, *In Harness: Yiddish Writers' Romance with Communism* (Syracuse: Syracuse Univ. Press, 2005); Alexandre Métraux, "Opening Remarks on the History of Science in Yiddish," *Science in Context* 20 (June 2007): 145–62; and Barry Trachtenberg, "Ber Borochov's 'The Tasks of Yiddish Philology,'" *Science in Context* 20 (June 2007): 341–52.

14. See, for example, Benny Morris, *The Birth of the Palestinian Refugee Problem, 1947–1949* (Cambridge: Cambridge Univ. Press, 1989); Gershon Shafir, *Land, Labor and the Origins of the Israeli-Palestinian Conflict, 1882–1914* (Cambridge: Cambridge Univ. Press, 1989); Ilan Pappé, *The Making of the Arab-Israeli Conflict, 1947–1951* (London: I. B. Tauris, 1992); Boas Evron, *Jewish State or Israeli Nation?* (Bloomington: Indiana Univ. Press, 1995); Zeev Sternhell, *The Founding Myths of Israel: Nationalism, Socialism, and the Making of the Jewish State,* trans. David Maisel (Princeton: Princeton Univ. Press, 1998); Avi Shlaim, *The Iron Wall: Israel and the Arab World* (New York: W. W. Norton, 2000); Ilan Pappé, *The Ethnic Cleansing of Palestine* (Oxford: Oneworld Publications, 2006); and Gabriel Piterberg, *The Returns of Zionism: Myths, Politics and Scholarship in Israel* (New York: Verso, 2008).

15. David N. Myers, "The Ideology of Wissenschaft des Judentums," in *History of Jewish Philosophy,* ed. Daniel H. Frank and Oliver Leaman (London: Routledge, 1997), 706–20.

16. Immanuel Wolf, "Über den Begriff einer Wissenschaft des Judentums," reprinted and translated in *The Jew in the Modern World: A Documentary History,* ed. Paul Mendes-Flohr and Jehuda Reinharz, 2nd ed. (Oxford: Oxford Univ. Press, 1995), 219–20.

17. Ismar Schorsch, *From Text to Context: The Turn to History in Modern Judaism* (Hanover, N.H.: Brandeis Univ. Press, 1994).

18. Ibid., 161.

19. N. Shtif, "Vegn a yidishn akademishn institut," *Di organizatsye fun der yidisher visnshaft* (Vilna: TsBK and VIL'BIG, 1925), 4.

20. Dovid Katz, "On Yiddish, in Yiddish, and for Yiddish: 500 Years of Yiddish Scholarship," in *Identity and Ethos: A Festschrift for Sol Liptzin on the Occasion of His Eighty-fifth Birthday,* ed. Mark H. Gelber (New York: Peter Lang, 1986), 23, 32.

21. Métraux, 146. Métraux also notes that the term often refers to "scholarship regarding the Yiddish language or studies on Jewish subject matter written in Yiddish or in any other language."

22. Ibid, 148. As Métraux puts it, "The guiding idea underlying our view on *yidishe visnshaft* therefore is that the Yiddish name for scholarship in Yiddish refers to work done in institutions by people operating materially upon data, samples, documents, and other means of research, and symbolically upon theories, hypotheses, opinions, ideologies, etc."

23. See, for example, Mikhail Krutikov, *Yiddish Fiction and the Crisis of Modernity, 1905–1914* (Stanford: Stanford Univ. Press, 2001); Sarah Abrevaya Stein, *Making Jews Modern: The Yiddish and Ladino Press in the Russian and Ottoman Empires* (Bloomington: Indiana Univ. Press, 2003); Barbara Henry, "Jewish Plays on the Russian Stage: St. Petersburg, 1905–1917" in *Yiddish Theatre: New Approaches,* ed. Joel Berkowitz (Oxford: Littman, 2003), 61–75; Joshua Zimmerman, *Poles, Jews, and the Politics of Nationality* (Madison: Univ. of Wisconsin Press, 2004); Fishman, *The Rise of Modern Yiddish Culture;* and Stefani Hoffman and Ezra Mendelsohn, eds., *The Revolution of 1905 and Russia's Jews* (Philadelphia: Univ. of Pennsylvania Press, 2008).

24. For example, Cecile Kuznitz, "The Origins of Yiddish Scholarship and the YIVO Institute for Jewish Research" (PhD diss., Stanford Univ., 2000); David Shneer, *Yiddish and the Creation of Soviet Jewish Culture;* Shneer, "A Study in Red: Jewish Scholarship in the 1920s Soviet Union," *Science in Context* 20 (2007): 197–213; and Samuel D. Kassow, *Who Will Write Our History?: Emanuel Ringelblum, the Warsaw Ghetto, and the Oyneg Shabes Archive* (Bloomington: Indiana Univ. Press, 2007).

25. In more recent years, this representation has been most forcefully asserted by Dovid Katz. See his "On Yiddish, in Yiddish, and for Yiddish." For contrasting representations of pre-Yiddishist scholarship, see Max Weinreich, *Geschichte der jiddischen Sprachforschung,* ed. Jerold Frakes (Atlanta: Scholars Press, 1992); and Hans Peter Althaus, "Yiddish," *Linguistics in Western Europe,* ed. Einar Haugen, et al. (The Hague: Mouton Publishers, 1972), 1345–82.

26. Ber Borochov, "Di oyfgabn fun der yidisher filologye," in *Der pinkes: yorbukh far der geshikhte fun der yidisher literatur un shprakh, far folklore, kritik un bibliografye,* ed. Shmuel Niger (Vilna: B. Kletskin, 1913), 1–22; and Borochov, "Di bibliotek funem yidishn filolog (400 yor yidishe shprakh-forshung)," in *Der pinkes,* 1–68 (separate pagination).

27. See Dovid Katz, *Lithuanian Jewish Culture* (Vilnius: Baltos Lankos, 2004), 282–85.

28. On the similarities between Jewish nationalist and socialist movements, see Yosef Gorny, *Converging Alternatives: The Bund and the Zionist Labor Movement, 1897–1985* (Albany: State Univ. of New York Press, 2006).

29. Benjamin Harshav, *Language in a Time of Revolution* (Berkeley: Univ. of California Press, 1993), chapter 5, "The Force of Negation."

30. Johann Gottfried Herder, *Abhandlung über den Ursprung der Sprache* (Berlin: C. F. Voss, 1772). Also see F. M. Barnard, *Herder on Nationality, Humanity, and History* (Montreal: McGill-Queen's Univ. Press, 2003); and the discussion "Hebrew, The Language of a

Nation," in Alain Dieckhoff, *The Invention of a Nation: Zionist Through and the Making of Modern Israel,* trans. Jonathan Derrick (New York: Columbia Univ. Press, 2003), 98–127.

31. Ivan T. Berend, *History Derailed: Central and Eastern Europe in the Long Nineteenth Century* (Berkeley: Univ. of California Press, 2003), 49.

32. Patrick J. Geary, *The Myth of Nations: The Medieval Origins of Europe* (Princeton: Princeton Univ. Press, 2002), 29–34.

33. Benedict Anderson, *Imagined Communities: Reflections on the Origin and Spread of Nationalism,* rev. ed. (London: Verso, 1996), 71.

34. Dieckhoff, 101.

35. On the idea of territory as a central component of national liberation movements in Eastern Europe, see Raymond Pearson, *National Minorities in Eastern Europe, 1848–1945* (London: Macmillan, 1983), 18–21.

36. Borochov, "Di oyfgabn," 1 (355). A full English translation of Borochov's "Di Oyfgabn" appeared as Ber Borochov, "The Tasks of Yiddish Philology," trans. Jacob Engelhardt and Dalit Berman, *Science in Context* 20 no. 2 (2007): 355–73, from which most of the quotes from this essay are taken. Page references refer to the original 1913 publication and translation references appear in parentheses following.

37. Max Weinreich, *Geshikhte fun der yidisher shprakh: bagrifn, faktn, metodn,* vol. 1 (New York: YIVO Institute for Jewish Research, 1973), 304.

1. The Jewish Revolution of 1905

1. Leon Trotsky, *1905,* trans. Anya Bostock (New York: Random House, 1971), 36.

2. Shlomo Lambroza, "The Pogroms of 1903–1906," in *Pogroms: Anti-Jewish Violence in Modern Russian History,* ed. John D. Klier and Shlomo Lambroza (Cambridge: Cambridge Univ. Press, 1992), 195–247; Edward H. Judge, *Easter in Kishinev: Anatomy of a Pogrom* (New York: New York Univ. Press, 1992); and Robert Weinberg, *The Revolution of 1905 in Odessa: Blood on the Steps* (Bloomington: Indiana Univ. Press, 1993).

3. An important exception to this is Jonathan Frankel, whose work on 1905 is an exploration of this transformative moment and which informs much of this work. See his *Prophecy and Politics;* "Jewish Politics and the Russian Revolution of 1905," *Spiegel Lectures in European Jewish History* 4 (Tel Aviv: Tel Aviv Univ., 1905); and "Ber Borokhov and the Revolutionary Generation of 1905," *Contemporary Jewry: Studies in Honor of Moshe Davis,* ed. Geoffrey Wigoder (Jerusalem: The Institute of Contemporary Jewry, 1984), 217–33.

4. Frankel, "The Crisis of 1881–1882 as a Turning Point in Modern Jewish History," in *The Legacy of Jewish Migration: 1881 and Its Impact,* ed. David Berger (New York: Brooklyn College Press, 1983), 10. The term "nationalist socialist" is Zeev Sternhell's, who employs it as a way of distinguishing from the "national socialism" of the Nazis. Sternhell, 7.

5. Hans Rogger, *Russia in the Age of Modernisation and Revolution 1881–1917* (New York: Longman, 1983), chapters 1, 2, 6, and 7; Ascher, *The Revolution of 1905: A Short History,* chapter 1.

6. Rogger, chapter 8.

7. Walter Sablinsky, *The Road to Bloody Sunday: Father Gapon and the St. Petersburg Massacre of 1905* (Princeton: Princeton Univ. Press, 1976), 261–68.

8. Frankel, "Jewish Politics and the Russian Revolution of 1905," 8.

9. In all, more than three thousand Jews are said to have been killed in Russia during 1905–6 as a result of pogroms. For a description of the pogroms that occurred during the 1905 Revolution, see Abraham Ascher, "Anti-Jewish Pogroms in the First Russian Revolution, 1905–1907," in *Jews and Jewish Life in Russia and the Soviet Union,* ed. Yaacov Ro'i (Ilford, Essex, England: Frank Cass, 1995), 127–45; Robert Weinberg, "The Pogrom of 1905 in Odessa: A Case Study," in Klier and Lambroza, 248–49; Lambroza, 195–247.

10. Quoted in Sophie Dubnov-Erlich, *The Life and Work of S. M. Dubnov,* 135–36.

11. Frankel, *Prophecy and Politics,* 157–58. Sidney Harcave, "The Jews and the First Russian National Election," *American Slavic and East European Review* 9, no. 1 (Feb. 1950): 33–41.

12. The term is Hans Rogger's. See his essay "The Ambiguous Revolution," *Russia in the Age of Modernisation and Revolution: 1881–1917,* 208–28.

13. Deutscher, *The Prophet Armed,* 175.

14. Geoffrey Hosking, *Russia and the Russians: A History* (Cambridge, Mass.: Harvard Univ. Press, 2001), 334.

15. Ibid.

16. Rogger, 182.

17. Ibid., 191.

18. Ibid., 188. Also see Zimmerman, 10–17.

19. David E. Fishman has suggested the comparison between the Ukrainian and Jewish cases. See "The Politics of Yiddish in Tsarist Russia," in *From Ancient Israel to Modern Judaism, Intellect in Quest of Understanding: Essays in Honor of Marvin Fox,* vol. 4, ed. Jacob Neusner et al. (Atlanta: Scholars Press, 1989), 155–71.

20. Piotr Wandycz, *The Lands of Partitioned Poland, 1795–1918* (Seattle: Univ. of Washington Press, 1974), 250.

21. Ibid., 253; and Timothy Snyder, *The Reconstruction of Nations: Poland, Ukraine, Lithuania, Belarus, 1569–1999* (New Haven: Yale Univ. Press, 2003), 122.

22. Rogger, 184.

23. Ibid.

24. Heinz-Dietrich Löwe, *The Tsars and the Jews: Reform, Reaction and Anti-Semitism in Imperial Russia 1772–1917* (Chur, Switzerland: Harwood Academic Publishers, 1993), 86. As Löwe states, this settlement distribution "was virtually an inversion of the usual Russian pattern."

25. The ambivalence that the Russian government had for the Jews is discussed in Stanislawski, *Tsar Nicholas I and the Jews: The Transformation of Jewish Society in Russia—1825–1855* (Philadelphia: Jewish Publication Society, 1983).

26. Rogger, 183.

27. Löwe, 27–54.

28. For a discussion of these pogroms, see Stephen M. Berk, *Year of Crisis, Year of Hope: Russian Jewry and the Pogroms of 1881–1882* (Westport, Conn.: Greenwood Press, 1985); Erich E. Haberer, *Jews and Revolution in Nineteenth-Century Russia* (Cambridge: Cambridge Univ. Press, 1995), 206–29; the essays by I. Michael Aronson, "The Anti-Jewish Pogroms in Russia in 1881"; John D. Klier and Shlomo Lambroza "The Pogroms of 1881–1884"; Moshe Mishkinsky, "'Black Repartition' and the pogroms of 1881–1882"; and Erich Haberer, "Cosmopolitanism, Antisemitism, and Populism: A Reappraisal of the Russian and Jewish Socialist Response to the Pogroms of 1881–1882," in Klier and Lambroza, 98–134.

29. Klier and Lambroza, 40.

30. Ibid., 41.

31. Kahan, *Essays in Jewish Social and Economic History*. For an early sociological examination of the effects of urbanization and industrialization, see Jacob Lestschinsky, "Statistika Shel Eyara Ahat," *Ha-Shiloah* 12 (1903): 87–96.

32. Löwe, 93.

33. On the Russian-Jewish integrationists, see Benjamin Nathans, *Beyond the Pale: The Jewish Encounter with Late Imperial Russia* (Berkeley: Univ. of California Press, 2002); and Nathans, "The Other Modern Jewish Politics: Integration and Modernity in *Fin de Siècle* Russia," in *The Emergence of Modern Jewish Politics: Bundism and Zionism in Eastern Europe,* ed. Zvi Gitelman (Pittsburgh: Univ. of Pittsburgh Press, 2003), 20–34.

34. The Bund's full name was finalized in 1901 as *Der algemeyner yidisher arbeter bund in lite, rusland un poyln* (The General Jewish Workers Union in Lithuania, Russia and Poland). On the early Jewish Social Democratic movement, see Zimmerman, chapter 2, "The First Sproutings of the Jewish Socialist Movement, 1890–1905."

35. Löwe, 170. As Löwe states, other estimates offer the more conservative number of 23,000.

36. Judge, *Easter in Kishinev;* and Lambroza, "The Pogroms of 1903–1906."

37. Judge, 50.

38. Ibid., 72–74.

39. *Prophecy and Politics,* 135. Frankel cites the figures that whereas in 1900, 37,011 Jews went from Russia to the United States, the number increased to 77,544 in 1904, 92,388 in 1905, and 125,234 in 1906.

40. David Vital, *A People Apart: The Jews in Europe 1789–1939* (Oxford: Oxford Univ. Press, 1999), 509–15. Also see the contemporary accounts by Elias Regensberg, *Kishinover hesped* (London: H. Gintsberg, 1903); and Michael Davitt, *Within the Pale: The True Story of Anti-Semitic Persecution in Russia* (New York: Barnes, 1903).

41. Simon Dubnow, "A Historic Moment (The Question of Emigration)," in *Nationalism and History: Essays on Old and New Judaism,* ed. Koppel S. Pinson (Philadelphia: Jewish Publication Society, 1958), 192–93.

42. Löwe, 178–83. Also see Zvi Halevy, *Jewish Schools under Czarism and Communism: A Struggle for Cultural Identity* (New York: Springer Publishing Company, 1976), 58–145.

43. Christoph Gassenschmidt, *Jewish Liberal Politics in Tsarist Russia, 1900–1914: The Modernization of Russian Jewry* (New York: New York Univ. Press, 1995), 13–16.

44. Leonard Schapiro, "The Role of the Jews in the Russian Revolutionary Movement," *Slavonic and East European Review* 40, no. 94 (Dec. 1961): 160.

45. The Hebrew press also suffered in this period. Both *Ha-Melitz* and *Ha-Zeman*, two prominent periodicals featuring the best of the new Hebrew writing, ceased publication in the years 1904 and 1906, respectively.

46. Herzl's 1903 call to establish Uganda as a Jewish homeland split the Seventh Zionist Congress, held in Basle in 1905.

47. Judge, 104.

48. Gideon Shimoni, *The Zionist Ideology* (Hanover, N.H.: Brandeis Univ. Press, 1995), 170–77; and Frankel, *Prophecy and Politics,* 288–328.

49. Frankel, *Prophecy and Politics,* 322.

50. Moshe Zilberfarb, "Di grupe 'vozrozhdenye,'" *Royter pinkes* 1 (1921): 116.

51. Ibid.; also see the group's short-lived journal *Vozrozhdenie* (1904); Ben-adir [A. Rosin], *Sotsialistisher teritorializm: zikhroynes un materialn tsu der geshikhte fun di parteyn s"s, y"s, un "fareynikte"* (Paris: Arkhiv-komisye fun di parteyn s"s, y"s un fareynikte, 1934), 21–43; in particular, see the essay by Nokhem Shtif, "Barikht fun der konferents 'vozrozhdenye,'" 130–33, for the group's criticisms of the Bund and the general Zionists; Alfred A. Greenbaum, *Tenu'at "ha-Tehiyah" ("Vozroz'denyah") u-Mifleget ha-Po'alim ha-Yehudit-Sotsyalistit (M.P.Y.S.): Mivhar Ketavim* (Jerusalem: Merkaz Dinur, 1988); Frankel, *Prophecy and Politics,* 278–83; and Jack Jacobs, *On Socialists and "the Jewish Question" after Marx* (New York: New York Univ. Press, 1992), 120.

52. Gassenschmidt, *Jewish Liberal Politics in Tsarist Russia.* There was also a strong liberal movement that arose in this period in opposition to the radicalism of the Bund and other Jewish revolutionary groups. Liberals included Dubnow's Folkspartey (People's Party) and the Evreiskaia Narodnaia Gruppa (Jewish People's Group). In contrast to the young radicals who focused their efforts on synthesizing the demands of class and nation while furthering the overall revolution, the (generally) older liberals openly promoted Jewish national unity in forums permitted by the constitutional changes. In Mar. 1905, mainstream Zionists and liberals together formed the Union for the Attainment of Full Equality for the Jewish People in an attempt to fend off attacks from the revolutionary Left. Among the Union's most eloquent spokespersons was Ahad Ha'am, Menachem Mendel Ussishkin (1863–1941), Vladimir Jabotinsky (1880–1940), and Simon Dubnow. With the exception of Jabotinsky, members of the Union were typically of an older generation who hoped to ally themselves with the liberal Russian Kadet party and also who supported the creation of a Jewish National Assembly. Stressing Jewish unity over class struggle, they hoped that such a body would

promote the program of Jewish autonomy within the imperial framework and provide a forum for Jewish cultural and national development.

53. A. Kirzshnits, "Di sotsialistishe fraktsyes in tsienizm," in *Der yidisher arbeter: khrestomatye tsu der geshikhte fun der yidisher arbeter, revolutsionerer un sotsialstsher bavegung in rusland,* vol. 2 (Moscow: Tsentraler farlag far di felker fun F.S.S.R., 1925), 377–404; N. A. Bukhbinder, *Di geshikhte fun der yidisher arbeter-bavegung in rusland: loyt nit-gedrukte arkhiv-materialn,* trans. Dovid Roykhel (Vilna: Tamar, 1931), 386–405; Ben-Adir, *Sotsialistisher teritorializm;* A. L. Patkin, *The Origins of the Russian-Jewish Labour Movement* (Melbourne: F. W. Cheshire, 1947); Gregor Aronson, "Ideological Trends Among Russian Jews," in *Russian Jewry (1860–1917),* ed. Jacob Frumkin, et al. (New York: T. Yoseloff, 1966), 162–65; and Jacobs, 118–24.

54. Known in Russian as the *Sionistko-sotsialisticheskaia Rabochaia Partiia.*

55. Jacobs, 120; Patkin, 224.

56. Prior to its founding as a cohesive political movement in early 1906, there were many circles throughout Russia that had taken on the name Poalei Zion as a way to assert their Zionist Socialist stance. See Samuel Gozhansky, *Der tsienizm fun "LNU": mit a bayloge: di poyle tsien un zayer teorye* (London: Algemeynem yidishen arbeter bund, 1903). Also see Zeev Abramovitch, "The Poalei Zion Movement in Russia, Its History and Development," in *Essays in Jewish Sociology, Labour and Co-operation: In Memory of Dr. Noah Barou, 1889–1955,* ed. Henrik F. Infield (London: T. Yoseloff, 1962), 63–72.

57. Known in Russia as the *Evreiskaia Sotsialisticheskaia Rabochaia Partiia.*

58. Jacobs, 120.

59. According to Jacobs, in 1906, the S.S. claimed 27,000 adherents in 1906, the SERP had about half of the S.S., and the Poalei Zion had 16,000 (118–22).

60. Frankel, "Jewish Politics and the Russian Revolution of 1905," 6.

61. Gassenschmidt, 70–71.

62. In 1917, with the Mar. revolution, socialist Zionist parties once again emerged. On Mar. 15, S.S. and SERP members met and formed the Fareynikte (United) party, which had a much stronger nationalist platform. Gregor Aronson, "Jewish Communal Life in 1917–1918," in *Russian Jewry: 1917–1967,* ed. Gregor Aronson, et al. (New York: T. Yoseloff, 1969), 18.

63. Frankel, "Jewish Politics and the Russian Revolution of 1905," 20.

64. Isaac Deutscher, "The Non-Jewish Jew," in *The Non-Jewish Jew and Other Essays* (Oxford: Oxford Univ. Press, 1968), 25–41.

65. Gassenschmidt, 45–56.

66. Matthew Hoffman, *From Rebel to Rabbi: Reclaiming Jesus and the Making of Modern Jewish Culture* (Stanford: Stanford Univ. Press, 2007), 90–116. Also see Nurith Govrin, *Meora Brener: Ha-Maavak al Hofesh Ha-Bitui* (Jerusalem: Yad Yitshak Ben Tsevi, 1985); and Yossi Goldstein, "Review of Meor'a Brener," *Studies in Contemporary Jewry, An Annual: The Jews and the European Crisis 1941–21* 4 (1988): 343–46. For a discussion on

Brenner's relationship to Judaism, see Menahem Brinker, "Brenner's Jewishness," *Studies in Contemporary Jewry* 4 (1988): 232–51.

67. Reprinted in Goldstein, 345.

68. Steven J. Zipperstein, *Elusive Prophet: Ahad Ha'am and the Origins of Zionism* (Berkeley: Univ. of California Press, 1993), 237–44.

69. Ibid., 241.

70. See the discussions of this turn in Gassenschmidt, chapter 4,"Jewish Liberal Politics from 1908 to 1911: Reorganization, Determination and the Beginning of 'Organic Work'"; and Zimmerman, chapter 9, "From Politics to the New Yiddish Culture: The Bund in the Period of Revolutionary Defeat, 1907–1911."

71. See, for example, the development of Polish national culture in the wake of the failed 1863 uprisings in Jerzy Jedlicki, *A Suburb of Europe: Nineteenth Century Polish Approaches to Western Civilization* (Budapest: Central European Univ. Press, 1999); and Brian Porter, *When Nationalism Began to Hate: Imagining Modern Politics in Nineteenth-Century Poland* (Oxford: Oxford Univ. Press, 2000), 48–74.

72. Berend, 44.

73. Raphael Abramovitsh, *In tsvey revolutsyes: di geshikhte fun a dor,* vol. 1 (New York: Arbeter Ring, 1944), 315.

74. See, for example, *Zamelbukh "Kultur": 1905* (Minsk: Kultur, 1905), which included works by figures such as Peretz, Avrom Reisen, Sarah Reisen, Dovid Frishman. The Minsk press Kultur also released original works in Yiddish as well as translations from Russian writers and school books in Yiddish on topics such as mathematics, geography, and history. Also see the monthly journal *Dos lebn: a monatlekher zhurnal far literatur, visnshaft un gezelshaftlekhe frages* (Jan.–Aug. 1905), which was a publication of the St. Petersburg Yiddish daily newspaper *Der fraynd.*

75. For a recent study of Jewish newspaper culture at the beginning of the twentieth century in Russia, see Stein, *Making Jews Modern,* 23–54. Also see A. Kirzshnits, *Di yidishe prese in der gevezener ruslendisher imperye (1823–1916)* (Moscow: Tsentral felker farlag fun F.S.S.R., 1930).

76. Noyekh Prilutski, *Yidish teater: 1905–1921,* 2 vols. (Bialystok: A. Albek, 1921); and Nokhem Oyslender, *Yidisher teater: 1887–1917* (Moscow: Der emes, 1940), 53–258; Henry, 61–75; and Zimmerman, 241.

77. Henry J. Tobias and Charles E. Woodhouse, "Political Reaction and Revolutionary Careers: The Jewish Bundists in Defeat, 1907–10," *Comparative Studies in Society and History* 19, no. 3 (July 1977), 378–80; Gassenschmidt, 99–101; Zimmerman, 239–41; Halevy, *Jewish Schools Under Czarism and Communism,* 78–81.

78. Itzik Nakhmen Gottesman, *Defining the Yiddish Nation: The Jewish Folklorists of Poland* (Detroit: Wayne State Univ. Press, 2003); and Adam Rubin "Hebrew Folklore and the Problem of Exile," *Modern Judaism* 25 (2005): 62–83.

79. Robert Alter, *The Invention of Hebrew Prose: Modern Fiction and the Language of Realism* (Seattle: Univ. of Washington Press, 1988), 45–95; Angelika Glau, *Jüdisches Selbstverständnis im Wandel: Jiddische Literatur zu Beginn des zwanzigsten Jahrhunderts* (Wiesbaden: Harrassowitz, 1999); and Krutikov, *Yiddish Fiction and the Crisis of Modernity.* As Krutikov states, the embrace of modern literary forms marked a new attitude among Russian Jewry who sought a more open approach to other European national groups while still maintaining their particularist identity, marking "the beginning of a new era that synchronized the movement of Jewish history with the universal historical process" (115). As Alter writes, "It is, however, a truth of hindsight, for what Mendele and his forerunners in the Hebrew Enlightenment had in mind (and—after Mendele—Gnessin, Berdichevsky, and most of their contemporaries) was the creation on Central and East European soil of an authentically European Hebrew fiction." Alter, *The Invention of Hebrew Prose,* 71. Also see Harshav, 97–98.

80. Gassenschmidt, 99.

81. Israel Bartal, "From Traditional Bilingualism to National Monolingualism," in *Hebrew in Ashkenaz: A Language in Exile,* ed. Lewis Glinert (Oxford: Oxford Univ. Press, 1993), 141–49.

82. Yehoshua A. Gilboa, "The Language Dispute in the Pre-Soviet Era," in *A Language Silenced: The Suppression of Hebrew Literature and Culture in the Soviet Union* (Rutherford, N.J.: Fairleigh Dickinson Univ. Press, 1982), 11–26; Hillel Halkin, "The Great Jewish Language War," *Commentary* 114, no. 5 (Dec. 2002): 48–55.

2. From Jargon to *Visnshaft*

1. Cited in Frankel, *Prophecy and Politics,* 134.

2. See, for example, Keith Ian Weiser, "The Politics of Yiddish: Noyekh Prilutski and the Folkspartey in Poland, 1900–1926" (PhD diss., Columbia Univ., 2001); Henry, "Jewish Plays on the Russian Stage: St. Petersburg, 1905–1917"; Krutikov, *Yiddish Fiction and the Crisis of Modernity;* Stein, *Making Jews Modern;* Zimmerman, *Poles, Jews, and the Politics of Nationality;* and Estraikh, *In Harness.*

3. The exact origins of the Yiddish language are unknown. There are two dominant theories regarding its creation. See John Myhill, *Language in Jewish Society: Towards a New Understanding* (Toronto: Multilingual Matters, 2004), 126–27.

4. See Jerold C. Frakes, ed., *Early Yiddish Texts 1100–1750: With Introduction and Commentary* (Oxford: Oxford Univ. Press, 2005).

5. See the discussions in Max Weinreich, *Geshikhte fun der yidisher shprakh: bagrifn, faktn, metodn,* 3:253–331; and Dovid Katz, *Words on Fire: The Unfinished Story of Yiddish* (New York: Basic Books, 2004), 45–77; and Robert Alter, "Introduction," in *Modern Hebrew Literature,* ed. Robert Alter (New York: Behrman House, 1975), 1.

6. Myhill, 109.

7. David Sorkin, *The Transformation of German Jewry, 1780–1840* (Oxford: Oxford Univ. Press, 1987), 131. Sorkin argues that the concern for "pure language" dates back even

further, to the late seventeenth century. "For the preachers and pedagogues High German was an integral part of their *Bildung.* Newly emerged from the ghetto, they felt that the felicity and grace of their High German were directly proportionate to their achievement of humanity."

8. For a discussion of Moses Mendelssohn's complicated relationship to Yiddish, see David Sorkin, *Moses Mendelssohn and the Religious Enlightenment* (Berkeley: Univ. of California Press, 1996), 53, n. 3; Jeffrey A. Grossman, *The Discourse on Yiddish in Germany: From the Enlightenment to the Second Empire* (Rochester, N.Y.: Camden House, 2000), 77–79; and Jeremy Dauber, *Antonio's Devils: Writers of the Jewish Enlightenment and the Birth of Modern Hebrew and Yiddish Literature* (Stanford: Stanford Univ. Press, 2004), 133–36.

9. Sorkin, *The Transformation of Germany Jewry,* 81.

10. Michael A. Meyer, ed., *German-Jewish History in Modern Times* (New York: Columbia Univ. Press, 1997), 2:93–94. However, Yiddish and Yiddish terms continued to be spoken by some German Jews into the twentieth century.

11. Jozeph Michman and Marion Aptroot, *Storm in the Community: Yiddish Political Pamphlets of Amsterdam Jewry, 1797–1798* (Cincinnati: Hebrew Union College Press, 2002). Also see the rejection of Mendel Levin's (1741–1819) attempts to use Yiddish to promote the Haskalah in Jacob S. Raisin, *The Haskalah Movement in Russia* (Philadelphia: Jewish Publication Society, 1913), 99–101.

12. The number of Jews in the Pale of Jewish settlement in the mid–nineteenth century is hard to gauge with accuracy, since the rolls were notoriously inaccurate. Stanislawski, *Tsar Nicholas I and the Jews,* 160–70. The more reliable census of 1897 reported 5.2 million Jews.

13. As quoted in Shmuel Feiner, *Haskalah and History: The Emergence of a Modern Jewish Historical Consciousness* (Oxford: Oxford Univ. Press, 2002), 181. As Stanislawski states, "All of the maskilim so far considered [1840s and earlier] despised Yiddish as a bastardized, corrupt jargon and placed its elimination on the top rung of their ladder of priorities." Stanislawski, *Tsar Nicholas I,* 117.

14. In 1841, Israel Aksenfeld raised the question of how to combat the superstition of the Hasidim without Yiddish if the Jewish masses could not read the Hebrew writings of the *maskilim.* Stanislawski, *Tsar Nicholas I,* 117.

15. On Tsederbaum and *Kol mevaser,* see Yisroel Tsinberg, "Der "kol mevaser" un zayn tsayt," *Di yidishe velt,* nos. 1–4 (1913): 89–98, 83–90, 72–80, 74–81; Sh. L. Tsitron, *Di geshikhte fun der yidisher prese I: Fun yor 1863 biz 1889* (Warsaw: Ahisfer, 1923), 5–74; A. R. Mlachi, "Der 'kol mevaser' un zayn redactor," in *Pinkes far der forshung fun der yidisher literatur un prese,* ed. Shloyme Bikl (New York: Alveltlekhn yidishn kultur-kongres, 1965), 49–121; Alexander Orbach, *New Voices of Russian Jewry: A Study of the Russian-Jewish Press of Odessa in the Era of the Great Reforms, 1860–1871* (Leiden: Brill, 1980). Tsitron has a negative view of Tsederbaum's practicality, referring to him as a "man of the

wind" *(vint-mentsh),* that is, a man without strong convictions and worldly beliefs. Tsitron, *Di geshikhte fun der yidisher prese I,* 13.

16. For a study of Jewish Odessa in the years before 1881–82, see Steven J. Zipperstein, *The Jews of Odessa: A Cultural History, 1794–1881* (Stanford: Stanford Univ. Press, 1986).

17. Tsitron, *Di geshikhte fun der yidisher prese I,* 1.

18. As Orbach notes, "Zederbaum himself was certain that Yiddish would disappear within a matter of a few years and he was only using it now as a means toward his ultimate goals." Orbach, 110.

19. Goldsmith, 45–46.

20. Frankel, *Prophecy and Politics,* 173–83. The use of Yiddish in the early stages of the Jewish labor movement has been told in Zimmerman, *Poles, Jews, and the Politics of Nationality.* In it, Zimmerman demonstrates that the use of Yiddish by the Bund (and the group's overall turn toward Jewish nationalism) was initially a consequence of its struggles against the PPS to capture the loyalties of Jewish workers in Congress Poland.

21. Frankel, *Prophecy and Politics,* 176. As Frankel states, Russian-Jewish revolutionaries were following a model established by others outside the empire: "The ability of the Russian-Jewish socialists in London—and much more spectacularly in New York—to create a self-supporting Yiddish press and Yiddish-speaking trade-union movement inspired growing respect. Nothing succeeds like success, and in the years 1891–95 socialists throughout eastern Europe sought to repeat what had been achieved in the East End and the Lower East Side." Also see Zimmerman, 50–51.

22. Y. Sh. Herts, "Di umlegale prese un literatur fun 'bund,'" in *Pinkes far der forshung fun der yidisher literatur un prese,* ed. Khaym Bas (New York: Alveltlekhn yidishn kultur-kongres, 1972), 294–366. Also see Zimmerman, chapters 6–8.

23. Goldsmith, 79.

24. Ibid., 83–84; and Chone Shmeruk, "Hebrew-Yiddish-Polish: A Trilingual Jewish Culture," in *The Jews of Poland Between Two World Wars,* ed. Y. Gutman, et al. (Hanover, N.H.: Brandeis Univ. Press, 1989), 285–311; Zimmerman, chapter 9.

25. See Ruth Wisse, "Not the 'Pintele Yid' but the Full-Fledged Jew," *Prooftexts* 15 (1995): 33–61.

26. Gottesman makes the important point that Yiddishism has often been mischaracterized as a political movement of its own, rather than as an ideology of Jewish nationalism that placed the Yiddish language at its center. Gottesman, *Defining the Yiddish Nation,* xii, xiv–xv.

27. Fishman, *The Rise of Modern Yiddish Culture,* 101–2.

28. As Ruth Wisse argues, with only slight exaggeration, "With the exception of Theodor Herzl, the founder of political Zionism, no Jewish writer had a more direct effect on modern Jewry than Isaac Leib (Yitskhok Leybush) Peretz." *I. L. Peretz and the Making of Modern Jewish Culture,* xiii.

29. Niger, *Y. l. perets: zayn lebn, zayn firndike perzenlekhkayt, zayne hebreyishe un yidishe shriften, zayn virkung* (Buenos Aires: Alveltlekhn yidishn kultur-kongres, 1952), 534 (emphasis in the original).

30. See, for example, ibid.; Bal-Makhshoves, "Di goldene keyt," in *Sekirot u-reshamim* (Warsaw: Hotsa'at Sifrut, 1911), 101–13; Nachman Meisel, *Yitskhok leybush perets un zayn dor shrayber* (New York: IKUF, 1951); Wisse, *I. L. Peretz*.

31. David G. Roskies, *A Bridge of Longing: The Lost Art of Yiddish Storytelling* (Cambridge, Mass.: Harvard Univ. Press, 1995), 99–146; and Wisse, *I. L. Peretz*, 52–59.

32. Bal-dimyen [Nokhem Shtif], "Khaim zhitlovski: tsu zayn 25 yoriker yoyvel," *Di Yidishe velt* 1 (1913): 88.

33. Ibid., 79.

34. Weinberg, 89.

35. Zhitlovski, "A yid tsu yidn," in *Gezamelte shriftn* (New York: Yoyvleum oysgabe, 1912), 6:13–55; "Tsienizm oder sotsializm," 5:47–76; "Farvos dafke yidish?," 5:31–43.

36. Frankel, *Prophecy and Politics*, 271–72.

37. Rabinovitch, 114.

38. Zhitlovski, "Farvos dafke yidish?" 36–37.

39. David E. Fishman, "The Politics of Yiddish in Tsarist Russia." By 1890, Tsederbaum's *Kol mevaser* and *Yidishes folksblat* had ceased publication and the tsarist authorities granted no other licenses.

40. Stein, *Making Jews Modern*.

41. Ibid., 34.

42. See Nathans, *Beyond the Pale*, "The Jews of St. Petersburg," 83–198.

43. Stein, 34.

44. D. Druk, *Tsu der geshikhte fun der yidishe prese* (Warsaw: Hacefira, 1920), 25–26.

45. Stein, 31.

46. Khayim-dov Horovits, "Unzer ershte teglikhe tsaytung (tsu der tsen-yorkiker geshikhte fun'm 'fraynd')," *Der pinkes*, 251.

47. Druk, 32–49; Stein, 41.

48. Stein, 33.

49. *Der nayer veg* changed its name twice, to *Dos vort* (The Word) and then to *Unzer vort* (Our Word) as a way of getting around press restrictions. Kirzshnits, *Di yidishe prese in der gevezener ruslendisher imperye*, 27.

50. The biographical information on Lestschinsky comes from B[orekh] Tsh[ubinski], "Lestschinsky, Yakov," in *Leksikon fun der nayer yidisher literatur*, 5:381–85; and Gennady Estraikh, "Jacob Lestschinsky: A Yiddish Dreamer and Social Scientist," *Science in Context* 20 (2007): 215–37.

51. Lestschinsky, "Statistika Shel Ayara Ahat."

52. On the turn to a modern scholarly approach in Hebrew letters see, David N. Myers, *Re-inventing the Jewish Past: European Jewish Intellectuals and the Zionist Return to*

History (Oxford: Oxford Univ. Press, 1995), 35; and Ali Mohamed Abd El-Rahman Attia, *The Hebrew Periodical Ha-Shiloah (1896–1919): Its Role In the Development of Modern Hebrew Literature* (Jerusalem: Magnes Press, 1991), 115–72.

53. Lestschinsky, "Di yidishe emigranten in london," *Di yidishe bibliotek* 2 (Feb. 1904): 29–53; this essay was subsequently expanded into the monograph *Der yidisher arbeter: in london* (Vilna: Tsukunft, 1907).

54. Lestschinsky, "Der yidisher arbeter," *Der nayer veg,* nos. 7–8 (1906): 269–74, 310–17; *Der yidisher arbeter (in rusland)* (Vilna: Tsukunft, 1906).

55. Lestschinsky, *Der yidisher arbeter (in rusland),* 4.

56. Sholem Aleichem, "A gringer tones," in *Ale verk fun sholem aleykhem* (New York: Forverts, 1942), 4:167–77. The use of Yiddish literary images to depict changing economic conditions were a theme Lestschinsky developed more thoroughly in his later work. See his *Dos yidishe ekonomishe lebn in der yidisher literatur,* vol. 1 (Warsaw: Kultur lige, 1921).

57. Lestschinsky, *Der yidisher arbeter (in rusland),* 114.

58. On the reception of *Di literarishe monatsshriftn,* see Kenneth Moss, "Jewish Culture Between Renaissance and Decadence: *Di Literarishe Monatsshriften* and Its Critical Reception," *Jewish Social Studies* 8, no. 1 (2001): 166–72.

59. The dates of *Eyropeyishe literatur* are uncertain. No dates were printed in the journal itself. Kirzshnits (1928) has them listed as 1910–11 while Prager lists them as 1909–10. Leonard Prager, *Yiddish Literary and Linguistic Periodicals and Miscellanies: A Selective Annotated Bibliography* (Darby, Pennsylvania—Haifa: Norwood Editions, 1982).

60. Moss, 154.

61. "Tsu di lezer," *Di literarishe monatsshriftn* 1 (Feb. 1908): 5–6.

62. Ibid.

63. Ibid., 7–8.

64. Moss., 166–72.

65. See Eliyohu Shulman, "A halber yorhundert nokh di literarishe monatsshriftn," in *Portretn un etyudn* (New York: Tsiko, 1979), 406–20.

66. It was held in Czernowitz in part because of the difficulty of gaining permission in the Russian empire for such a conference and because the city was Birnbaum's base. Goldsmith, 185.

67. *Di ershte yidishe shprakh-konferents: barikhtn, dokumentn un opklangen fun der tshernovitser konferents, 1908* (Vilna: YIVO, 1931).

68. Zhitlovski, *Gezamelte Shriften,* 4:118, as quoted in Goldsmith, 212.

69. It was Peretz himself who first made this claim. Since that time, scholars such as Dovid Katz have also echoed it; see Dovid Katz, "On Yiddish, in Yiddish, and for Yiddish," 23–36.

70. Following Shulman, in describing these journals, I use the Yiddish term *gezelshaftlekh,* which, like its German cognate *gesellschaftlich,* signifies something more inclusive than its English equivalent: "societal." In this case, the term implies not only an interest in community

affairs but also incorporates all aspects of Jewish communal life, including politics, news, culture, language, education, and science. See Eliyohu Shulman, "Di tsaytshrift di yidishe velt," *Pinkes fun der forshung fun der yidisher prese* (New York: Alveltlekhn yidishn kultur-kongres, 1965), 122–70. For a discussion on the new Russian press at the turn of the twentieth century, see Beth Holmgren, *Rewriting Capitalism: Literature and the Market in Late Tsarist Russia and the Kingdom of Poland* (Pittsburgh: Univ. of Pittsburgh Press, 1998).

71. Meyer Waxman, *A History of Jewish Literature: From the Close of the Bible to Our Own Days* (New York: Bloch Publishing Co., 1945), 3:158.

72. Noyekh Prilutski, "Materialen far yidisher gramatik un ortografye," *Lebn un visnshaft* 5 (Sept. 1909): 61.

73. A. Litvin, "Tsu di lezer," *Lebn un visnshaft* 1 (1909): 3.

74. Ibid., 2.

75. Ibid.

76. Imported words from modern German that have a Yiddish equivalent.

77. Rabinovitch, 177. See his discussion, "From *Evreiskii mir* to *Di yidishe velt*: The Battle against Assimilation and the Yiddishization of Folkism," 162–79.

78. Quoted in Shulman, 123.

79. Rabinovitch, 177. Rabinovitch further states, "The publication catered rather explicitly to 'der yidisher inteligents' with the aim of building a bridge between modern culture and the culture of the folk. The editors were aware of the difficulties of conducting such a task in St. Petersburg, a city they described as 'remote from every Jewish tradition, dry in daily Jewish life, and only in the least aware of the noise of the true poetry that surrounds folk-life and folk-custom.' David Fishman points to the reconstitution of *Evreiskii mir* in the form of *Di yidishe velt* as emblematic of the rise of Yiddish high culture. Certainly the Jewish intelligentsia became less interested in publishing Jewish literature in Russian, than Yiddish literature in the original. The failure of a *Jewish World* in Russian and its replacement by a *Jewish World* in Yiddish can also, however, be seen as a symbol of the refashioning of Jewish intellectual life from Russian to the vernacular of the majority of East European Jewry."

80. *Di yidishe velt* traveled a circuitous route. After the new edition appeared in Vilna dated Jan. 1913 under Niger's editorial direction, it was reprinted in the United States as *Literatur un lebn (Literature and Life)*. With the onset of World War I and the consequent government crackdown and general chaos, Niger was forced in 1916 to edit the journal from St. Petersburg (and under heavy censorship) and under titles that changed monthly, including *Dos yidishe vort, Fun tog tsu tog, In unzere teg,* and *Lebns-klangen*. It finally folded at the end of 1916.

81. Zalmen Reisen, *Yidishe gramatik* (Warsaw: Progres, 1908), 3 (emphasis in the original).

82. For an extended discussion of the range of Prilutski's efforts in the post–1905 revolutionary period (which included philology, theater criticism, folklore, and poetry in Yiddish), see Weiser, "The Politics of Yiddish," 131–89.

83. Noyekh Prilutski, *Noyekh prilutski's zamelbikher far yidishen folklore, filologye un kulturgeshikhte* 1 (Warsaw: Nayer farlag, 1912): 7–8. For an extended discussion of Yiddish folkloristics, see Mark W. Kiel, "Vox Populi, Vox Dei: The Centrality of Peretz in Jewish Folkloristics," *Polin* 7 (1992): 88–120; Weiser, "The Politics of Yiddish"; and Gottesman, *Defining the Yiddish Nation.*

84. For example, see Weinreich, *History of the Yiddish Language,* 298. Dovid Katz, "On Yiddish, in Yiddish, and for Yiddish," 33–35; ibid., "Preface: On the First Winter Symposium," *Origins of the Yiddish Language,* ed. Dovid Katz (Oxford: Pergamon Press, 1987), 1; and Kuznitz, 26.

85. Borochov, "Di oyfgabn."

86. Simon Dubnow, Yankev Dinezon (1856–1919), and Ben-Ami (1854–1932), for example, made significant contributions. The generational shift inherent in the pages of *Der pinkes* was noted in its own time as well. See the review by "Mevaker," "Ha-pinkes," *Ha-Zeman* (1913): 276, 277, 278.

87. Niger, "Fun der redaktsye," *Der pinkes,* 2

88. Ibid., 1.

89. See, for instance, the value that Shtif placed on *Der pinkes* in his 1924 essay, "Vegn a yidishn akademishn institut," 9. Shtif's assessment of *Der pinkes* in 1924 was far more laudatory than his review a decade prior. See chapter 4.

90. For example, Niger's own "Shtudyes: Tsu der geshikhte fun der yidisher literatur" continues to be cited as a pioneering work in the area of gender and Yiddish publishing. See the discussion in chapter 3. On Horovits' contribution, "Unzer ershte teglikhe tsaytung," see Stein, 31–36. On the lasting impact of Borochov's contribution, see chapter 4.

3. Shmuel Niger and the Making of Yiddish High Culture

1. Ber Borochov, "Letter to Shmuel Niger," (14 Dec. 1912), published in *Yivo bleter* 6 (Feb. 1934): 13 (emphasis in original).

2. Shmuel Niger, *Mendele moykher sforim: zayn lebn, zayn gezelshaftlekhe un literarishe oyftuungen* (Chicago: L. M. Shtayn, 1936); Niger, *Y. l. perets: zayn lebn, zayn firndike perzenlekhkayt, zayne hebreyishe un yidishe shriftn, zayn virkung;* Niger, *Sholem aleykhem: zayne vikhtigste verk, zayn humor, un zayn ort in der yidisher literatur* (New York: IKUF, 1928); Niger, *Sholem ash, zayn lebn, zayn verk: biografie, opshatsungen, polemik, briv, bibliografye* (New York: Alveltlekhn yidishn kultur-kongres, 1960); Niger, *H. leyvik: zayn opshtam, zayne kinder- un yugnt-yorn, zayne lirishe un dramatishe verk, zayn dikhterisher gang* (Toronto: H. Leyvik yoyvl-komitet, 1951).

3. For example, see Niger, *Shmuesen vegn bikher* (New York: Yidish, 1922); Niger, *Yidishe shrayber in sovet-rusland* (New York: Alveltlekhn yidishn kultur-kongres, 1958); Niger, *Yidishe shrayber fun tsvantsikstn yorhundert,* 2 vols. (New York: Alveltlekhn yidishn kultur-kongres, 1972).

4. P. Berman [Maks vaynraykh], "Sh. Niger: der kritiker, der klal-tuer, der bal-seykhl," *Der forverts* (1 Jan. 1956), sec. 2: 5.

5. Niger, *Vegn yidishe shrayber: kritishe artikln*, 2 vols. (Warsaw: Z. S. Sreberk, 1912).

6. Ephim H. Jeshurin, *Shmuel niger bibliografye* (New York: YIVO, 1956).

7. Ibid., "Shmuel niger bibliografye (oprufn af zayn toyt)," in *Shmuel niger-bukh*, ed. Shlomo Bikl and Leybush Lehrer (New York: YIVO, 1958), 31–42.

8. H. Leyvik, "Der kritiker un der shrayber (shtrikhn tsu der perzenlekhkayt fun Sh. Niger e"h)," in Bikl and Lehrer, 18.

9. See Khayim Bez, "Sh. Niger: der kritiker un der mentsh," in *Fun mayn togbukh*, Sh. Niger (New York: Alveltlekhn yidishn kultur-kongres, 1973), 7–99; N. B. Minkov, *Zeks yidishe kritiker* (Buenos Aires: Yidbukh, 1954), 293–344.

10. P. Berman [Maks vaynraykh], 5.

11. The biographical information on Niger comes from L. V. "Niger Shmuel," in *Leksikon fun der yidisher literatur, prese un filologye*, ed. Zalmen Reisen (Vilna: B. Kletskin, 1928–29), 2:539–51; L. V., "Niger, Shmuel," in *Leksikon fun der nayer yidisher literatur*, 6:190–210; Minkov, *Zeks yidisher kritiker*; Bikl and Lehrer, *Shmuel niger-bukh*; and Bez's introduction of Niger's *Fun mayn togbukh*. Further information on the early life of the Tsharny brothers can be found in Daniel Tsharny, *Barg aroyf: bletlekh fun a lebn* (Warsaw: Literarishe bleter, 1935); and *Dukor: memuarn* (Toronto: Pomer, 1951).

12. Niger, "Vos iz der yidisher arbeter," *Der nayer veg* 1, 2, 3, (1906); later that year it was republished (twice) as *Vos iz azoyns der yidisher arbeter?* (Vilna: Tsukunft, 1906), from which I cite.

13. Niger, *Vos iz azoyns der yidisher arbeter?* 3.

14. Ibid., 20. Niger further articulated these themes in another essay, "Klas un natsion," *Der nayer veg*, nos. 14–15 (1906).

15. Niger, *Vos iz azoyns der yidisher arbeter?*, 3; I. L. Peretz, "Bontshe shvayg," *Literatur un lebn* (1894): 11–22.

16. Niger, *Vos iz azoyns der yidisher arbeter?* 7.

17. Ibid., 9.

18. Niger, "Di yidishe shprakh and di yidishe inteligents," *Der nayer veg* 5 (1906): 167–78.

19. Ibid., 168.

20. Ibid., 174.

21. Ibid., 178.

22. Bez, 33, 40–41.

23. Ibid., 41.

24. Shmuel Niger, "Vegn di tragedye fun goles," *Dos vort*, no. 1 (1907) (continued in nos. 2 and 3); Sholem Asch, *Meshiekh's tsaytn* (Vilna: Tsukunft, 1906).

25. Also perhaps to posit himself (and to claim Sholem Asch as his own) over his one competitor, the literary critic Bal-Makhshoves, who had earlier written on Asch's 1903 collection of short stories, *In a shlekhter tsayt*.

26. Niger, "Vegn di tragedye fun goles," 31.

27. Ibid., no. 2, p. 32 (emphasis in the original).

28. Ibid., "A yunger folks-dikhter," *Unzer veg* 3 (1907).

29. Ibid., 34. On Danilevitsh as a Yiddish folklorist, see Gottesman, *Defining the Yiddish Nation*, 51–56.

30. Niger, "Shmuesen vegn der yidisher literatur," *Unzer veg* 6 (1907): 30.

31. Bez, 26–32.

32. Niger, "Vegn y. l. perets," *Di literarishe monatsshriftn* 1 (Feb. 1908): 84.

33. Niger, "Der novi fun der erd: sholem ash," *Di literarishe monatsshriftn* 4 (May 1908): 113–56.

34. Ibid., 120.

35. Ibid., 133.

36. Ibid., 102.

37. Niger, "Kneytshn: avrom reyzen's gezamlete lider," *Di literarishe monatsshriftn* 3 (Apr. 1908): 79.

38. Niger, "Bal-Makhshoves," *Di tsukunft* 40 (1934): 171.

39. See the memoirs of Ben-Zion Dinur, *Be-'Olam she-Shaka': Zikhronot u-Reshumot mi-Derekh Hayim* (Jerusalem: Mosad Byalik, 1958), 375–94.

40. As recounted in Bez, 32–42.

41. See the records at Staatsarchiv des Kantons Bern, Erziehungswesen (B.15) 1831 ff. BBIIIb. My thanks to Shifra Kuperman for locating Niger's course records. As Kuperman has confirmed, no record of his dissertation exists. Private correspondence with Kuperman, 1 July 2003.

42. See, "Ayzik Meir Dik," *He-evar* 2 (1913): 140–54; "Vegn hebreyish un kh. n. bialk," *Dos naye land* 1, nos. 9–12 (1909).

43. Niger, "Kultur un bildung: vegn der yidisher inteligents," *Dos naye lebn* 3, no. 7 (1911): 27–33.

44. Niger, "Kultur un bildung," 32–33.

45. Niger, "Daytshmerish," *Lebn un visnshaft,* no. 11–12 (1912): 49–66.

46. Ibid., 50.

47. Ibid.

48. Ibid., 55.

49. Zalmen Reisen, *Leksikon fun der yidisher literatur un prese,* ed. Shmuel Niger (Warsaw: Tsentral, 1914).

50. "Fun der redaktsye," *Di yidishe velt* 1 (Jan. 1913): 146.

51. A vilner [Niger], "Tsu dem rayen tsu shafn a yidisher universitet," *Di yidishe velt* 2, no. 2 (1914): 126–34.

52. Ibid., 127.

53. At the Eleventh Zionist Congress in Vienna (1913), proponents of the university project declared that they wanted to build a new Yavne. This was a reference to the great center of Jewish learning believed to have been established by Rabbi Yochanan ben Zakkai after the fall of the second Temple in the year 70 CE.

54. A vilner [Niger], "Tsu dem rayen tsu shafn a yidisher universitet," 131 (emphasis in original).

55. Niger and Borochov's connection dated back to the days leading up to the 1905 Revolution. According to Niger, the two first met either in Odessa or Ekaterinoslav for a public debate on the question of Jewish self-determination. It may have actually taken place in Berdichev, where, according to Mitchell Cohen, Borochov "matched wits" with the Vozrozhdenie in late 1905. Mitchell Cohen, "Introduction," in *Class Struggle and the Jewish Nation: Selected Essays in Marxist Zionism,* Ber Borochov, ed. Mitchell Cohen (New Brunswick, N.J.: Transaction Books, 1994), 1–34.

56. Niger, "Shtudyes: Tsu der geshikhte fun der yidisher literatur: di yidishe literatur—un di lezerin," *Der pinkes,* 85–138.

57. On Niger's plans for future chapters, see Naomi Seidman, *A Marriage Made in Heaven: The Sexual Politics of Hebrew and Yiddish* (Berkeley: Univ. of California Press, 1997), 4, n. 13.

58. This essay was reprinted as *Di yidishe literatur—un di lezerin* (Vilna: B. Kletskin, 1919).

59. Niger, "Shtudyes," 85.

60. Ibid.

61. Ibid.

62. Noyekh Prilutski, *Yidishe folkslider* (Warsaw: Bikher far ale, 1910)

63. Niger, "Shtudyes," 87.

64. Ibid., 91 (emphasis in original).

65. Ibid., 118.

66. Ibid., 98–99 (emphasis in original).

67. For a discussion of women's Yiddish prayers, see Chava Weissler, *Voices of the Matriarchs: Listening to the Prayers of Early Modern Jewish Women* (Boston: Beacon Press, 1999).

68. As Frieda Forman, et al., state, "To counteract their distance from what they considered holy, women designated a *zogerin*—a speaker or teller—a position which was highly respected and admired. The *zogerin* read the prayers aloud to the women, leading them in the service. The *zogerin* had a special significance in representing the illiterate. Individual women would also ask her to intercede on their behalf for something personal. This could include anything from the serious, like the health of a child, to the more material or frivolous. Frieda Forman, et al., eds., *Found Treasures: Stories by Yiddish Women Writers* (Toronto: Second Story Press, 1994), 85.

69. Niger, "Shtudyes," 99.

70. See Jerold C. Frakes's emendation of this claim in his introduction to *Early Yiddish Texts.*

71. Niger, "Shtudyes," 105, 101.

72. See Weissler, *Voices of the Matriarchs;* Seidman, *A Marriage Made in Heaven;* and Zucker's summarized translation of Niger's essay in *Women of the Word: Jewish Women and Jewish Writing,* ed. Judith R. Baskin (Detroit: Wayne State Univ. Press, 1994), 70–90.

73. Zalmen Reisen, *Leksikon* (1914).

74. Zalmen Reisen, "Forrede," *Leksikon* (1914), unpaginated first page.

75. On Pines' text, see chapter 5; on Borochov's, see chapter 4.

76. Although in his autobiography Nokhem Shtif claimed that he did most of the work. Nokhem Shtif, "Oytobiografye," *Yivo bleter* 5 nos. 3–5 (Mar.–May 1933): 208–9; and Prager, 318.

4. Ber Borochov: Science in Service of the Revolution

1. Shmuel Niger, "Vegn der alter un der nayer yidisher literatur," *Bleter geshikhte fun der yidisher literatur* 2: 295.

2. In particular, see Matityahu Mintz, *Ber Borokhov: Ha-Ma'gal Ha-Rishon* (1900–1906) (Tel Aviv: Tel Aviv Univ. Press, 1976) and *Zemanim Hadashim-Zemirot Hadashot: Ber Borokhov 1914–1917* (Tel Aviv: Tel Aviv Univ. Press, 1988); Frankel, *Prophecy and Politics,* 329–63; and Cohen, "Introduction."

3. The biographical information on Borochov comes from B. Tsh[ubinski] and Y[ehezkel]. K[eitelman], "Ber borokhov" in *Leksikon fun der nayer yidisher literatur,* 1:235–38; Nachman Meisel, "Ber borochov: filolog un literatur-historiker," introduction to *Shprakh-forshung un literatur-geshikhte,* Ber Borokhov, ed. Nachman Meisel, (Tel Aviv: I. L. Peretz, 1966), 9–38; Mintz, *Ber Borokhov: Ha-Ma'gal Ha-Rishon;* Frankel, *Prophecy and Politics,* 329–63; and Cohen, "Introduction."

4. Borochov, "Letter to Shmuel Niger," (12 Oct. 1912), *Yivo bleter* 6: 8–9.

5. Cohen, 5.

6. Frankel, *Prophecy and Politics,* 336.

7. Reprinted in Borochov, *Class Struggle and the Jewish Nation,* 51–74.

8. Frankel, "Ber Borochov and the Revolutionary Generation of 1905," 222.

9. Reprinted in Borochov, *Class Struggle and the Jewish Nation,* 75–103.

10. Frankel, *Prophecy and Politics,* 338–44; Borochov, "Ber Borochov and the Revolutionary Generation of 1905," 218. Kassow describes this split as between a "prognostic" stance toward Jewish settlement in Palestine and a "voluntarist" one. Kassow, 31–33.

11. Frankel, "Ber Borochov and the Revolutionary Generation of 1905," 219.

12. Borochov, "Our Platform," 92.

13. Gabriele Kohlbauer-Fritz, "Yiddish as an Expression of Jewish Cultural Identity in Galicia and Vienna," *Polin* 12 (1999): 164–76.

14. Tsitron, *Dray literarishe doyres,* 3:55 (emphasis in the original). Frankel mentions that Borochov referred to his Yiddish as "abominable" in 1905. *Prophecy and Politics,* 332. Borochov himself claimed that he only learned Yiddish at age twenty-six. "Letter to Shmuel Niger," (12 Oct. 1912), *Yivo bleter* 6: 9.

15. Ya'akov Zerubavel, "Vi azoy iz ber borokhov gekumen tsu yidish un yidish-forshung," *Literarishe bleter* (8 Jan. 1926): 24–25.

16. Borochov, "Tsu der natsyonaler frage in belgyen," *Di yugend-shtime: zamelbukh* (Warsaw, 1908), 63–84. Borochov's vision for Yiddish was clearly inspired by the Flemish model, and he is reported to have stated, "I read somewhere that not long ago Belgians celebrated the hundredth birthday of their writer [Henrik] Conscience. . . . He taught his people to read and I want to teach my people to write!" (Tsitron, *Dray literarishe doyres,* 3:56).

17. "'Motke Ganev' fun Sholem Asch"; "Y. Opatoshu"; "An ofener briv tsu di 'yunge'"; and "Vegn di 'yunge'" in *Sprakh forshung un literatur geshikhte.* "A por verter," in Morris. Basin, *Antologye: finf hundert yor yidishe poezye* (New York: Dos bukh, 1917), iii–vi.

18. An exception to this was Shiper, who, in a mostly laudatory review of *Der pinkes* in *Poalei Zion,* praised Borochov's manifesto as marking a new stage in the language war between Yiddish and Hebrew." Yitskhok Shiper, "A naye tkufe in unzer kamf far yidish," *Der yidisher arbeter* 10, no. 49–50 (25 Dec. 1913): 17–24. His review is dedicated to "My dear Borochov—a gift."

19. "Di oyfgabn" was reprinted in 1920 in the Soviet Union (Odessa) by *Dos naye lebn* and again in 1966 in the compendium edited by Nachman Meisel. Despite Borochov's insistence on his own orthography, different from that in the rest of *Der pinkes,* his orthography is not replicated exactly in the 1920 republication but instead contains additional diacritical marks not present in the 1913 publication. There are also slight orthographic variations in the 1966 volume.

20. *Di literarishe monatsshriftn* 1:7–8; Borochov, "Di oyfgabn," 4, n. 3 (356).

21. Borochov, "Di Oyfgabn," 1 (355).

22. See, for example, the cases of Polish, Ukrainian, Lithuanians, and Belarusian nationalism as discussed in Pearson, *National Minorities in Eastern Europe;* and Snyder, *The Reconstruction of Nations.*

23. Borochov, "Di oyfgabn," 5.

24. Maurice Olender, *The Languages of Paradise: Race, Religion, and Philology in the Nineteenth Century,* trans. Arthur Goldhammer (Cambridge: Harvard Univ. Press, 1992), 5.

25. Karl D. Uitti, "Philology," *The Johns Hopkins Guide to Literary Theory and Criticism,* ed. Michael Groden and Martin Kreiswirth (Baltimore: Johns Hopkins Univ. Press, 1994), 570.

26. See "Letter to Shmuel Niger" (14 Dec. 1912), *Yivo bleter* 6: 13–14.

27. Olender, 6–9.

28. Geary, 30–32.

29. Borochov, "Letter to Shmuel Niger," (14 Dec. 1912), *Yivo bleter* 6: 14. Borochov was echoing a line of thinking that stretched back to Herder and was continued throughout the nineteenth and early twentieth centuries. As the Bulgarian Ljuben Karavelov wrote, "Every nation should take pride in its language . . . [and] purify it of foreign garbage." Quoted in Berend, 51.

30. Borochov, "Di Oyfgabn," 8.

31. Borochov, "Letter to Shmuel Niger" (14 Dec. 1912), *Yivo bleter* 6: 13 (emphasis in original).

32. Borochov, "Di Oyfgabn," 11.

33. He argued that both German and Yiddish are corrupted. Yiddish was corrupted in the marketplace, where it became infused with other non-Yiddish words, and the Yeshiva, where it became infused with too many words taken from religious life. On the other hand, German became corrupted in the universities and the bureaucracy, where it was distanced artificially from the German people. "Di Oyfgabn," 11.

34. Borochov, "Di Oyfgabn," 15–16.

35. Zalmen Reisen, *Yidishe gramatik.*

36. Ibid., "Forvort" (unpaginated). Later in this introduction, Reisen goes on to praise some of the elements that Borochov later condemns. He acknowledges the help he received from *Der fraynd,* with its "true Yiddish language, . . . its pure enduring orthography." The orthography that Reisen lauds is what Borochov would later chide as heavily influenced by contemporary German. For other examples of scholarly activity in and on Yiddish that predate Borochov's call, one could look to the United States and find the multilingual dictionaries of Alexander Harkavy (1863–1939) and the linguistic work of Jehuda Joffe.

37. Borochov, "Di Oyfgabn," 17–18 (369–70).

38. Ibid (370) (emphasis in the original).

39. "Mendele discovered the language. . . . Peretz brought it to new countries." Ibid., 18.

40. Ibid., 18 (370).

41. Ber Borochov, "Di bibliotek funem yidishn filolog (400 yor yidishe shprakh-forshung)," in *Der pinkes,* unpaginated first two columns.

42. Katz, "On Yiddish, in Yiddish, and for Yiddish," 36.

43. Borochov, "Di bibliotek," col. 20, entry 118. Mansch's study was never reprinted from its serialized form. Borochov also discussed Mansch's contribution in a Russian-language encyclopedia entry on Yiddish. "Di yidishe shprakh," trans. N. Heykin, *Sprakh forshung un literatur geshikhte,* 151.

44. Joffe, "Review of *Der pinkes,*" *Di tsukunft* 19 (1914): 972.

45. Ibid., 973.

46. Joffe, "Review of *Der pinkes*" (part 2), *Di tsukunft* 19 (1914): 1074.

47. Shtif's criticisms are discussed at length in chapter 5, as are Borochov's assessment of Shtif's contribution to *Der pinkes.*

48. Tsitron, *Dray literarishe doyres,* 3:53.

49. Ibid., 54–55.

50. Ibid., 59–61.

51. Borochov, "Letter to Shmuel Niger, 19 May 1913," in "Plan far a geshikhte fun yidish," in *Landoy bukh: filologishe shriftn,* ed. Max Weinreich (Vilna: B. Kletskin, 1926), 28–38.

52. Ibid.

53. First published in *Di yidishe velt,* it was reprinted that same year in *Literatur un lebn* and in Meisel's 1966 anthology, from which the references below are taken.

54. Borochov, "Di geshikhte," 182. Leo Weiner, *The History of Yiddish Literature in the Nineteenth Century* (New York: C. Scribner's Sons, 1899).

55. Borochov, "Geshikhte," 185.

56. Ibid., 179.

57. Ibid., 180.

58. Ibid. (emphasis in the original).

59. Ibid., 181, 212.

60. Borochov, "Geshikhte," 212.

61. Ibid., 192–94.

62. Ibid., 194–95.

63. See his "Bamerkungen vegn der alt-yidisher shprakh," in ibid., 197–207.

64. Ibid., 208.

65. Borochov's explanation for this was that "the wanderer has more natural energy than when he is at home." Ibid., 208.

66. Ibid., 209.

67. Ibid., 210.

5. Nokhem Shtif: A Contrarian's Yiddishism

1. Sh. Niger, "Der umruiger gayst," *Der tog* (23 Apr. 1933).

2. Max Weinreich, "Nokhem shtif: tsu der kharakteristik fun dem forshtorbenem yidishistishem forsher un shrifshteler," *Di tsukunft* 38, no. 6 (June 1933): 346.

3. Ibid., 347.

4. Niger, "Der umruiger gayst."

5. Among some of his most significant works are *Yidn un yidish: oder ver zaynen 'yidishistn' un vos vilen zey?* (Kiev: Onheyb, 1919); *Humanizm in der elterer yidisher literatur: a kapital literatur-geshikhte* (Berlin: Klal-Farlag, 1922); *Pogromen in ukreyne: di tsayt fun der frayviliger armey* (Berlin: Vostok, 1923); "Ditrikh fun bern," *Yidishe filologye* 1, nos. 2–3 (1924): 1–11, 112–22; "A geshribene yidishe bibliotek in a yidish hoyz in venetsye in mitn dem zekhtsntn yorhundert," *Tsaytshrift* (Minsk) 1, nos. 2–3 (1926): 141–50, 525–44; "Ven den: bindverter in der yidisher shprakh dos XV–XVI yorhundert," in *Landoy bukh,* 95–128; and *Yidishe stilistik* (Kharkov: Tsentraler farlag far di felker fun F. S. R. R., 1930).

6. Yoysef Tsherniak, "Nokhem shtif (zikhroynes fun aynem fun zayne yorshim)," *Goldene keyt* 59 (1967): 220–22; Khayim Loytsker, "Zayn baytrog in unzer kultur-oytser," *Sovietishe heymland* 2 (Dec. 1969): 127–31; Rakhmiel Peltz, "The Dehebraization Controversy in Soviet Yiddish Language Planning: Standard or Symbol?" *Readings in the Sociology of Jewish Languages,* ed. J. A. Fishman (Leiden: E. J. Brill, 1985), 125–50; Kuznitz, "The Origins of Yiddish Scholarship and the YIVO Institute for Jewish Research"; and Shneer, 75–77. An exception to this is Chone Shmeruk, "Nokhem shtif, mark shagal, un di yidishe kinder-literatur in vilner B. Kletskin 1916–1917," *Di pen* 26 (Sept. 1996): 1–19.

7. The bulk of this information is from Shtif, "Oytobiografye fun Nokhem Shtif," *YIVO-bleter* 5, nos. 3–5 (1933): 195–225; and L.[eonard] P.[rager], "Shtif, Nokhem," *Leksikon fun der nayer yidisher literatur,* 8:637–41.

8. Shtif, *Pinkhusa Dashevskogo* (London: Molodoi Izrail, 1903) and in Yiddish as *Pinkhes Dashevsky* (London: Yung Yisroel, 1903); Shtif, *Chemu nas uchit pokushenie Pinkhusa Dashevskogo* (London: Molodoi Izrail, 1903) and in Yiddish as *Vos lernt undz der atentat fun dashevski* (London: Yung Yisroel, 1903). Dashevsky (1879–1934) was a Zionist Socialist activist in Kiev who attempted to assassinate one of the chief instigators of the Kishinev pogrom, P. Krushevan, in St. Petersburg. His actions and subsequent trial were an inspiration for Jewish youths who quickly followed his example and arranged many of the Jewish self-defense organizations in the wake of his attempt on Krushevan's life. *Pinkhes dashevsky: biografye* (London: Yung Yisroel, 1903); Moshe Mishkinsky, "Dashewski, Pinhas," *Encyclopedia Judaica,* 5:1310. Also Frankel, *Prophecy and Politics,* 323.

9. Shtif, "Oytobiografye," 200.

10. Ibid., 201.

11. Bal-dimyen, "Khaim zhitlovski: tsu zayn 25 yoriker yoyvel," 80.

12. Shtif, "Oytobiografye," 202–3.

13. For a discussion of Shtif's views on territorialism and the attempt to separate it from the idea of Jewish emigration from Russia, see Nsh"f [Nokhem Shtif], "Teritorializm, emigratsye, un di yidishe virklikhkayt," *Di shtime* 2 (1908): 141–60.

14. Shtif, "Di val-kampanye," *Di folksshtime* 2 (25 Dec. 1906).

15. Voting restrictions had excluded large numbers of Jewish workers from casting ballots in the election (the government only recognized voting councils in those factories with more than fifty workers and most Jewish laborers were employed in small shops), and many radical parties chose instead to denounce the entire process.

16. This strategy brought mixed results for the Jewish revolutionary parties. Jewish participation in the Duma dropped from twelve to four deputies, yet the second Duma was more radical in its overall composition.

17. Shtif, "Di val-kampanye," 1.

18. Shtif, "Fun minsk biz helzingford," *Di folksshtime* 3 (18 Jan. 1907): 82–96.

19. Ibid., 84–85.

20. On Herzl's proposal to colonize Uganda as a Jewish homeland, see Walter Laqueur, *A History of Zionism* (London: Weidenfeld and Nicolson, 1972), 122–23, 126–29.

21. Ibid., 93.

22. Ibid., 82.

23. Ibid., 93.

24. Shtif, "Tsu der boykot-frage," *Di folksshtime* 11 (11 July 1907): 1–12; and "Der internatsionaler sotsialisten-kongres in shtutgart," *Di folksshtime* 14 (3 Aug. 1907): 1–10.

25. Ibid., "Oytobiografye," 198.

26. Bal-dimyen [Shtif], "Sholem-aleykhem, der folks shrayber," *Dos naye lebn* 1 (1908): 48.

27. Lucy Dawidowicz, *The Golden Tradition: Jewish Life and Thought in Eastern Europe* (New York: Holt, Rinehart and Winston, 1967), 257.

28. For a thorough discussion of tensions between liberals and radicals in St. Petersburg in the wake of the 1905 Revolution, see Gassenschmidt, 72–109. Also Rabinovitch, 129–93.

29. Bal-dimyen, "'Yidish' un di 'khevres far yidish,'" *Der fraynd,* (24 Mar. 1908): 1–2. Several years later, Shtif also engaged in a famous debate with Bialik on the potential of Yiddish as a Jewish national language. See Gilboa, "The Language Dispute in the Pre-Soviet Era," in *A Language Silenced,* 11–26; and Adam Rubin, "Hebrew Folklore and the Problem of Exile," 65–66.

30. Ibid., "Di yidishe shprakh un dos yidishe teater," *Der fraynd* (19 Dec. 1907).

31. Mechtatel [Nokhem Shtif], "Konets 'Frainda,'" *Razsvet* 41 (1908).

32. Shtif, "Oytobiografye," 203.

33. Mechtatel [Nokhem Shtif], "Literarishe Monatshriften," *Razsvet* 10 (1908). As Moss relates, "though he hailed the journal as something to be 'welcomed by all to whom the interests of Jewish literature and art are dear,' he charged that 'our 'modernism' offered little to Jewish literature and certainly did not constitute the cornerstone of cultural renaissance." Moss, 169.

34. Shtif, "Oytobiografye," 206–7. Kuznitz reinforces this point in her discussion of Shtif's relationship to other Yiddish activists during this interrevolutionary era. See Kuznitz, 44–45. On Shtif's criticisms of Rosenfeld and Reisen, see Bal-dimyen, "Di yidishe poezye," *Dos naye lebn* (Apr.–July 1908).

35. Bal-dimyen, "Sholem-aleykhem, der folks shrayber," 45, 48.

36. Bal-dimyen, "Vegn unzere 'yunge,'" *Dos naye lebn* (May 1909): 353–61.

37. Ibid., 354.

38. Ibid., 358.

39. Ibid., 359, 361.

40. Nokhem Shtif, "Betokhn," *Dos naye lebn* 5 (May 1911): 237–42.

41. Sholem Aleichem, *Tevye der milkhiker* (Warsaw: Progres, 1895).

42. Shtif, "Oytobiografye," 211. Shtif was referring to Moshe Esrim Vearba's *Shmuel bukh* (Augsburg, 1544).

43. Ibid.

44. *Responsa* (Hebrew: *She'elot u' teshuvot*) is the term for rabbinic decisions over matters of Jewish law.

45. Shtif, "Oytobiografye," 212.

46. M. Pines, *L'Histoire de la Littérature Judéo-Allemande* (Paris: Jouve et Cie, 1911).

47. Despite the opprobrium with which this work was met by its Yiddish critics (see Shmuel Niger's review, "Der ershter prub," *Di yidishe velt* 1 [1912]: 69–82; and Ber Borochov, "Di bibliotek funem yidish filolog," 22–23), the volume found favor in its original form with Franz Kafka, who greatly admired the text. He wrote in his diary: "read, and indeed greedily, Pines's L'Histoire de la littérature Judéo-Allemande, 500 pages, with such thoroughness, haste, and joy as I have never yet shown in the case of similar books." (24 Jan. 1912). Franz Kafka, *The Diaries of Franz Kafka 1910–1913,* ed. Max Brod, trans. Joseph Kresh (New York: Schocken, 1948), 223.

48. Bal-Makhshoves, "Forrede fun der redaktsye," in *Geshikhte fun der yidisher literatur,* i.

49. Bal-dimyen, "Dr. m. pines—di geshikhte fun der yidisher literatur," *Der pinkes,* 313–48, a review of M. Pines, *Di geshikhte fun der yidisher literatur* (Warsaw: B. Shimin, 1911). The quote is from column 336 of the review. Pines's work was also translated into German and Russian. On Pines, see Kh. L. F. "Pines, meyer," *Leksikon fun der nayer yidisher literatur* 7:149–52; Leonard Prager, "Pines, Meyer Isser," *Encyclopedia Judaica,* 13:533–34.

50. Bal-dimyen, "Dr. m. pines," 319.

51. Ibid., 314.

52. Ibid., 335.

53. Ibid.

54. Ibid.

55. Ibid., 336.

56. Bal-dimyen, "Der pinkes," *Di yidishe velt* 1. nos. 2–3 (1914): 247–60, 395–411.

57. Ibid., 248; M. [Khayim Eliezer-Moyshe] Tshemerinski, "Di yidishe fonetik," *Der pinkes,* 48–78; S.[arah] Reisen, "Avrom reisen (tsum 20 yoriken yoyvelye)" *Der pinkes,* 197–202.

58. Bal-dimyen, "Review of *Der pinkes,*" 250.

59. Ibid., 408.

60. See Shmuel Niger, "Vegn '*pinkes,*'" *Literatur un lebn* 5 (May 1914): 458–61.

61. His attack may have been motivated in part by Borochov's highly critical opinion of Shtif's submission to *Der pinkes*. In a letter to Niger, Borochov strongly criticized Shtif's review, finding many errors of dates and attribution, and argued that instead of simply demonstrating

what was wrong about Pines's study, Shtif should have written an even more programmatic piece, outlining the tasks for future Yiddish scholarship. See Shmuel Niger, "Briv fun ber borokhov: mit an araynfir un onmerkungen," *Gedank un lebn* 5 (1948): 117–19.

62. Bal-dimyen, "Review of *Der pinkes*," 251.

63. Ibid., 254.

64. Ibid., 249.

65. Borochov's response to Shtif was not made public until long after his death. Shtif relates that soon after the publication of his review, Borochov sent him an angry denouncement, filled with curses. As Shtif relates, however, Borochov did not counter any of Shtif's claims. Shtif, "Oytobiografye," 212.

66. Several years later, Shtif reflected upon the development of *Yidishe visnshaft* and its tumultuous pre–World War I period. He demonstrated a much more sympathetic stance toward *Der pinkes* and Borochov's contributions, seeing them as among the first building blocks for the new science. In an obituary for Borochov, in Dec. 1917, Shtif took a sympathetic stance toward Borochov and acknowledged the value of his achievement. Bal-dimyen, "Dov ber borokhov," *Folksblat* 9 (12 Dec. 1917): 5–7. Later, when writing the essay that founded the YIVO, he even praised Borochov essays as a "monumental bibliographical work, a key to all of Yiddish research." Shtif, "Vegn a yidishn akademishn institut," 10.

67. Shtif, "Oytobiografye," 213.

Conclusion

1. The scholarly literature on interwar Yiddish in Poland and the Soviet Union is much too great to enumerate here. However, a list of recent studies on the period includes Abraham Novershtern, "Yung Vilne: The Political Dimension of Literature," in *The Jews of Poland Between Two World Wars*, ed. Yisrael Gutman, et al., 383–98; Chone Shmeruk, "Hebrew-Yiddish-Polish: A Trilingual Jewish Culture," in *The Jews of Poland Between Two World Wars*, ed. Yisrael Gutman, et al., 285–311; Shmeruk, "Yiddish Literature in the U.S.S.R," in *The Jews in Soviet Russia Since 1917*, ed. Lionel Kochan (Oxford: Oxford University Press, 1978), 242–80; Chone Shmeruk and Shmuel Werses, eds., *Ben Shete Milhamot Olam: Perakim me-Haye ha-Tarbut shel Yehude Polin li-Leshonotehem* (Jerusalem: Magnes Press, 1997), 157–283; Jeffrey Veidlinger, *The Moscow State Yiddish Theater: Jewish Culture on the Soviet Stage* (Bloomington: Indiana Univ Press, 2000); Anna Shternshis, *Soviet and Kosher: Jewish Popular Culture in the Soviet Union, 1923–1939* (Bloomington: Indiana Univ. Press, 2006); and Kassow, *Who Will Write Our History?*

2. Ezra Mendelsohn, *The Jews of East Central Europe Between the World Wars* (Bloomington: Indiana Univ. Press), 48.

3. See Elias Schulman, *A History of Jewish Education in the Soviet Union* (New York: Ktav, 1971); Zvi Y. Gitelman, *Jewish Nationality and Soviet Politics: The Jewish Sections of the CPSU, 1917–1930* (Princeton: Princeton Univ. Press, 1972) 321–71. Also see Shneer, *Yiddish and the Creation of Soviet Jewish Culture*, 162–65.

4. See Alfred A. Greenbaum, *Jewish Scholarship and Scholarly Institutions in Soviet Russia, 1918–1953* (Jerusalem: Hebrew Univ. of Jerusalem Centre for Research and Documentation of East European Jewry, 1978); Estraikh, *Soviet Yiddish: Language Planning and Linguistic Development;* Kuznitz, "The Origins of Yiddish Scholarship and the YIVO Institute for Jewish Research"; and Shneer, *Yiddish and the Creation of Soviet Jewish Culture.*

5. The full name of *Tsaytshrift* was *Tsaytshrift: far yidisher geshikhte, demografye un ekonomik, literatur-forshung, shprakh-visnshaft un etnografye.*

6. Marcus Moseley, "Autobiographies of Jewish Youth in Interwar Poland," *Jewish Social Studies* 7, no. 3 (2001): 14.

7. As can be seen in the case of Emanuel Ringelblum. See Kassow, chapter 2, "Borochov's Disciple," *Who Will Write Our History?* 27–18. Sternhell argues, however, that in the political sphere, Borochov's actual influence was sharply limited, as the realities of state building could not accommodate to the continually competing demands of socialism and nationalism. Sternhell, 18.

8. "In retrospect, one gets the impression that only after his death was the magnitude of his personality really appreciated." Matityahu Mintz, "Ber Borokhov," *Studies in Zionism* 5 (Apr. 1982): 33.

9. For two brief discussions of the mythmaking, see Mintz, "Ber Borokhov" 33; and Frankel, *Prophecy and Politics,* 330–31. Borochov's admirers have now moved to the Internet, where there exist several sites dedicated to his political achievements.

10. Mintz, *Ber borokhov: Ha-Ma'gal Ha-rishon (1900–1906)* and *Zemanim Hadashim-Zemirot Hadashot: Ber Borokhov 1914–1917;* Frankel, *Prophecy and Politics;* Cohen, "Introduction." In his introduction, Cohen gives us perhaps the broadest descriptor of Borochov as a "renaissance man" yet does not spend more than a portion of a paragraph discussing what Yiddish language research actually meant to Borochov. Cohen, 3.

11. Zalmen Reisen, "In rekhtn oyfbli: ber borokhovs tsenter yortsayt," *Literarishe bleter* 51 (23 Dec. 1927): 998. Elias Tcherikower, "Ber borokhov—vi ikh ken im," *Literarishe bleter* 52 (30 Dec. 1927): 1023. Niger, "Vegn der alter un nayer yidisher literatur," 296. Weinreich, *History of the Yiddish Language,* 299. See, for example, the laudatory descriptions of Borochov by his one-time critics Nokhem Shtif, *Vegn a yidishn akademishn institute;* and Joffe, "Borokhov, ber."

12. Ber Borochov, *Sprakh-forshung un literatur-geshikhte,* ed. Nachman Meisel (Tel Aviv: I. L. Peretz, 1966).

13. Nachman Meisel, "Ber borokhov—filolog un literatur-historiker," *Sprakh-forshung un literatur-geshikhte,* ed. Nachman Meisel (Tel Aviv, 1966), 9–38. Much of the 1966 introduction is taken from *Ber borokhov: der goen fun der yidisher filologye* (New York: IKUF, 1963). As an editor at *Di yidishe velt* in 1912–14, Meisel was one of the first to publish Borochov's works on Yiddish.

14. The contemporary scholar Dovid Katz, who has written about Borochov on several occasions, has declared that Borochov founded the field of Yiddish linguistics, wrote its

"Declaration of Independence," set the standards for later Yiddish orthography, and created a research agenda that later scholars have followed nearly to the letter. He hails Borochov as "the most brilliant Yiddish scholar of the twentieth century, who single-handedly fashioned Yiddish studies as a new field of academic research." Dovid Katz, "Ber Borokhov, Pioneer of Yiddish Linguistics," *Jewish Frontier* 47 (1980): 10–20; "On Yiddish, in Yiddish, and for Yiddish"; *Words on Fire*, 274–78; *Lithuanian Jewish Culture*, 282–85. A more complicated portrayal of Borokhov has been offered by the scholar Rakhmiel Peltz, who, in a talk entitled, "The Politics of Ber Borokhov's Research on Yiddish Language," situates Borochov's efforts in the social sciences that were emerging in Central Europe at the turn of the twentieth century. Paper delivered at the Thirty-fourth Annual Conference of the Association for Jewish Studies, 12 Dec. 2002, Los Angeles. Also see Trachtenberg, "Ber Borochov's 'The Tasks of Yiddish Philology,'" 341–52.

15. Kuznitz, 45.

16. For example, Bal-dimyen, "Mendele moykher sforim z"l," *Folksblat* 9 (12 Dec. 1917). Also see his essays, "Di vegn fun der yidisher oytonomye," and "Partey un parteyishkayt," *Fun tsayt tsu tsayt* 1 (3 Sept. 1918).

17. See Estraikh, *In Harness*, 30–36.

18. Shtif, *Pogromen in ukreyne*.

19. Kuznitz, 56–59.

20. Peltz, "The Dehebraization Controversy," 133. Also see Estraikh, *Soviet Yiddish*, 68–70, 74.

21. See Avrom Nowersztern, "Yiddish Research after the Holocaust: From the Folk to the Academic," *Encyclopedia Judaica Yearbook 1988–9*, ed. G. Wigoder (Jerusalem: Keter Publishing House, 1989), 14–24.

Bibliography

Archival Sources

Archives of the YIVO Institute for Jewish Research, New York
RG 360: Shmuel Niger Collection

Works Cited

A. Vayter [Ayzik Meir Devenishski]. *Ksovim.* Edited by A. Y. Goldshmidt. Vilna: B. Kletskin, 1922.

Abramovitch, Zeev. "The Poalei Zion Movement in Russia, Its History and Development." In *Essays in Jewish Sociology, Labour and Co-operation: In Memory of Dr. Noah Barou, 1889–1955,* edited by Henrik F. Infield, 63–72. London: T. Yoseloff, 1962.

Abramovitsh, Rafael. *In tsvey revolutsyes: di geshikhte fun a dor.* New York: Arbeter Ring, 1944.

Alter, Robert. *The Invention of Hebrew Prose: Modern Fiction and the Language of Realism.* Seattle: Univ. of Washington Press, 1988.

Alter, Robert, ed. *Modern Hebrew Literature.* New York: Behrman House, 1975.

Althaus, Hans Peter. "Yiddish." In *Linguistics in Western Europe,* edited by Einar Haugen, et al., 1345–82. The Hague: Mouton, 1972.

Anderson, Benedict. *Imagined Communities: Reflections on the Origin and Spread of Nationalism.* Rev. ed. London: Verso, 1996.

Aronson, Gregor. "Ideological Trends Among Russian Jews." In *Russian Jewry (1860–1917),* edited by Jacob Frumkin, et al., 162–65. New York: T. Yoseloff, 1966.

———. "Jewish Communal Life in 1917–1918." In *Russian Jewry: 1917–1967,* edited by Gregor Aronson, et al., 13–38. New York: T. Yoseloff, 1969.

Asch, Sholem. *Meshiekh's tsaytn.* Vilna: Tsukunft, 1906.

Ascher, Abraham. "Anti-Jewish Pogroms in the First Russian Revolution, 1905–1907." In *Jews and Jewish Life in Russia and the Soviet Union,* edited by Yaacov Ro'i, 127–45. Ilford, Essex, England: Frank Cass, 1995.

———. *The Revolution of 1905: A Short History.* Stanford: Stanford Univ. Press, 2004.

Attia, Ali Mohamed Abd El-Rahman. *The Hebrew Periodical Ha-Shiloah 1896–1919: Its Role in the Development of Modern Hebrew Literature.* Jerusalem: Magnes Press, 1991.

Bal-Makhshoves. *Sekirot u-Reshamim.* Warsaw: Hotsa'at Sifrut, 1911.

———. "Forrede fun der redaktsye." In *Geshikhte fun der yidisher literatur,* by I. M. Pines. Warsaw: B. Shimin, 1911.

Barnard, F. M. *Herder on Nationality, Humanity, and History.* Montreal: McGill-Queen's Univ. Press, 2003.

Bartal, Israel. "From Traditional Bilingualism to National Monolingualism." In *Hebrew in Ashkenaz: A Language in Exile,* edited by Lewis Glinert, 141–49. Oxford: Oxford Univ. Press, 1993.

Baumgarten, Jean. *Introduction to Old Yiddish Literature.* Edited and translated by Jerold C. Frakes. Oxford: Oxford Univ. Press, 2005.

Ben-adir [Avrom Rosin]. *Sotsialistisher teritorializm: zikhroynes un materialn tsu der geshikhte fun di parteyn s"s, y"s, un fareynikte".* Paris: Arkhiv-komisye fun di parteyn s"s, y"s, un fareynikte, 1934.

Berend, Ivan T. *History Derailed: Central and Eastern Europe in the Long Nineteenth Century.* Berkeley: Univ. of California Press, 2003.

Berger, Shlomo. "The Beginnings of Yiddish Journalism." *Khulyot* 6 (2002): 363–71.

Berk, Stephen M. *Year of Crisis, Year of Hope: Russian Jewry and the Pogroms of 1881–1882.* Westport, Conn.: Greenwood Press, 1985.

Berkowitz, Joel, ed. *Yiddish Theatre: New Approaches.* Oxford: Littman, 2003.

Bez, Khayim. "Sh. niger: der kritiker un der mentsh," Introduction to *Fun mayn togbukh,* by Shmuel Niger. New York: Alveltlekhn yidishn kultur-kongres, 1973.

Borochov, Ber. "Di bibliotek funem yidishn filolog (400 yor yidishe shprakh-forshung)." In *Der pinkes: yorbukh far der geshikhte fun der yidisher literatur un shprakh, far folklore, kritik un bibliografye,* edited by Shmuel Niger, 1–66. Vilna: B. Kletskin, 1913.

———. "Briv fun ber borochov." *Yivo bleter* 6 (Feb. 1934): 5–24.

———. *Class Struggle and the Jewish Nation: Selected Essays in Marxist Zionism.* Edited by Mitchell Cohen. New Brunswick, N.J.: Transaction Books, 1994.

———. "Di oyfgabn fun der yidisher filologye." In *Der pinkes: yorbukh far der geshikhte fun der yidisher literatur un shprakh, far folklore, kritik un bibliografye*, edited by Shmuel Niger, 1–22. Vilna: B. Kletskin, 1913.

———. "Plan far a geshikhte fun yidish." In *Landoy bukh: filologishe shriftn*, edited by Max Weinreich, 22–28. Vilna: B. Kletskin, 1926.

———. "A por verter." In *Antologye: finf hundert yor yidishe poezye*, edited by Basin Morris, iii–vi. New York: Dos yidishe bukh, 1917.

———. *Sprakh-forshung un literatur-geshikhte*. Edited by Nachman Meisel. Tel Aviv: I. L. Peretz, 1966.

———. "The Tasks of Yiddish Philology." Translated by Jacob Engelhardt and Dalit Berman. *Science in Context* 20, no. 2 (2007): 355–37.

Branover, Herman. *The Encyclopedia of Russian Jewry: Biographies A–I*. Northvale, N.J.: Jason Aronson, 1998.

Brinker, Menahem. "Brenner's Jewishness." *Studies in Contemporary Jewry, An Annual: The Jews and the European Crisis 1941–21* 4 (1988): 232–51.

Bukhbinder, N. A. *Di geshikhte fun der yidishe arbeter-bavegung in rusland: loyt nitgedrukte arkhiv-materialn*. Translated by Dovid Roykhel. Vilna: Tamar, 1931.

Cohen, Mitchell. "Introduction: Ber Borochov and Socialist Zionism." In *Class Struggle and the Jewish Nation: Selected Essays in Marxist Zionism*, by Ber Borochov. New Brunswick, N.J.: Transaction Books, 1994.

Dauber, Jeremy. *Antonio's Devils: Writers of the Jewish Enlightenment and the Birth of Modern Hebrew and Yiddish Literature*. Stanford: Stanford Univ. Press, 2004.

Davitt, Michael. *Within the Pale: The True Story of Anti-Semitic Persecution in Russia*. New York: Barnes, 1903.

Dawidowicz, Lucy. *The Golden Tradition: Jewish Life and Thought in Eastern Europe*. New York: Holt, Rinehart and Winston, 1967.

Deutscher, Isaac. *The Non-Jewish Jew and Other Essays*. Oxford: Oxford Univ. Press. 1968.

———. *The Prophet Armed: Trotsky, 1879–1921*. Oxford: Oxford Univ. Press, 1954.

Dieckhoff, Alain. *The Invention of a Nation: Zionist Thought and the Making of Modern Israel*. Trans. Jonathan Derrick. New York: Columbia Univ. Press, 2003.

Dinur, Ben-Zion. *Be-'Olam she-Shaka': Zikhronot u-Reshumot mi-Derekh Hayim*. Jerusalem: Mosad Byalik, 1958.

Druk, D. *Tsu der geshikhte fun der yidishe prese*. Warsaw: Hacefira, 1920.

Dubnov-Erlich, Sophie. *The Life and Work of S. M. Dubnov: Diaspora Nationalism and Jewish History.* Edited by Jeffrey Shandler and translated by Judith Vowles. Bloomington: Indiana Univ. Press, 1991.

Dubnow, Simon. *Fun "zhargon" tsu yidish un andere artiklen: literarishe zikhroynes.* Vilna: B. Kletskin, 1929.

———. *Nationalism and History: Essays on Old and New Judaism.* Edited by Koppel S. Pinson. Philadelphia: Jewish Publication Society, 1958.

———. *Weltgeschichte des jüdischen Volkes: von seinen Uranfängen bis zur Gegenwart.* Berlin: Jüdischer Verlag, 1925–30.

Estraikh, Gennady. *In Harness: Yiddish Writers' Romance with Communism.* Syracuse: Syracuse Univ. Press, 2005.

———. "Jacob Lestschinsky: A Yiddish Dreamer and Social Scientist." *Science in Context* 20 (2007): 215–37.

———. *Soviet Yiddish: Language Planning and Linguistic Development.* Oxford: Clarendon Press: 1999.

Evron, Boas. *Jewish State or Israeli Nation?* Bloomington: Indiana Univ. Press, 1995.

Feiner, Shmuel. *Haskalah and History: The Emergence of a Modern Jewish Historical Consciousness.* Oxford: Oxford Univ. Press, 2002.

Fishman, David E. "The Politics of Yiddish in Tsarist Russia." In *From Ancient Israel to Modern Judaism: Intellect in Quest of Understanding: Essays in Honor of Marvin Fox,* 155–71. Vol. 4 of *The Modern Age: Theology, Literature, History.* Edited by Jacob Neusner, et al. Atlanta: Scholars Press, 1989.

———. *The Rise of Modern Yiddish Culture.* Pittsburgh: Univ. of Pittsburgh Press, 2005.

Fishman, Joshua A. *Ideology, Society, and Language: The Odyssey of Nathan Birnbaum.* Ann Arbor, Mich.: Karoma Publishers, 1987.

———. *Language and Nationalism: Two Integrative Essays.* Rowley, Mass.: Newbury House, 1972.

———. "Nosn birnboym 'di avodes fun mizrekh-eyropeyishe yidn.'" *YIVO Bleter, naye serie* 1 (1991): 109–27.

Forman, Frieda, et al., eds. *Found Treasures: Stories by Yiddish Women Writers.* Toronto: Second Story Press, 1994.

Frakes, Jerold, ed. *Early Yiddish Texts 1100–1750: With Introduction and Commentary.* Oxford: Oxford Univ. Press, 2005.

Frankel, Jonathan. "Ber Borokhov and the Revolutionary Generation of 1905." In *Contemporary Jewry: Studies in Honor of Moshe Davis,* edited by Geoffrey Wigoder, 217–33. Jerusalem: Institute of Contemporary Jewry, 1984.

———. "The Crisis of 1881–1882 as a Turning Point in Modern Jewish History." In *The Legacy of Jewish Migration: 1881 and Its Impact,* edited by David Berger, 9–22. New York: Brooklyn College Press, 1983.

———. "Jewish Politics and the Russian Revolution of 1905." *Spiegel Lectures in European Jewish History,* no. 4. Tel Aviv: Tel Aviv Univ., 1905.

———. *Prophecy and Politics: Socialism, Nationalism and the Russian Jews, 1862–1917.* Cambridge: Cambridge Univ. Press, 1981.

———. "S. M. Dubnov: Historian and Ideologist." In *The Life and Work of S. M. Dubnov: Diaspora Nationalism and Jewish History,* by Sophie Dubnov-Erlich, edited by Jeffrey Shandler, translated by Judith Vowles, 1–33. Bloomington: Indiana Univ. Press, 1991.

Frieden, Ken. *Classic Yiddish Fiction: Abramovitsh, Sholem Aleichem, and Peretz.* Albany: State Univ. of New York Press, 1995.

Gassenschmidt, Christoph. *Jewish Liberal Politics in Tsarist Russia, 1900–1914: The Modernization of Russian Jewry.* New York: New York Univ. Press, 1995.

Geary, Patrick J. *The Myth of Nations: The Medieval Origins of Europe.* Princeton: Princeton Univ. Press, 2002.

Gilboa, Yehoshua A. *A Language Silenced: The Suppression of Hebrew Literature and Culture in the Soviet Union.* Rutherford, N.J.: Fairleigh Dickinson Univ. Press, 1982.

Glau, Angelika. *Jüdisches Selbstverständnis im Wandel: Jiddische Literatur zu Beginn des zwanzigsten Jahrhunderts.* Wiesbaden: Harrassowitz, 1999.

Goldsmith, Emanuel S. *Architects of Yiddishism at the Beginning of the Twentieth Century: A Study in Jewish Cultural History.* Rutherford, N.J.: Fairleigh Dickinson Univ. Press, 1976.

Goldshmidt, A. Y. "Ayzik-meyr devenishski: zayn lebn un virkn." In A. Vayter, *Ksovim,* ed. A. Y. Goldshmidt (Vilna: B. Kletskin, 1922), v–clxv.

Goldstein, Yossi. Review of *"Meor'a Brener": Ha-Maavak 'al Hofesh Habitui,* by Nurit Guvrin. *Studies in Contemporary Jewry, An Annual: The Jews and the European Crisis 1941–21* 4 (1988): 343–46.

Gordon-Mlotek, Khana. "Der toyt fun a. vayter un zayne nokhfolgn." *Yivo bleter, naye serie* 2 (1994): 43–65.

Gorny, Yosef. *Converging Alternatives: The Bund and the Zionist Labor Movement, 1897–1985.* Albany: State Univ. of New York Press, 2006.

Gottesman, Itsik Nakhmen. *Defining the Yiddish Nation: The Jewish Folklorists of Poland.* Detroit: Wayne State Univ. Press, 2003.

Govrin, Nurith. *"Meor'a Brenner": Ha-Maavak 'al Hofesh Habitui.* Jerusalem: Yad Yitshak Ben Tsevi, 1985.

Gozhansky, Samuel. *Der tsienizm fun "LNU": mit a bayloge: di poyle tsien un zayer teorye.* London: Algemeynem yidishen arbeter bund, 1903.

Greenbaum, Alfred Abraham. *Jewish Scholarship and Scholarly Institutions in Soviet Russia, 1918–1953.* Jerusalem: Hebrew Univ. of Jerusalem Centre for Research and Documentation of East European Jewry, 1978.

———. *Tenu'at "ha-Tehiyah" ("Vozroz'denyah") u-Mifleget ha-Po'alim ha-Yehudit-sotsyalistit (M.P.Y.S.): Mivhar Ketavim.* Jerusalem: Merkaz Dinur, 1988.

Grossman, Jeffrey A. *The Discourse on Yiddish in Germany: From the Enlightenment to the Second Empire.* Rochester, N.Y.: Camden House, 2000.

Grünbaum, Max. *Jüdischdeutsche Chrestomathie: Zugleich ein Beitrag zur Kunde der hebräischen Literatur.* Leipzig: F. A. Brockhaus, 1882.

Haberer, Erich. "Cosmopolitanism, Antisemitism, and Populism: A Reappraisal of the Russian and Jewish Socialist Response to the Pogroms of 1881–1882." In *Pogroms: Anti-Jewish Violence in Modern Russian History,* edited by John D. Klier and Shlomo Lambroza, 98–134. Cambridge: Cambridge Univ. Press, 1992.

———. *Jews and Revolution in Nineteenth-Century Russia.* Cambridge: Cambridge Univ. Press, 1995.

Halevy, Zvi. *Jewish Schools under Czarism and Communism: A Struggle for Cultural Identity.* New York: Springer Publishing Company, 1976.

Halkin, Hillel. "The Great Jewish Language War." *Commentary* (Dec. 2002): 48–55.

Harcave, Sidney. "The Jews and the First Russian National Election." *American Slavic and East European Review* 9, no. 1. (Feb. 1950): 33–41.

Harshav, Benjamin. *Language in a Time of Revolution.* Berkeley: Univ. of California Press, 1993.

———. *The Meaning of Yiddish.* Berkeley: Univ. of California Press, 1990.

Henry, Barbara. "Jewish Plays on the Russian Stage: St. Petersburg, 1905–1917." In *Yiddish Theatre: New Approaches,* edited by Joel Berkowitz, 61–75. Oxford: Littman, 2003.

Herder, Johann Gottfried. *Abhandlung über den Ursprung der Sprache.* Berlin: C. F. Voss, 1772.

Herts, Y. Sh. "Di umlegale prese un literatur fun 'bund.'" In *Pinkes far der for-shung fun der yidisher literatur un prese,* edited by Khaym Bas, 294–366. New York: Alveltlekhn yidishn kultur-kongres, 1972.

Hoffman, Matthew. *From Rebel to Rabbi: Reclaiming Jesus and the Making of Modern Jewish Culture.* Stanford: Stanford Univ. Press, 2007.

Hoffman, Stefani, and Ezra Mendelsohn, eds. *The Revolution of 1905 and Russia's Jews: A Turning Point?* Philadelphia: Univ. of Pennsylvania Press, 2008.

Holmgren, Beth. *Rewriting Capitalism: Literature and the Market in Late Tsar-ist Russia and the Kingdom of Poland.* Pittsburgh: Univ. of Pittsburgh Press, 1998.

Horovits, Khayim-dov. "Unzer ershte teglikhe tsaytung (tsu der tsen-yorkiker geshikhte fun'm 'fraynd')." In *Der pinkes: yorbukh far der geshikhte fun der yidisher literatur un shprakh, far folklore, kritik un bibliografye,* edited by Shmuel Niger, 243–64. Vilna: B. Kletskin, 1913.

Hosking, Geoffrey. *Russia and the Russians: A History.* Cambridge, Mass.: Harvard Univ. Press, 2001.

Howe, Irving, Ruth R. Wisse, Khone Shmeruk, eds. *The Penguin Book of Modern Yiddish Verse.* New York: Penguin, 1987.

Hroch, Miroslav. "Real and Constructed: The Nature of the Nation." In *The State of the Nation: Ernest Gellner and the Theory of Nationalism,* edited by John A. Hall, 91–106. Cambridge: Cambridge Univ. Press, 1998.

———. *Social Preconditions of National Revival in Europe: A Comparative Anal-ysis of the Social Composition of Patriotic Groups among the Smaller Euro-pean Nations.* Cambridge: Cambridge Univ. Press, 1985.

Hughes, H. Stuart. *Consciousness and Society: The Reorientation of European Social Thought, 1890–1914.* New York: Octagon Books, 1976.

Jacobs, Jack. *On Socialists and "the Jewish Question" after Marx.* New York: New York Univ. Press, 1992.

Jedlicki, Jerzy. *A Suburb of Europe: Nineteenth Century Polish Approaches to Western Civilization.* Budapest: Central European Univ. Press, 1999.

Jeshurin, Ephim H. *Shmuel niger bibliografye.* New York: Kultur un 'ertsiung, 1912.

———. "Shmuel niger bibliografye (oprufn af zayn toyt)." In *Shmuel niger-bukh,* edited by Shlomo Bikl and Leybush Lehrer, 31–42. New York: YIVO, 1958.

Joffe, Yehuda A. "Review of *Der pinkes.*" *Di tsukunft* (1914): 971–75, 1074–76.

Judge, Edward H. *Easter in Kishinev: Anatomy of a Pogrom.* New York: New York Univ. Press, 1992.

Kafka, Franz. *The Diaries of Franz Kafka, 1910–1913.* Edited by Max Brod, translated by Joseph Kresh. New York: Schocken, 1948.

Kahan, Arcadius. *Essays in Jewish Social and Economic History.* Edited by Roger Weiss. Chicago: Univ. of Chicago Press, 1986.

Katz, Dovid. "Ber Borokhov, Pioneer of Yiddish Linguistics." *Jewish Frontier* 47 (1980): 10–20.

———. *Lithuanian Jewish Culture.* Vilnius: Baltos Lankos, 2004.

———. "On Yiddish, in Yiddish, and for Yiddish: 500 Years of Yiddish Scholarship." In *Identity and Ethos: A Festschrift for Sol Liptzin on the Occasion of His Eighty-fifth Birthday,* edited by Mark H. Gelber, 23–36. New York: Peter Lang, 1986.

———. *Words on Fire: The Unfinished Story of Yiddish.* New York: Basic Books, 2004.

Katz, Dovid, ed. *Origins of the Yiddish Language.* Oxford: Pergamon Press, 1987.

Kerler, Dov-Ber. *The Origins of Modern Literary Yiddish.* Oxford: Clarendon Press, 1999.

Kiel, Mark W. "Vox Populi, Vox Dei: The Centrality of Peretz in Jewish Folkloristics." *Polin* 7 (1992): 88–120.

Kirzshnits, A. *Di yidishe prese in der gevezener ruslendisher imperye (1823–1916).* Moscow: Tsentral felker farlag fun F.S.S.R., 1930.

———. *Der yidisher arbeter: khrestomatye tsu der geshikhte fun der yidisher arbeter, revolutsionerer un sotsialistsher bavegung in rusland.* Moscow: Tsentraler farlag far di felker fun F.S.S.R., 1925.

Klier, John D., and Shlomo Lambroza, eds. *Pogroms: Anti-Jewish Violence in Modern Russian History.* Cambridge: Cambridge Univ. Press, 1992.

Kohlbauer-Fritz, Gabriele. "Yiddish as an Expression of Jewish Cultural Identity in Galicia and Vienna." *Polin* 12 (1999): 164–76.

Krutikov, Mikhail. "Reading Yiddish in a Post-Modern Age: Some Trends in Literary Scholarship of the 1990s." *Shofar: An Interdisciplinary Journal of Jewish Studies* 20, no. 3 (2002): 1–13.

———. *Yiddish Fiction and the Crisis of Modernity, 1905–1914.* Stanford: Stanford Univ. Press, 2001.

Kuznitz, Cecile. "The Origins of Yiddish Scholarship and the YIVO Institute for Jewish Research." PhD diss., Stanford Univ., 2000.

Lambroza, Shlomo. "The Pogroms of 1903–1906." In *Pogroms: Anti-Jewish Violence in Modern Russian History*, edited by John D. Klier and Shlomo Lambroza, 195–247. Cambridge: Cambridge Univ. Press, 1992.

Landau, Alfred. *Jüdische privatbriefe aus dem jahre 1619: nach den originalen des K. u. K. Haus-, hof- und staatsarchivs im auftrage der Historischen kommission der Israelitischen kultusgemeinde in Wien.* Leipzig: W. Braumüller, 1911.

Laqueur, Walter. *A History of Zionism.* London: Weidenfeld and Nicolson, 1972.

Lestschinsky, Jacob. *Dos yidishe ekonomishe lebn in der yidisher literatur.* Warsaw: Kultur lige, 1921.

———. "Dubnow's Autonomism and His 'Letters on Old and New Judaism." In *Simon Dubnow: The Man and His Work*, edited by Aaron Steinberg, 73–91. Paris: Section Française du Congrés Juif Mondial, 1963.

———. "Statistika Shel Ayara Ahat." *Ha-Shiloah* 12 (1903): 87–96.

———. "Di yidishe emigranten in london." *Di yidishe bibliotek* (Feb. 1904): 29–53.

———. "Der yidisher arbeter." *Der nayer veg* 7–8 (1906): 269–74, 310–17.

———. *Der yidisher arbeter: in london.* Vilna: Tsukunft, 1907.

———. *Der yidisher arbeter (in rusland).* Vilna: Tsukunft, 1906.

Leyvik, H. "Der kritiker un der shrayber (shtrikhn tsu der perzenlekhkayt fun Sh. Niger e"h)." In *Shmuel niger-bukh*, edited by Shlomo Bikl and Leybush Lehrer, 31–42. New York: YIVO, 1958.

Litvin, A. "Tsu di lezer." *Lebn un visnshaft* 1 (1909): 3.

Löwe, Heinz-Dietrich. *The Tsars and the Jews: Reform, Reaction and Anti-Semitism in Imperial Russia, 1772–1917.* Chur, Switzerland: Harwood Academic Publishers, 1993.

Loytsker, Khayim. "Zayn baytrog in unzer kultur-oytser." *Sovietishe heymland* 2 (Dec. 1969): 127–31.

Medem, Vladimir. *Vladimir Medem: The Life and Soul of a Legendary Jewish Socialist.* Translated by Samuel A. Portnoy. New York: Ktav, 1979.

Meisel, Nachman. *Ber borokhov: der goen fun der yidisher filologye.* New York: IKUF, 1963.

———. "Ber borokhov: filolog un literatur-historiker," Introduction to *Sprakhforshung un literatur-geshikhte*, by Ber Borochov, edited by Nachman Meisel, 9–38. Tel Aviv: I. L. Peretz, 1966.

———. "Ber borokhov—vi ikh ken im." *Literarishe bleter* 51–52 (1927): 999–1000, 1023–24.

———. *Yitskhok leybush perets un zayn dor shrayber.* New York: IKUF, 1951.

Métraux, Alexandre. "Opening Remarks on the History of Science in Yiddish," *Science in Context* 20, no. 2 (2007): 145–65.

Mevaker. "Ha-pinkes," *Ha-Zeman* 276, 277, 278 (1913).

Meyer, Michael A. "Two Persistent Tensions Within *Wissenschaft des Judentums*." *Modern Judaism* 24, no. 2 (2004): 105–19.

Meyer, Michael A., ed. *German-Jewish History in Modern Times*. 4 vols. New York: Columbia Univ. Press, 1997.

Michman, Jozeph, and Aptroot, Marion. *Storm in the Community: Yiddish Political Pamphlets of Amsterdam Jewry, 1797–1798*. Cincinnati: Hebrew Union College Press, 2002.

Minkov, N. B. *Zeks yidishe kritiker*. Buenos Aires: Yidbukh, 1954.

Mintz, Matityahu. "Ber Borokhov." *Studies in Zionism* 5 (Apr. 1982): 33.

———. *Ber Borokhov: Ha-Ma'gal Ha-Rishon (1900–1906)*. Tel Aviv: Tel Aviv Univ. Press, 1976.

———. *Zemanim Hadashim-Zemirot Hadashot: Ber Borokhov 1914–1917*. Tel Aviv: Tel Aviv Univ. Press, 1988.

Miron, Dan. *The Image of the Shtetl and Other Studies of Modern Jewish Literary Imagination*. Syracuse: Syracuse Univ. Press, 2000.

———. *A Traveler Disguised: The Rise of Modern Yiddish Fiction in the Nineteenth Century*. New York: Schocken, 1972.

Mishkinsky, Moshe. "'Black Repartition' and the Pogroms of 1881–1882." In *Pogroms: Anti-Jewish Violence in Modern Russian History*, edited by John D. Klier and Shlomo Lambroza, 62–90. Cambridge: Cambridge Univ. Press, 1992.

Mlachi, A. R. "Der 'kol mevaser' un zayn redactor." In *Pinkes far der forshung fun der yidisher literatur un prese*, edited by Shloyme Bikl, 49–121. New York: Alveltlekhn yidishn kultur-kongres, 1965.

Morris, Benny. *The Birth of the Palestinian Refugee Problem, 1947–1949*. Cambridge: Cambridge Univ. Press, 1989.

Moseley, Marcus. "Autobiographies of Jewish Youth in Interwar Poland." *Jewish Social Studies* 7, no. 3 (2001): 14.

Moser, Charles A. "Russian Theory and Criticism: Nineteenth Century." In *The Johns Hopkins Guide to Literary Theory and Criticism*, edited by Michael Groden and Martin Kreiswirth, 638–41. Baltimore: Johns Hopkins Univ. Press, 1994.

Moss, Kenneth. "Jewish Culture Between Renaissance and Decadence: *Di Literarishe Monatsshriften* and Its Critical Reception." *Jewish Social Studies* 8, no. 1 (2001): 153–98.

Myers, David N. "From Zion Will Go Forth Torah": Jewish Scholarship and the Zionist Return to History." PhD diss., Columbia Univ., 1991.

———. "The Ideology of Wissenschaft des Judentums." In *History of Jewish Philosophy*, edited by Daniel H. Frank and Oliver Leaman, 706–20. London: Routledge, 1997.

———. *Re-inventing the Jewish Past: European Jewish Intellectuals and the Zionist Return to History*. Oxford: Oxford Univ. Press, 1995.

Nathans, Benjamin. *Beyond the Pale: The Jewish Encounter with Late Imperial Russia*. Berkeley: Univ. of California Press, 2002.

———. "The Other Modern Jewish Politics: Integration and Modernity in *Fin de Siècle* Russia." In *The Emergence of Modern Jewish Politics: Bundism and Zionism in Eastern Europe*, edited by Zvi Gitelman, 20–34. Pittsburgh: Univ. of Pittsburgh Press, 2003.

Niger, Shmuel. "Ayzik Meir Dik." *He-evar* 2 (1913): 140–54.

———. "Bal-makhshoves: der publitsist un kritiker." *Lebn un visnshaft* 2, nos. 3–5 (1912): 23–25, 25–29, 25–28.

———. "Briv fun ber borokhov: mit an araynfir un onmerkungen." *Gedank un lebn* 5 (1948): 114–37.

———. "Daytshmerish." *Lebn un visnshaft* 11–12 (1912): 49–66.

———. "Dr. khaym zhitlovsky: tsu zayn zekhtsik-yorikn yoyvelum." *Zhitlovski-zamlbukh*. Warsaw: Kh. Bzhaza, 1929.

———. "Der ershter prub." *Di yidishe velt* 1 (1912): 69–82.

———. "Fun der redaktsye." In *Der pinkes: yorbukh far der geshikhte fun der yidisher literatur un shprakh, far folklore, kritik un bibliografye*, edited by Shmuel Niger, i–iv. Vilna: B. Kletskin, 1913.

———. *Fun mayn togbukh*. Edited by Khayim Bez. New York: Alveltlekhn yidishn kultur-kongres, 1973.

———. *H. leyvik: zayn opshtam, zayne kinder-un yugnt-yorn, zayne lirishe un dramatishe verk, zayn dikhterisher gang*. Toronto: H. Leyvik yoyvl-komitet, 1951.

———. "Klas un natsion." *Der nayer veg* 14–15 (1906).

———. "Kneytshn: avrom reyzen's gezamlete lider." *Di literarishe monatsshriftn* 3 (Apr. 1908): 78–95.

———. "Kultur un bildung: vegn der yidisher inteligents." *Dos naye lebn* 3, no. 7 (1911): 27–33.

———. *Mendele moykher sforim: zayn lebn, zayn gezelshaftlekhe un literarishe oyftungen*. Chicago: L. M. Shtayn, 1936.

———. "Shmuesen vegn der yidisher literatur." *Unzer veg* 6 (1907): 30–37.

———. *Shmuesen vegn literatur.* New York: Yiddish, 1922.

———. *Sholem aleykhem: zayne vikhtigste verk, zayn humor, un zayn ort in der yidisher literatur.* New York: IKUF, 1928.

———. *Sholem ash, zayn lebn, zayn verk: biografie, opshatsungen, polemik, briv, bibliografye.* New York: Alveltlekhn yidishn kultur-kongres, 1960.

———. "Shtudyes: Tsu der geshikhte fun der yidisher literatur: di yidishe literatur-cun di lezerin." In *Der pinkes: yorbukh far der geshikhte fun der yidisher literatur un shprakh, far folklore, kritik un bibliografye*, edited by Shmuel Niger, 85–138. Vilna: B. Kletskin, 1913.

———. [A vilner]. "Tsu dem rayen tsu shafn a yidisher universitet." *Di yidishe velt* 2, no. 1 (Apr. 1914): 126–34.

———. "Der umruiger gayst." *Der tog* 23 (Apr. 1933).

———. "Vaysnberg." *Lebn un visnshaft* 1, nos. 3–4 (1909): 66–87.

———. "Vegn di tragedye fun goles." *Dos vort,* nos. 1–2 (1907): 31–37, 30–36.

———. "Vegn hebreyish un kh. n. bialk." *Dos naye land* 1, nos. 9–12 (1909).

———. "Vegn 'pinkes.'" *Literatur un lebn* 5 (May 1914): 458–61.

———. *Vegn yidishe shrayber: kritishe artikln.* 2 vols. Warsaw: Z. S. Sreberk, 1912.

———. *Vos iz azoyns der yidisher arbeter?* Vilna: Tsukunkft, 1906.

———. "Vos iz der yidisher arbeter." *Der nayer veg* 1–3 (1906).

———. *Di yidishe literatur—un di lezerin.* Vilna: Kletskin, 1919.

———. *Yidishe shrayber fun tsvantsikstn yorhundert.* 2 vols. New York: Alveltlekhn yidishn kultur-kongres, 1972.

———. *Yidishe shrayber in sovet-rusland.* New York: Alveltlekhn yidishn kultur-kongres, 1958.

———. *Y. l. perets: zayn lebn, zayn firndike perzenlekhkayt, zayne hebreyishe un yidishe shriften, zayn virkung.* Buenos Aires: Alveltlekhn yidishn kultur-kongres, 1952.

———. "A yunger folks-dikhter." *Unzer veg* 3 (1907): 34–37.

Niger, Shmuel, and Zalmen Reisen, eds. *Vayter-bukh: tsum ondenk fun a. vayter.* Vilna: Br. Rozental, 1920.

Niger, Shmuel, and Yankev Shatski, eds. *Leksikon fun der nayer yidisher literatur.* New York: Alveltlekhn yidishn kultur-kongres, 1956–81.

Nowersztern, Avrom. "Yiddish Research After the Holocaust: From the Folk to the Academic." In *Encyclopedia Judaica Yearbook 1988–89*, edited by G. Wigoder, 14–24. Jerusalem: Keter Publishing House, 1989.

————. "Yung Vilne: The Political Dimension of Literature." In *The Jews of Poland Between Two World Wars,* edited by Yisrael Gutman, et al., 383–98. Hanover, N.H.: Brandeis Univ. Press, 1989.

Olender, Maurice. *The Languages of Paradise: Race, Religion, and Philology in the Nineteenth Century.* Translated by Arthur Goldhammer. Cambridge, Mass.: Harvard Univ. Press, 1992.

Orbach, Alexander. *New Voices of Russian Jewry: A Study of the Russian-Jewish Press of Odessa in the Era of the Great Reforms, 1860–1871.* Leiden: Brill Academic Publishers, 1980.

Oyslender, Nokhem. *Yidisher teater: 1887–1917.* Moscow: Der emes, 1940.

Pappe, Ilan. *The Making of the Arab-Israeli Conflict, 1947–1951.* London: I. B. Tauris, 1992.

Patkin, A. L. *The Origins of the Russian-Jewish Labour Movement.* Melbourne: F. W. Cheshire, 1947.

Pearson, Raymond. *National Minorities in Eastern Europe, 1848–1945.* London: Macmillan, 1983.

Peltz, Rakhmiel. "The Dehebraization Controversy in Soviet Yiddish Language Planning: Standard or Symbol?" In *Readings in the Sociology of Jewish Languages,* edited by J. A. Fishman, 125–50. Leiden: E. J. Brill, 1985.

Penkower, Monty Noam. "The Kishinev Pogrom of 1903: A Turning Point in Jewish History." *Modern Judaism* 24, no. 3 (2004): 187–225.

Peretz, I. L. "Bontshe shvayg." *Literatur un lebn* (1894): 11–22.

Pines, Meyer. *Di geshikhte fun der yidisher literatur: biz'n yor 1890.* Warsaw: B. Shimin, 1911.

————. *L'Histoire de la Littérature Judéo-Allemande.* Paris: Jouve et Cie, 1911.

Pinsker, Leon. *Autoemancipation! Mahnruf an seine Stammesgenossen von einem russischen Juden.* Berlin: W. Issleib, 1882.

Piterberg, Gabriel. *The Returns of Zionism: Myths, Politics and Scholarship in Israel.* New York: Verso, 2008.

Porter, Brian. *When Nationalism Began to Hate: Imagining Modern Politics in Nineteenth-Century Poland.* Oxford: Oxford Univ. Press, 2000.

Prager, Leonard. *Yiddish Literary and Linguistic Periodicals and Miscellanies: A Selective Annotated Bibliography.* Darby, Pa.: Norwood Editions, 1982.

Prilutski, Noyekh. "Materialen far yidisher gramatik un ortografye." *Lebn un visnshaft* 5 (Sept. 1909): 61–68.

————. *Noyekh prilutski's zamelbikher far yidishen folklore, filologye un kulturgeshikhte.* 2 vols. Warsaw: Nayer farlag, 1912.

———. *Yidishe folkslider.* 2 vols. Warsaw: Bikher far ale, 1910.

———. *Yidish teater: 1905–1921.* 2 vols. Bialystok: A. Albek, 1921.

Rabinovitch, Simon. "Alternative to Zion: The Jewish Autonomist Movement in Late Imperial and Revolutionary Russia." PhD diss., Brandeis Univ., 2007.

Raisin, Jacob S. *The Haskalah Movement in Russia.* Philadelphia: Jewish Publication Society, 1913.

Regensberg, Elias. *Kishinover hesped.* London: H. Gintsberg, 1903.

Reisen, Sarah. "Avrom reyzen (tsum 20yoriken yoyvelye)." In *Der pinkes: yorbukh far der geshikhte fun der yidisher literatur un shprakh, far folklore, kritik un bibliografye,* edited by Shmuel Niger, 197–202. Vilna: B. Kletskin, 1913.

Reisen, Zalmen. "In rekhtn oyfbli: ber borokhovs tsenter yortsayt." *Literarishe bleter* 51 (23 Dec. 1927): 998.

———. *Yidishe gramatik.* Warsaw: Progress, 1908.

Reisen, Zalmen, ed. *Leksikon fun der yidisher literatur, prese un filologye.* 4 vols. Vilna: B. Kletskin, 1926.

Rogger, Hans. *Russia in the Age of Modernisation and Revolution 1881–1917.* London: Longman, 1983.

Roskies, David G. *A Bridge of Longing: The Lost Art of Yiddish Storytelling.* Cambridge, Mass.: Harvard Univ. Press, 1995.

Roth, Cecil, ed. *Encyclopedia Judaica.* Jerusalem: Encyclopaedia Judaica; New York: Macmillan, 1971.

Rubin, Adam. "Hebrew Folklore and the Problem of Exile." *Modern Judaism* 25 (2005): 62–83.

Sablinsky, Walter. *The Road to Bloody Sunday: Father Gapon and the St. Petersburg Massacre of 1905.* Princeton: Princeton Univ. Press, 1976.

Saunders, David. "Russia and Ukraine under Alexander II: The Valuev Edict of 1863." *The International History Review* 17 (1995): 23–50.

———. "Russia's Ukrainian Policy (1847–1905): A Demographic Approach." *European History Quarterly* 25, no. 2 (Apr. 1995): 181–201.

Schapiro, Leonard. "The Role of the Jews in the Russian Revolutionary Movement." *Slavonic and East European Review* 40, no. 94 (Dec. 1961): 148–67.

Seidman, Naomi. *A Marriage Made in Heaven: The Sexual Politics of Hebrew and Yiddish.* Berkeley: Univ. of California Press, 1997.

Shafir, Gershon. *Land, Labor and the Origins of the Israeli-Palestinian Conflict, 1882–1914.* Cambridge: Cambridge Univ. Press, 1989.

Shandler, Jeffrey. *Adventures in Yiddishland: Postvernacular Language and Culture.* Berkeley: Univ. of California Press, 2006.

Shimoni, Gideon. *The Zionist Ideology*. Hanover, N.H.: Brandeis Univ. Press, 1995.

Shlaim, Avi. *The Iron Wall: Israel and the Arab World*. New York: W. W. Norton, 2000.

Shmeruk, Chone. "Hebrew-Yiddish-Polish: A Trilingual Jewish Culture." In *The Jews of Poland Between Two World Wars*, edited by Yisrael Gutman, et al., 285–311. Hanover, N.H.: Brandeis Univ. Press, 1989.

———. "Nokhem shtif, mark shagal, un di yidishe kinder-literatur in vilner b. Kletskin 1916–1917." *Di pen* 26 (Sept. 1996): 1–19.

Shmeruk, Chone, and Shmuel Werses, eds. *Ben Shete Milhamot 'Olam: Perakim me-Haye ha-Tarbut shel Yehude Polin li-Leshonotehem*. Jerusalem: Magnes Press, 1997.

Shneer, David. *Yiddish and the Creation of Soviet Jewish Culture, 1918–1930*. Cambridge: Cambridge Univ. Press, 2004.

Sholem Aleichem. *Ale verk fun sholem aleykhem*. 5 vols. New York: Forverts, 1942.

———. *Tevye der milkhiker*. Warsaw: Progres, 1895.

Shternshis, Anna. *Soviet and Kosher: Jewish Popular Culture in the Soviet Union, 1923–1939*. Bloomington: Indiana Univ. Press, 2006.

Shtif, Nokhem [Bal-dimyen, N-sh]. "Barikht fun der konferents 'vozrozhdenye.'" In *Sotsialistisher teritorializm: zikhroynes un materialn tsu der geshikhte fun di parteyn s"s, y"s, un "fareynikte,"* edited by Ben-adir, 130–33. [A. Rosin]. Paris: Arkhiv-komisye fun di parteyn s"s, y"s un fareynikte, 1934.

———. "Betokhn." *Dos naye lebn* 5 (May 1911): 237–42.

———. "Ditrikh fun bern." *Yidishe filologye* 1–2/3 (1924): 1–11, 112–22.

———. "Dov ber borokhov." *Folksblat* 9 (12 Dec. 1917): 5–7.

———. "Dr. m. pines—di geshikhte fun der yidisher literatur." In *Der pinkes: yorbukh far der geshikhte fun der yidisher literatur un shprakh, far folklore, kritik un bibliografye*, edited by Shmuel Niger, 313–48. Vilna: B. Kletskin, 1913.

———. "Fun minsk biz helzingford." *Di folksshtime* 3 (18 Jan. 1907): 82–96.

———. "A geshribene yidishe bibliotek in a yidish hoyz in venetsye in mitn dem zekhtsntn yorhundert." *Tsaytshrift* (Minsk) 1–2/3 (1926).

———. *Humanizm in der elterer yidisher literatur*. Berlin: Klal-Farlag, 1922.

———. "Der internatsionaler sotsialisten-kongres in shtutgart." *Di folksshtime* 14 (3 Aug. 1907): 1–10.

———. "Khaim zhitlovski: tsu zayn 25 yoriker yoyvel." *Di yidishe velt* 1 (1913): 78–88.

————. "Mendele moykher sforim z"l." *Folksblat* 9 (12 Dec. 1917): 7–13.

————. "Oytobiografye." *Yivo bleter* 5 (1933): 195–225.

————. "Di partey-diferentsirung fun der yidisher burzshuazye un der nayer feld-marsh fun der asimilatsye." *Di folksshtime* 4 (Feb. 1907): 9–27.

————. "Partey un parteyishkayt." *Fun tsayt tsu tsayt* 1 (3 Sept. 1918): 31–38.

————. "Der pinkes." *Di yidishe velt* 1, nos. 2–3 (1914): 247–60, 395–411.

————. *Pinkhes dashevsky: biografye.* London: Yung Yisroel, 1903. Also published as *Pinkhusa Dashevskogo.* London: Molodoi Izrail, 1903.

————. *Pogromen in ukreyne.* Berlin: Vostok, 1923.

————. "Sholem-aleykhem, der folks shrayber." *Dos naye lebn* (1908): 38–49.

————. "Teritorializm, emigratsye, un di yidishe virklikhkayt." *Di shtime* 2 (1908): 141–60.

————. "Tsu der boykot-frage." *Di folksshtime* 11 (11 July 1907): 1–12.

————. "Di val-kampanye." *Di folksshtime* 2 (25 Dec. 1906): 1–22.

————. "Vegn a yidishn akademishn institut." In *Di organizatsye fun der yidisher visnshaft,* 3–33. Vilna: TsBK and VIL"BIG, 1925.

————. "Di vegn fun der yidisher oytonomye." *Fun tsayt tsu tsayt* 1 (3 Sept. 1918): 13–38.

————. "Vegn unzere 'yunge.'" *Dos naye lebn* (May 1909): 353–61.

————. "Ven den: bindverter in der yidisher shprakh dos XV–XVI yorhundert." In *Landoy bukh,* edited by Max Weinreich, 95–128. Vilna: YIVO, 1926.

————. *Vos lernt undz der atentat fun dashevski.* London: Yung Yisroel, 1903. Also published as *Chemu nas uchit pokushenie Pinkhusa Dashevskogo.* London: Molodoi Izrail, 1903.

————. "Di yidishe shprakh un dos yidishe teater." *Der fraynd* (19 Dec. 1907).

————. *Yidishe stilistik.* Kharkov: Tsentraler farlag far di felker fun F. S. R. R., 1930.

————. "'Yidish' un di 'khevres far yidish.'" *Der fraynd* 24–25 (Mar. 1908).

————. *Yidn un yidish: oder ver zaynen 'yidishistn' un vos vilen zey?* Kiev: Onheyb, 1919.

Shulman, Eliyohu. *Portretn un etyudn.* New York: CYCO, 1979.

————. "Di Tsaytshrift 'Di yidishe velt.'" In *Pinkes fun der forshung fun der yidisher prese,* edited by Shlomo Bikl, 122–70. New York: Alveltlekhn yidishn kultur-kongres, 1965.

Snyder, Timothy. *The Reconstruction of Nations: Poland, Ukraine, Lithuania, Belarus, 1569–1999.* New Haven: Yale Univ. Press, 2003.

Sorkin, David. *Moses Mendelssohn and the Religious Enlightenment.* Berkeley: Univ. of California Press, 1996.

———. *The Transformation of German Jewry, 1780–1840.* Oxford: Oxford Univ. Press, 1987.

Stanislawski, Michael. *For Whom Do I Toil? Judah Leib Gordon and the Crisis of Russian Jewry.* Oxford: Oxford Univ. Press, 1988.

———. *Tsar Nicholas I and the Jews: The Transformation of Jewish Society in Russia 1825–1855.* Philadelphia: Jewish Publication Society, 1983.

Stein, Sarah Abrevaya. *Making Jews Modern: The Yiddish and Ladino Press in the Russian and Ottoman Empires.* Bloomington: Indiana Univ. Press, 2003.

Steinschneider, Moritz. "Jüdisch-Deutsche Literature nach einem handschriftlichen Katalog der Oppenheim'schen Bibliothek (in Oxford) mit Zusätzen und Berichtigungen." *Serapeum* 9 (1848–1849).

Sternhell, Zeev. *The Founding Myths of Israel.* Translated by David Maisel. Princeton: Princeton Univ. Press, 1998.

Tcherikower, Elias. "Ber borokhov—vi ikh ken im." *Literarishe bleter* 52 (30 Dec. 1927): 1023.

Tobias Henry J., and Charles E. Woodhouse. "Political Reaction and Revolutionary Careers: The Jewish Bundists in Defeat, 1907–10." *Comparative Studies in Society and History* 19, no. 3 (July 1977): 367–96.

Trachtenberg, Barry. "Ber Borochov's 'The Tasks of Yiddish Philology.'" *Science in Context* 20 (June 2007): 341–52.

———. "The Revolutionary Origins of Yiddish Scholarship." In *The Revolution of 1905 and Russia's Jews,* edited by Stephanie Hoffman and Ezra Mendelsohn, 174–84. Philadelphia: Univ. of Pennsylvania Press, 2008.

Trotsky, Leon. *1905.* Translated by Anya Bostock. New York: Random House, 1971.

Tsharny, Daniel. *Barg aroyf: bletlekh fun a lebn.* Warsaw: Literarishe bleter, 1935.

———. *Dukor: memuarn.* Toronto: Pomer, 1951.

Tshemerinski, M. [Khayim Eliezer-Moyshe]. "Di yidishe fonetik." In *Der pinkes: yorbukh far der geshikhte fun der yidisher literatur un shprakh, far folklore, kritik un bibliografye,* edited by Shmuel Niger, 48–78. Vilna: B. Kletskin, 1913.

Tsherniak, Yoysef. "Nokhem shtif (zikhroynes fun aynem fun zayne yorshim)." *Goldene keyt* 59 (1967): 220–22.

Tsinberg, Yisroel. *Di geshikhte fun der literatur by yidn.* 10 vols. Vilna: Farlag Tamar, 1929–1970.

———. "Der "kol mevaser" un zayn tsayt." *Di yidishe velt* 1–4 (1913): 89–98, 83–90, 72–80, 74–81.

Tsitron, Sh. L. *Dray literarishe doyres.* 2 vols. Vilna: Z. S. Sreberk, 1921.

———. "Erinerungen vegn a. vayter." *Lebn* 2 (Apr. 1920): 22–26.

———. *Di geshikhte fun der yidisher prese I: Fun yor 1863 biz 1889.* Warsaw: Ahisfer, 1923.

Uitti, Karl D. "Philology." In *The Johns Hopkins Guide to Literary Theory and Criticism,* edited by Michael Groden and Martin Kreiswirth, 567–74. Baltimore: The Johns Hopkins Univ. Press, 1994.

Veidlinger, Jeffrey. *The Moscow State Yiddish Theater: Jewish Culture on the Soviet Stage.* Bloomington: Indiana Univ. Press, 2000.

Vital, David. *A People Apart: The Jews in Europe 1789–1939.* Oxford: Oxford Univ. Press,1999.

———. *Zionism: The Formative Years.* Oxford: Oxford Univ. Press, 1982.

Wandycz, Piotr Stefan. *The Lands of Partitioned Poland, 1795–1918.* Seattle: Univ. of Washington Press, 1974.

Waxman, Meyer. *A History of Jewish Literature: From the Close of the Bible to Our Own Days.* 4 vols. New York: Bloch Publishing, 1945.

Weinberg, David H. *Between Tradition and Modernity: Haim Zhitlowsky, Simon Dubnow, Ahad Ha'am, and the Shaping of Modern Jewish Identity.* New York: Holmes & Meier, 1996.

Weinberg, Robert. "The Pogrom of 1905 in Odessa: A Case Study." In *Pogroms: Anti-Jewish Violence in Modern Russian History,* edited by John D. Klier and Shlomo Lambroza, 248–89. Cambridge: Cambridge Univ. Press, 1992.

———. *The Revolution of 1905 In Odessa: Blood on the Steps.* Bloomington: Indiana Univ. Press, 1993.

Weiner, Leo. *The History of Yiddish Literature in the Nineteenth Century.* New York: C. Scribner's Sons, 1899.

Wiener, Meir. *Tsu der geshikhte fun der yidisher literatur in 19-tn yorhundert (etyudn un materiyaln).* New York: IKUF, 1945–46.

Weinreich, Max. *Bilder fun der yidisher literatur geshikhte: fun di onheybn biz mendele moykher-sforim.* Vilna: Tamar, 1928.

———. *Geschichte der jiddischen Sprachforschung.* Edited by Jerold C. Frakes. Atlanta: Scholars Press, 1996. Original: "Studien zur Geschichte und dialektischen Gliederung der jiddischen Sprache, Erster Teil: Geschichte und gegenwärtiger Stand der jiddischen Sprachforschung." PhD diss., Universität Marburg, 1923.

———. *Geshikhte fun der yidisher shprakh: bagrifn, faktn, metodn.* 4 vols. New York: YIVO, 1973.

———. "Nokhem shtif: tsu der kharakteristik fun dem forshtorbenem yidishis-tishem forsher un shrifshteler." *Di tsukunft* 38, no. 6 (June 1933): 345–48.

———. [P. Berman]. "Sh. Niger: der kritiker, der klal-tuer, der bal-seykhl." *Der forverts* 2 (1 Jan. 1956): 5.

Weiser, Keith Ian. "The Politics of Yiddish: Noyekh Prilutski and the Folkspartey in Poland, 1900–1926." PhD diss., Columbia Univ., 2001.

Weissler, Chava. *Traditional Yiddish Literature: A Source for the Study of Women's Religious Lives.* Cambridge, Mass.: Harvard Univ. Library, 1988.

White, James D. "The Revolution in the Baltic Provinces." In *The Russian Revolution of 1905: Centenary Perspectives,* edited by Jonathan D. Smele and Anthony Heywood, 55–78. London: Routledge, 2005.

Wisse, Ruth. *I. L. Peretz and the Making of Modern Jewish Culture.* Seattle: Univ. of Washington Press, 1991.

———. "Not the 'Pintele Yid' but the Full-Fledged Jew." *Prooftexts* 15 (1995): 33–61.

Wisse, Ruth, ed. *The I. L. Peretz Reader.* New York: Schocken Books, 1990.

Wohl, Robert. *The Generation of 1914.* Cambridge, Mass.: Harvard Univ. Press, 1979.

Wynn, Charters. *Workers, Strikes, and Pogroms: The Donbass-Dnepr Bend in Late Imperial Russia, 1870–1905.* Princeton: Princeton Univ. Press, 1992.

Zamelbukh "Kultur": 1905. Minsk: Kultur, 1905.

Zerubavel, Ya'akov. "Vi azoy iz ber borokhov gekumen tsu yidish un yidish-forshung." *Literarishe bleter,* no. 88 (8 Jan. 1926): 24–25.

Zhitlowsky, Chaim. *Gezamelte shriften.* New York: Yoyvleum oysgabe, 1912–19.

Zilberfarb, Moshe. "Di grupe 'vozrozhdenye.'" *Royter pinkes* 1 (1921): 113–29.

Zipperstein, Steven J. *Elusive Prophet: Ahad Ha'am and the Origins of Zionism.* Berkeley: Univ. of California Press, 1993.

———. *The Jews of Odessa: A Cultural History, 1794–1881.* Stanford: Stanford Univ. Press, 1986.

Index

Italic page number denotes illustration.

OTHER TITLES IN JUDAIC TRADITIONS IN LITERATURE, MUSIC, AND ART

American Artists, Jewish Images
  Matthew Baigell

Classic Yiddish Stories of S. Y. Abramovitsh, Sholem Aleichem, and I. L. Peretz
  Ken Frieden, Ted Gorelick, and Michael Wex, trans.; Ken Frieden, ed.

Finding the Jewish Shakespeare: The Life and Legacy of Jacob Gordin
  Beth Kaplan

God, Man, and Devil: Yiddish Plays in Translation
  Nahma Sandrow, trans. and ed.

Here and Now: History, Nationalism, and Realism in Modern Hebrew Fiction
  Todd Hasak-Lowy

In Harness: Yiddish Writers' Romance with Communism
  Gennady J. Estraikh

Neither With Them nor Without Them: The Russian Writer
and the Jew in the Age of Realism
  Elena M. Katz

Recovering "Yiddishland": Threshold Moments in American Literature
  Merle L. Bachman

Representing the Immigrant Experience: Morris Rosenfeld
and the Emergence of Yiddish Literature in America
  Marc Miller

What Must Be Forgotten: The Survival of Yiddish Writing in Zionist Palestine
  Yael Chaver